Noël Coward

Related Titles available from Methuen Drama

Blithe Spirit
Noël Coward
ISBN: 978-1-4725-8947-7

Coward Plays: Nine
Noël Coward
ISBN: 978-1-3500-4132-5

Hay Fever
Noël Coward
ISBN: 978-0-4135-4090-4

The Letters of Noël Coward
Noël Coward
ISBN: 978-1-4081-0675-4

Gielgud, Olivier, Ashcroft, Dench: Great Shakespeareans: Volume XVI
Russell Jackson
ISBN: 978-1-4742-5339-0

Shakespeare in the Theatre: Trevor Nunn
Russell Jackson
ISBN: 978-1-4742-8958-0

Noël Coward
The Playwright's Craft in a Changing Theatre

Russell Jackson

methuen | drama
LONDON • NEW YORK • OXFORD • NEW DELHI • SYDNEY

METHUEN DRAMA
Bloomsbury Publishing Plc
50 Bedford Square, London, WC1B 3DP, UK
1385 Broadway, New York, NY 10018, USA
29 Earlsfort Terrace, Dublin 2, Ireland

BLOOMSBURY, METHUEN DRAMA and the Methuen Drama logo are trademarks of
Bloomsbury Publishing Plc

First published in Great Britain 2022
This paperback edition published 2023

Copyright © Russell Jackson, 2022, 2023

Russell Jackson has asserted his right under the Copyright,
Designs and Patents Act, 1988, to be identified as Author of this work.

Unpublished material from the Noël Coward archives, ©
N.C. Aventales AG successor in title to The Noël Coward Estate c/o Alan Brodie
Representation Ltd abr@alanbrodie.com

For legal purposes the Acknowledgements on pp. ix–x constitute an
extension of this copyright page.

Cover image: Noël Coward, Blue Harbour in Jamaica, April 1951.
Photography by Cecil Beaton, Vogue (© Condé Nast / Noël Coward Archive Trust)

All rights reserved. No part of this publication may be reproduced or transmitted in
any form or by any means, electronic or mechanical, including photocopying,
recording, or any information storage or retrieval system, without prior
permission in writing from the publishers.

Bloomsbury Publishing Plc does not have any control over, or responsibility for, any
third-party websites referred to or in this book. All internet addresses given in this book
were correct at the time of going to press. The author and publisher regret any
inconvenience caused if addresses have changed or sites have ceased to exist,
but can accept no responsibility for any such changes.

A catalogue record for this book is available from the British Library.

Library of Congress Cataloging-in-Publication Data

Names: Jackson, Russell, 1949- author.
Title: Noël Coward : the playwright's craft in a changing theatre / Russell Jackson.
Description: London ; New York : Methuen Drama, 2022. |
Includes bibliographical references and index. |
Identifiers: LCCN 2021050810 (print) | LCCN 2021050811 (ebook) |
ISBN 9781350246065 (hardback) | ISBN 9781350246102 (paperback) |
ISBN 9781350246072 (epub) | ISBN 9781350246089 (ebook)
Subjects: LCSH: Coward, Noël, 1899–1973—Criticism and interpretation.
Classification: LCC PR6005.O85 Z637 2022 (print) | LCC PR6005.O85 (ebook) |
DDC 822/.912—dc23/eng/20220110
LC record available at https://lccn.loc.gov/2021050810
LC ebook record available at https://lccn.loc.gov/2021050811

ISBN:	HB:	978-1-3502-4606-5
	PB:	978-1-3502-4610-2
	ePDF:	978-1-3502-4608-9
	eBook:	978-1-3502-4607-2

Typeset by RefineCatch Limited, Bungay, Suffolk

To find out more about our authors and books visit www.bloomsbury.com
and sign up for our newsletters.

For Patricia

CONTENTS

Preface viii
Acknowledgements ix
Notes on references and play extracts xi

Introduction 1

1 The 1920s: From the 'best side of youth' to the international set 9

2 The 1930s: Old and new designs for living 43

3 The 1940s: Wartime entertainment, post-war discontent 81

4 The 1950s: Keeping a public, losing the critics 111

5 The 1960s: A 'rendezvous with the past' and new directions 153

Conclusion 185

Notes 187
Bibliography 203
Index 209

PREFACE

The Noël Coward archives are divided between London, where they are administered by the Noël Coward Archive Trust, and the Noël Coward Collection at Birmingham University's Cadbury Research Library. Between them these collections are rich in manuscript and typescript drafts, personal and professional correspondence, scrapbooks of press cuttings, logbooks of telegrams sent and received by Coward's London office, programmes, photographs and other memorabilia. This study draws on these, as well as on published sources, of which the most important – indeed, indispensable – are *The Letters of Noël Coward*, edited by Barry Day (London, Methuen Drama, 2007) and *The Noël Coward Diaries* (London, Macmillan, 1982), edited by Graham Payn and Sheridan Morley.

The diaries begin in 1941 and end in 1969, three years before Coward's death. The Cadbury Research Library holds a transcript, typed in Coward's London office, of the manuscript diaries and journals whose originals are now at Yale. There are entries not present in the published edition, and in some cases personal comments were omitted by Payn and Morley to avoid offence to persons still living in 1982. Some entries were removed as being repetitive and of little interest to the general reader, but the typescript's inclusion of these has proved valuable in tracing Coward's day-to-day progress. The editors also omitted references to plays not published or produced at the time of publication, notably *Salute to the Brave* and *Volcano*, both now be to be found, edited by Barry Day, in the ninth volume of the Methuen Drama *Collected Plays*.

ACKNOWLEDGEMENTS

I owe special thanks to the staff of the Cadbury Research Library at the University of Birmingham, particularly Mark Eccleston, for access to published and unpublished material and expert advice. I have benefitted greatly from Jess Worthington's comprehensive catalogue of this collection. (Before this became available, Holly Saunders, under a University of Birmingham scheme providing experience for undergraduates as assistants for research projects, made an invaluable preliminary survey of the collection's script materials.) In London, at the Noël Coward Room and Library, my work has been supported by Robert Hazle, the Learning and Archive Officer, and Carrie Kruitwagen, the collection's archivist. Alan Brodie, chair of the Noël Coward Archive Trust, has been supportive of this project from the beginning. I am also grateful to Mary Huelsbeck, at the Wisconsin Historical Society Archives for copies of script material held there, and to the Beinecke Rare Book and Manuscript Library, Yale University, for access to material in the John C. Wilson Collection. Research for this book has been facilitated by the Society for Theatre Research's Denning Award.

Mark Dudgeon, Lara Bateman and Ella Wilson at Bloomsbury Publishing Plc have given attentive and patient editorial guidance, and Mark Fisher has been a meticulous and perceptive copy-editor. I have greatly enjoyed conversations with and advice from Christopher Luscombe and Stanley Wells. My wife Patricia Lennox, an unfailing source of encouragement and acute critical insight, has shared with me the invariably enlivening company of Noël Coward.

* * *

Every effort has been made to trace copyright holders and to obtain their permission for the use of copyright material. The publisher apologizes for any errors or omissions and would be grateful if notified of any corrections that should be incorporated in future reprints or editions of this book.

The third party copyrighted material displayed in the pages of this book is done so on the basis of 'fair dealing for the purposes of criticism and review' or 'fair use for the purposes of teaching, criticism, scholarship or research' only in accordance with international copyright laws, and is not intended to infringe upon the ownership rights of the original owners.

NOTES ON REFERENCES AND EXTRACTS

In-text references are to both the Methuen series of Coward's *Collected Plays* (as 'M1' etc.) and (as '*PP1*,' etc.) the '*Play Parade*' volumes overseen and introduced by the author and published between 1934 and 1962. Where appropriate, reference is also made to the first editions and (as 'Fr.') to Samuel French's Acting Editions of individual plays: for details, see Bibliography, pp. 203–208.

In quotations from manuscripts and typescripts, the use of underlining for stage directions has been retained, as have the spelling and punctuation of the originals. In the typescripts, act- and scene-numbers are sometimes rendered in Roman rather than Arabic numerals; thus 'I-II' rather than '1-2' for 'Act One, Scene Two.'

Introduction

In September 1932, *Play Pictorial* and *Plays and Players* announced an essay competition on the question 'Noël Coward – Craftsman or Genius?' The prize was £5, and the winning entry and a selection from the runners-up were to be printed in the November issue of both magazines. In the winning essay, Joan Littlefield (of 4, Alexandra Avenue, N.22) began by suggesting it would perhaps have been better for him 'if he had not been a child of theatre' who had 'lived so long in the world of make-believe, and mastered so easily the arts and crafts that go to the making of a play, [had], in fact, so infallible a sense of what is "good theatre," that it [was] difficult for him to get away from the merely theatrical'. As for 'genius', Coward 'had it in abundance' if it was defined as the gift of recognizing 'the psychological moment for writing and producing a given work'. But if the criterion was 'depth as well as brilliance', he had yet to prove himself: 'The stuff, I think, is there but unless Mr. Coward puts up a stiff fight against his craftsmanship, he will continue to remain the playboy of the West End world.'[1]

Arguments of this kind, weighing the relative degrees of 'depth' (if not genius) and craftsmanship, would recur throughout a career spanning another four decades as author, composer, performer and (whenever possible) director. From the 'boy playwright' of the early 1920s to the 'Master' of his later career, Coward was aware of the dangers as well as advantages of labels he regarded with appreciative but ironic amusement. A compulsively industrious writer, he was also a voracious reader, even though the sense of him as a constant frequenter of 'marvellous parties' was an important and cultivated element of his persona as a celebrity. Coward was a happily social being rather than a socialite, worked hard at his craft, and dedicated himself to writing for the professional theatre and its public rather than the critics. As John Lahr points out in *Coward the Playwright* (1999), he 'managed to steer his career between the two poles of public adulation and hard work'.[2] He experienced two periods of post-war upheaval, after 1918 and 1945–6, the first being a decade characterized by Richard Overy as marked by a 'widespread culture of decline or crisis [. . .] regularly replenished by evidence of conflict, economic crisis, international disputes and occasional war'.[3]

The present study examines a number of his major plays in the light of archival evidence that reflects both the speed with which he could write when he was in the vein, and the care with which he revised. His dramatic work was almost invariably shaped to suit the demands of the professional, mainstream theatre, often with particular actors in mind. For one reason or another, some plays remained unproduced during his lifetime: notable examples are *Semi-Monde* (1927), *Post-Mortem* (1931), *Long Island Sound* (1947) and *Volcano* (1957). The archive's script material, especially in the earliest manuscript drafts, conveys the impression of a playwright who is also an actor and director, seeing characters decisively from the outset, hearing the lines as he writes them and already directing the play in the theatre of his mind.

Coward strove to balance attention to dramaturgical structure with his facility in writing dialogue, and aspired to be taken seriously as a dramatist, even in his comedies. Early and late in his career he engaged with the demands of the well-made play as practised by his long-time friend and mentor, W. Somerset Maugham. John Russell Taylor, in *The Rise and Fall of the Well-Made Play* (1967), points out that 'the decisive step Noël Coward took, whether in comedy or drama, was a drastic lightening of the plot-load'.[4] His attitude to the methods of older plays was one of respect combined with the desire to do things differently while keeping a grip on the attention of audiences. A crucial difference lay in the definition of the social misdemeanours that in the older dispensation were handled in comedy by the revelation of one or more mistakes (so that in fact there had been no transgression), or in drama by punishment of some kind. One imperative remained important: there should be a series of crises to push action forward, with each act and scene predicating the need for resolution or development. Each act would include one or more scenes of confrontation, and these 'scenes' – as in 'making a scene' socially – would build towards the 'obligatory scene.' In an analysis of French nineteenth-century theory and practice, William Archer had identified such a scene as 'one which the audience (more or less clearly and conscientiously) foresees and desires, and the absence of which it may with reason resent'.[5]

On 6 August 1956, prompted by dissatisfaction with a number of new plays, Coward wrote in his diary: 'as long as I continue to write plays to be acted in theatres, I shall strain every fibre to see that they are clear, well constructed and strong in content, either serious or funny, to keep an average paying audience interested from 8.30 until 11.15'.[6] Plays should be made well, but not necessarily in the conventional manner. In *Semi-Monde* he attempted an unusual number of plot lines; *Private Lives* pares the dramatic structure down to the bone; and the manuscripts of *Design for Living* (1935), show him fashioning a radically decentred structure to show the vagaries of the central characters' emotional and sexual attachments. The example of Maugham was often before him, but not for imitation, and Coward ranged freely across dramatic genres, flirting with farce, engaging effectively with the family chronicle, and occasionally veering into melodrama.

By the late 1940s reviewers were all too ready to point out that far from being ahead of the times, he was now some distance behind them. His responses to reviews regularly invoked the evidence of the box-office to defend his self-esteem. In the 1950s he was perplexed by changes in received definitions of 'serious' drama. The diaries suggest that he found the success of contemporaries writing for the West End stage – such as Christopher Fry, Terence Rattigan, N.C. Hunter and Enid Bagnold – less troubling than the more radical emerging talents of Arnold Wesker, John Osborne and Harold Pinter. Although in diaries and letters he often inveighed against the social milieu, obtrusive 'messages', and lack of attention to formal technique in the plays of new writers, he was generous in his responses to what he perceived as genuine originality. Harold Pinter is a notable example of this open-mindedness. In March 1960 he had 'loathed' *The Dumb Waiter* and *The Room*, as part of 'the surrealist school of non-playwriting', but in May he decided he was 'onto Pinter's wavelength' after seeing his latest play: '*The Caretaker* is, on the face of it, everything I hate most in the theatre – squalor, repetition, lack of action, etc. – but something seizes hold of you. [. . .] The writing is at moments brilliant and quite unlike anyone else's.'[7]

Lahr suggests that 'only when Coward is frivolous does he become in any sense profound', while frivolity, 'as Coward embodied it', was 'an act of freedom, of disenchantment'. He had been 'among the first popular entertainers to give a shape to his generation's sense of absence. His frivolity celebrates a metaphysical stalemate, calling it quits with meanings and certainties'.[8] After Coward's death, Kenneth Tynan wrote that he 'took the fat off English comic dialogue: he was the Turkish bath in which it slimmed'.[9] One element of this was the avoidance of epigrams, of which Maugham's comedies included some prime examples. In *The Constant Wife* (1926; first produced in England 1927) Mrs. Culver's worldly wisdom is expressed entirely in them, although they tend to be less economical than Oscar Wilde's. She declares that 'of course truth is an excellent thing, but before one tells it one should be quite sure that one does so for the advantage of the person who hears it rather than for one's own advantage'.[10] In *How to Write a Play* (1929), the critic and dramatist St John Ervine accused Coward of 'paying the heavy price of our interest in what is said' by reducing his dialogue to 'the bare mumbles which pass for conversation today'.[11] Maugham took issue with Ervine in the preface to the third volume of his *Collected Plays* (1931) but admitted that 'the current fashion to be slangy, brief and incoherent [had] blinded the dramatists to the fact that a great many people do talk grammatically, do choose their words, and do make use of well-turned phrases'.[12]

The most amusing effects in Coward's dialogue, such as 'Very flat, Norfolk', (*Private Lives*) and 'This haddock's disgusting' (*Hay Fever*), often come from the placing of a line or a word and the rhythm of the scene rather than any intrinsic comic value. Lahr comments that such moments 'have the divine silliness of an agile mind'.[13] As for flippancy (or 'frivolity'), defined as speaking lightly of serious matters, he was happy to challenge the social and dramatic criteria applied by his detractors. Sos Eltis has observed that, as an element of camp humour, it is one of the gay elements of his writing. At least in the public prints, most of those who disliked its tone identified it as the hallmark of a new generation's irreverence, with 'a recurrent emphasis [. . .] on control, on style rooted in restriction and indirection'.[14] As well as sharing the ironic detachment from conventions inherent in 'camp', Coward's humour was in tune with what Cyril Connolly, in a review of Evelyn Waugh's

Decline and Fall (1928), described as being 'of that subtle metallic kind which, more than anything else, seems a product of this generation'.[15] Later in his career, in *After the Ball* (1954), the musical adaptation of Wilde's *Lady Windermere's Fan*, and *Look after Lulu* (1958–9), his version of Georges Feydeau's *Occupe-toi d'Amélie*, Coward's approach to comic dialogue is at odds with the methods of the originals. By the time *After the Ball* was into its pre-London tour, he had decided that 'the more Coward we can get into the script and the more Wilde we can eliminate, the happier we shall all be'.[16]

A vivid picture of the collaborative nature of his work emerges from the letters and cables that circulated among Coward and his London associates, particularly during the periods of residence abroad necessitated by his tax situation in the 1950s and 1960s. With a mixture of respect and affectionate irony, he was commonly referred to and addressed among this professional family as 'father' and 'Master', and his occasional 'finger-waggings' were accepted as part of the job. In *Present Laughter* (first produced in 1942) the tightly-knit group of friends and associates, led by his secretary Monica, that supports the star actor Gary Essendine is a comic version of the playwright's own team. The archive's letters, journals, cables, and business documents show him at the centre of a remarkable 'family' of assistants, intimate friends and colleagues. Their names will occur frequently in the chapters that follow. Cole Lesley and Graham Payn graduated from being lovers to membership of a group presided over, from 1924 until her death in 1967, by Coward's formidable and much-loved personal assistant, Lorn Loraine. Other influential figures were the designer Gladys Calthrop, the actress Joyce Carey, John C. Wilson, his business partner in the United States (another former lover), and Hugh ('Binkie') Beaumont, with whom Coward had been associated since 1937. As co-founder and managing-director of the producing firm H.M. Tennent Ltd, Beaumont was a dominant figure in West End theatre from the mid-1930s to the 1960s. In the words of his biographer Richard Huggett, what attracted him was 'the good, pleasant commercial play, preferably a comedy which he could cast easily, which would attract one or two stars and which would appeal to the middlebrow and middle-class audiences in the home counties who kept the theatre alive'.[17] Although not all his productions were comedies of this kind, Beaumont was a shrewd judge of what would appeal to the clientèle that he cultivated. (Coward and he were of a mind in this, arguably to the detriment of his later plays.)

The chapters that follow focus on Coward's working methods in what used to be called 'straight' plays, to distinguish them from musicals, revues or variety shows. Between the revue *London Calling!* in 1922 and the musical *Sail Away* in 1961, Coward was responsible as sole author or collaborator on some notable productions in both genres, among them the musical plays *Bitter Sweet* (1929), *Conversation Piece* (1934), *Pacific 1860* (1946) and *After the Ball* (1954), and the revues *This Year of Grace!* (1928), *Words and Music* (1932) and *Sigh no More* (1945). He also wrote songs and incidental music for his own plays and films, as well as those of others. An indispensable guide to this aspect of his career is *Noël Coward, the Complete Lyrics*, edited by Barry Day (1988), and there is archival material to document thoroughly this aspect of Coward's output, but it calls for musicological as well as dramaturgical analysis beyond the scope of the present study.

I have adopted a chronological approach, in order to reflect the ways in which Coward's working practice responded to changing circumstances. In a generous 'appreciation' published in 1957, his friend and rival Terence Rattigan deprecated the tendency of criticism to look for 'development' in his work: 'A playwright writes the best play of which he is capable at any given time, and he writes it in the style and the method which best fit his own particular talent. [. . .] Throughout his career Noël Coward has most wisely continued to write like Noël Coward, and like nobody else.'[18] Especially in his earliest work, changes of direction, no less than those in the theatre and society in general, do not respect the arbitrary pattern of decades. Nevertheless, the part played in his work by attention to structure, the increased interest in the fluidity of sophisticated personal relationships, and responses to two successive post-war situations suggest that a chronological approach is appropriate. One turning point, at the beginning of the 1960s, has particular significance.

In a seminal article in 1991, Alan Sinfield pointed out that 'Coward's major plays all offer some flirtation with unorthodox sexuality', and the topic has since been pursued with effective thoroughness, notably in Sean and Julia O'Connor's *Straight Acting* (1997).[19] As a gay man, Coward exercised discretion in his public persona, and as a playwright until the last decade of his career he was constrained by the theatrical censorship of the Lord Chamberlain's Office from directly addressing male and female homosexuality. By the early 1960s the prohibition of references to homosexuality was in abeyance, and the representation of gay and lesbian characters on public stages would soon be possible. (Technically 'private' performances, with audiences paying for membership of a 'club', were a means of circumventing the law, and in 1968 pre-censorship of the drama was at last abolished.) The archive includes hitherto unpublished evidence of a plan from 1960 for a drama in which homosexual relationships would play a significant role. In *A Song at Twilight* (1965), an ageing novelist is obliged to face up to evidence of his concealed homosexuality. In an unpublished scene from the comedy *Age Cannot Wither*, left incomplete in 1967, homophobic prejudice is confronted directly by an independent-minded grandmother in her sixties. Coward was at last able to take advantage of the demise of prohibition that forty years earlier precluded the public performance – at least in the United Kingdom – of *Semi-Monde*.

Certain recurring themes emerge from an overview of Coward's plays. In several of them, characters either escape from the restrictions of conventional society or attempt to do so, while in others (notably *Private Lives* and *Design for Living*) the protagonists have already cut themselves free. In *Hay Fever* the conventional characters even have to make a furtive escape from the world of the blithely 'abnormal' Bliss family. Recurrent character types include detached, sophisticated witty observers; older ladies with either an independence of mind derived from social class or an endearing lack of connection with the modern world and its fashions; and uncomprehending and stolid members of the upper classes who act as a foil for the witty and sophisticated. All are carefully designed to suit the talents of leading actors, who are also given the entrances and exits appropriate to the prevailing conventions of commercial theatre. Although certain characteristics, notably in his comic dialogue, led critics to write of a 'typical Noël Coward play', his engagement with the playwright's craft can be described as restless, refracting if not always directly reflecting changes in theatre and society.

1

The 1920s: From the 'best side of youth' to the international set

Olive Do you think his work is really clever?

Sheila He has a wonderful sense of the dramatic, which of course is most important, and his dialogue is exceedingly witty. He may fail a bit in construction, but that won't matter a bit if he shows sincerity.

The Rat Trap, PP3, 372

The order in which Coward wrote (or in some cases, revised) the plays staged in the mid-1920s did not correspond to the order in which they were produced, suggesting not so much a traceable line of development as the work of a playwright trying out different approaches, variously comic and/or serious, to material that challenged dramatic and social convention. *The Rat Trap*, written in 1918, was not published until 1924 and was first performed in 1926. By then, he would already have read comments on his own plays resembling these on the work of the play's aspiring dramatist Martin Keld. 'Wit' would often be praised above the 'construction' that Coward was so anxious to achieve, while 'sincerity' – or, more generally, seriousness – would prove problematic throughout his career. The range of themes – sometimes touched on, sometimes central to the plays – included some pervasive topics of post-war culture: the shift in moral attitudes, generational conflict, and the very rapidity of change. 'Living modernly's living quickly', says

Lucy in Aldous Huxley's *Point Counter Point* (1928): 'You can't cart a waggon-load of ideals and romanticism about with you these days. When you travel by aeroplane, you must leave your heavy baggage behind'.[1] In a *Spectator* article in 1929, Evelyn Waugh wrote that 'the social subsidence that resulted from the War' had divided Europe 'into three perfectly distinct classes between whom none but the most superficial sympathy can ever exist'. He enumerated them as '(a) the wistful generation who grew up and formed their opinions before the War and who were too old for military service; (b) the stunted and mutilated generation who fought; and (c) the younger generation'.[2] As well as being in itself a topic for discussion within plays, the generational question also provided the terms of comic or dramatic confrontations essential to the well-made play, in which crises would be precipitated, questions left in the air at the end of each act and scene, and resolution sought or denied. The plays of the 1920s show Coward trying new variations on the formula; capitalizing on the 'younger generation' theme (including depictions of a decadent older generation); and, in the case of the unproduced *Semi-Monde*, combining the sense of social modernity with a complex plotting of intersecting lives.

Beginnings: 'Making scenes'

Coward's debut in the West End was a determinedly 'light' comedy with 'youthfulness' to the fore. *I'll Leave It to You* was first presented at the Gaiety Theatre in Manchester before its London transfer to the New Theatre (now the Noël Coward) in St Martin's Lane. He was reported in the local press as having written it 'in three days, transcribed direct from his brain to his typewriter'.[3] An eccentric family, with artistically gifted children and a somewhat scatter-brained mother, has been dependent since the father's death on remittances from a rich uncle in America. He arrives in due course, supposedly mortally ill, and promises to leave his fortune to whichever of the children makes the most effort to turn their talents to the family's material advantage. Hence the proposition, 'I'll Leave It to You!' They take up the challenge, but at the end of the second act he reveals that in fact there is no money, and the promise was a ruse to energize them. The play might well have ended here, with the achievement of Daniel's stratagem and the family now able to support itself by its collective talent and initiative. In the third act Daniel, unwilling to face the children's hostility, decamps to the local inn, but Mrs. Dermott insists that he be brought back, and they are reconciled. She still believes his impoverishment was a hoax, and opportunely Daniel receives a telegram announcing that his mine has struck gold. Just before the final curtain Sylvia, the aspiring actress who has always been the most sympathetic of the children to Daniel, asks him quietly whether he sent the telegram himself, and he answers 'Yes!!!' as the curtain falls. Apart from the reconciliation between the family members, the unfinished business left for this act is the resolution of the meagre love interest: Bobbie's intended, Faith, having been told by her mother that he is no longer likely to inherit a fortune, decides life with a songwriter is not for her.

Although some London reviewers suggested that comic effect was supplied as much by the vivacity of the younger cast members as the writing, there was applause for the 'bright, nippy dialogue, interesting characters, and the breezy wisdom of health, optimism and the best side of youth generally'.[4] There was also rather avuncular advice for the 'boy playwright'. The *Daily Telegraph* asked why he left himself 'absolutely no material out of which to make his last act'.[5] The most encouraging notice was Rebecca West's in *Time and Tide*, which pointed to what would become a vital element of Coward's dramatic strategy in years to come: the refashioning of existing dramatic modes. Unlike many of the young writers who had emerged from the war with imitations of the decadents of the nineties, 'as if the intervening quarter of a century in which Shaw and Wells and Bennett came to their own had not existed for them', Coward was among those 'who have run about among their elders and picked up all their most useful tricks and set about their own pretty wits to find new uses for them'.[6]

The Young Idea, 'a comedy of youth in three acts' written in 1921 and produced at the Savoy Theatre in 1923, was chosen by J.W. Marriott for his collection of *Great Modern Plays* as representative of one of the 'standard-bearers in the modern British drama movement'.[7] A brother and sister return from their mother's home in Italy to rescue their father from a faithless second wife and her frivolous social world, and reconcile him with their mother. The crucial turn in the plot, freeing the ex-husband to seek a reconciliation with his first wife, is the revelation of the second wife's flagrant adultery. The third act is a humorous celebration of the artistic life, and the appeal of Italy as a place of greater freedom. George Bernard Shaw did not fail to notice the play's indebtedness to *You Never Can Tell* (1897), with its theme of young people bringing about the reconciliation of their estranged parents. Returning a copy of the script 'scribbled all over with alterations and suggestions', he advised Coward that he 'showed every indication of becoming a good playwright, providing that [he] never again in [his] life read another word that he, Shaw, had ever written'.[8]

Coward told reporters that his next play to be produced in London would be *The Rat Trap*. This was written in 1918 but did not appear in print for another four years, receiving its first production (12 performances) in 1926. The marriage of Keld Maxwell and Sheila Brandreth – he a playwright, she a novelist – falls apart as their careers diverge. Their friend Olive Lloyd-Kennedy has warned that they will be like rats in a trap. By the second act he is working on his new play while Sheila is suffering from his selfishness, being left to cope with household matters, and Keld is being snared by an ambitious actress, Ruby Raymond. In the third act, his play has been successful, but as they celebrate, Sheila, who has learned of his flirtation with Ruby, tells him she never wants to see him again. In the short fourth act, Olive brings Keld down to the cottage in Cornwall where Sheila has been living for four months. She has been writing hard, and her publisher is pleased with the completed novel. The play ends with her asking 'Why aren't we ordinary, normal people without these beastly analytical minds?' (A question Gilda, Otto and Leo would address, with refreshing insouciance, in *Design for Living*.) Although she no longer loves Keld, she will return to him because she is going to have a baby and is 'so alone – and so dreadfully frightened' (*PP3*, 458). The main interest of this semi-conventional play – with no actual adultery, a chain of more or less predictable events, and a sentimental ending Ibsen's heroines would have scorned – lies in its self-referential elements. In Act Two, when Sheila and Keld have their 'scene' over his involvement with Ruby, he comments that it is 'a pity that there isn't a stenographer here to take all this down in shorthand, it would have made an excellent scene in a domestic comedy' (*PP3*, 397). In the corresponding 'obligatory scene' in Act Three, Sheila tells Keld that she realizes that they have 'to face facts, beastly, incredible facts – this situation we've so often refused to write about because it was too hackneyed. Now we're living it and we can't get away' (*PP3*, 424).

In several plays the social necessity of 'making a scene' is itself an issue of contention. As Dan Rebellato has pointed out, 'by making a scene out of not making a scene, Coward reveals the rules of etiquette as little more than scripts, guidelines for performance'.[9] In *Home Chat* (1927) Paul Ebony insists that his wife Janet must inevitably have committed adultery if she had to share a sleeping car compartment with another man, and claims that in any case if she had confessed the supposed affair they might have 'talked things over, and all this unpleasantness might have been avoided'. He tells her that he does not believe in 'making scenes' when 'much more can be achieved by sense and understanding' (*PP3*, 565). The upshot is that she resolves to teach her priggish husband and his domineering mother a lesson by pretending that she and the prospective co-respondent have indeed been having an affair, thus staging a 'scene' of her own devising. Refusal to accept the appropriateness of 'making a scene' in life as in the theatre is also central to *This Was a Man*, written in 1926 but refused a licence by the Lord Chamberlain's Office. 'Every character in this play, presumably ladies and gentlemen', wrote the examiner, 'leads an adulterous life and glories in doing so'. Given the current circumstances of social unrest, 'what better propaganda could the Soviet instigate and finance?'[10] Edward Churt, 'a successful modern portrait painter', is being betrayed by his wife. Admitting that he 'suffer[s] from a pre-war conscience', he blames his failure to confront her on this new age that he 'loathes'. He is neither 'primitive enough to thrash Carol and drive her out of [his] life forever' or 'strong enough to hold her' (*PP3*, 459/*M8*, 159). A friend, Evelyn Bathhurst, decides to teach Carol a lesson by letting her think he is trying to seduce her over dinner together in what the act's initial stage direction identifies as his 'manly apartment'. She turns the tables on him, and as the act ends she is seen stealing into his bedroom. Everything is prepared for the confrontation between husband and wife, but Edward insists that it is 'not a scene – it's a process of readjustment', pointing out that the situation is 'what's known, I believe, as the eternal triangle' (*PP3*, 531/*M8*, 216). He refuses to respond in the expected manner: either he will leave the county so that she can conveniently divorce him (the accepted 'gentlemanly' course of action), or he will sue her for divorce, naming Evelyn as co-respondent. He goes off to the

Berkeley, a fashionable nightclub, leaving them to decide for themselves:

> **Edward** *goes out.* **Evelyn** *and* **Carol** *look after him and then at each other.* **Carol** *after a pause walks over and sits next to* **Evelyn**.
>
> **Carol**   Evie.
>
> **Evelyn**   What?
>
> **Carol** (*sweetly*)   There's still time for you to shoot yourself!
>
> **Curtain.**
>
> PP3, 535/M8, 219

The play thus ends with Evelyn being offered sardonically one of the traditional 'manly' ways out of a situation, while Edward's behaviour asserts the title's radical claim that 'this was a man'.

The Vortex, 1923 (produced 1924): Revisiting the 'obligatory scene'

In *Present Indicative* Coward recalled that in 1923 his 'creative impulse was suffering from the monotony of eight performances a week' after almost seven months of 'hopping about' in *London Calling*, a revue for which his 'spontaneous enthusiasm had died ages ago'. But during the run he had found time to write two plays, *The Vortex* and *Fallen Angels*.[11] The first of these has a variation on the 'obligatory scene' in its final act, while the latter ends with the comic anticipation of one – or two, given the situation of the two married couples.

As if to put audiences off its scent, *The Vortex* begins in the vein of sophisticated and fashionably amoral social comedy, but soon develops into a near-tragedy, with some hope in the ending for both drug-addicted son and dissolute mother. *Fallen Angels*, a comedy, challenges the old double standard by which a woman was expected to be faithful to her husband not only during but even before marriage. Both plays encountered complaints that the very depiction of such irregularities was not only distasteful but harmful, and both were carefully constructed, and designed to provide roles that would attract and satisfy established actors. *The Vortex* brought Coward the overnight fame vividly described in *Present Indicative*: 'Success altered the face of London for me [. . . .] Every minute of every day was occupied and I relaxed, rather indiscriminately, into a welter of publicity'.[12] As with *I'll Leave It to You*, his youth was a significant element of the critical reception. Under the headline 'PLAY OF THE YEAR' and the sub-head 'Young Author's Big Achievement in "The Vortex,"' the *Daily Sketch*'s reviewer, 'P.P.', remarked that he started by 'counting, in rather peevish fashion, the number of times the words "adorable" and "too divine" were used'. His mood soon changed as the play darkened: 'Long before the end [. . .] I was wondering whether this wasn't the most interesting play I had seen for ages, and had decided, without wondering or hesitation, that Noël Coward is the cleverest young man that has arisen in the British theatre for at least a generation'.[13] There was 'much that is annoying' in the play, but the inevitable conclusion was that Coward had 'shed precocity for uncanny observation and a sense of the dramatic that is irresistible'. James Agate, in his *Sunday Times* notice, declared that the play had 'the imprint of truth' and that even though its 'creatures' were as 'nauseating as *animalculæ* in a pond', they 'interested'. A judgement that must have been especially gratifying to Coward followed immediately: 'The craftsmanship is beyond reproach, and the dialogue is taut and spare, and of an admirable *vraisemblance*'.[14] An anonymous review in the *Illustrated Sunday Herald* promised great things: 'If Coward continues, he'll be the Somerset Maugham of his generation'.[15] Coward recalled that 'Everyone but Somerset Maugham said I was a second Somerset Maugham, with the exception of a few who preferred to describe me as a second Sacha Guitry' – the comparison with the Parisian actor, dramatist and *boulevardier* had been made as early as *I'll Leave It to You*. As Christopher Innes points out, Coward was 'as much Maugham's follower as his rival.[16]

After West End managements failed to show interest in either play, both *The Vortex* and *Hay Fever* were offered to Norman MacDermott at the Everyman Theatre in Hampstead. In his account of the theatre's history, published in 1975, MacDermott noted that Kate Cutler, initially cast as Florence Lancaster, had championed the play.[17] In *Present Indicative* Coward describes the 'horrible setbacks' encountered in getting it on: the challenge of finding leading actors who would accept the theatre's rule of a fixed salary of five pounds a week for the whole cast; a dispute over the employment of Gladys Calthrop as designer; and the news that MacDermott would need an extra two hundred pounds to finance the production. This apparently insuperable obstacle was removed when Michel Arlen, whose *The Green Hat* had recently been a 'triumphant Best Seller' and who 'knew all the makeshifts of a struggling author', wrote a cheque for the amount. At a late stage in rehearsals a serious casting problem arose when Kate Cutler 'suddenly refused to go on rehearsing'. Coward had 'never quite known to this day what strange devil got into her'.[18] MacDermott recalled her as having walked out because of the author's 'studied rudeness' to her in front of the company. According to Coward, the immediate cause of her becoming 'surprisingly angry' was that 'upon realising that the last act was too short, [he] had rewritten it, enlarging [his] own part considerably in the process'. Rather than give in to her 'by reverting to the original last act which [he] knew to be too short and lacking the correct emotional balance in the conflict between mother and son', another leading lady had to be found. Lilian Braithwaite accepted the challenge of an abbreviated rehearsal period and the Everyman's meagre terms. Some reviewers claimed to detect the influence of Maugham's *Our Betters* (1923), which depicts a dissolute *milieu* of the kind inhabited by Nicky Lancaster's mother in *The Vortex*. Agate had described *Our Betters* as a 'brilliant and almost heartless comedy' in which Maugham had 'rewritten one of Henry James's short stories in the manner of Congreve'.[19]

The plot of *The Vortex* turns once again on generational conflict, but this time with an erring parent, Florence Lancaster, who is having an affair with a vacuous young man, Tom Vyvyan. When her son Nicky returns from his musical studies in Paris, it emerges that he has become a cocaine addict. He quarrels with his fiancée, Bunty Mainwearing, who has discovered that she knew Tom when they were children. At the end of the second act Nicky and his mother simultaneously discover Bunty in Tom's arms. Florence orders Bunty out of the house, and declares she will never see Tom again, but immediately relents and follows him upstairs as Nicky plays the piano furiously and the curtain falls. In the third act, Nicky insists on knowing whether Tom has been his mother's lover, and she confesses and admits to other affairs. Confronting her with the iniquity and folly of her desperate attempts to regain her youth,

Nicky denounces the 'civilisation' that 'makes rottenness so much easier': 'How can we help ourselves? We swirl about in a vortex of beastliness – this is a chance – don't you see – to realize the truth – our only chance' (*PP1*, 239/M1, 132). To her horror, he admits that he has become a drug addict. In the final moments, as he kneels by her and she strokes his hair – an image reminiscent of both *Hamlet* and Ibsen's *Ghosts* – they resolve to reform.

Coward's work on the play reflects his careful marshalling of Nicky's possessive and protective attitude towards her, intensified by his discovery of the truth about Tom Vyvyan and Bunty, and the appalled realization that both he and his mother are, as he puts it, 'rotten'.

The principal manuscript materials, in two of the archive's forty-nine notebooks, reflect Coward's working methods.[20] Writing in pencil, he sometimes began at the front of a notebook, and then turned it upside down and began writing from the back. The front of the foolscap (approx. 8 by 13 inches) Notebook 41 contains a draft of all three acts, identified here as the 'complete' manuscript of the play. The back of this book has a list of 'completed short stories', and 'revisions' to Acts 1 and 2, and a cancelled note on Florence Lancaster,

> In the old days whenever Flo Lancaster came into a room, there was a sudden hush, as tho everyone's breath had been abruptly taken away – it had been wonderful that feeling of predominance by sheer ~~beauty~~ loveliness – she had always been perfectly conscious of every effect she obtained – hers was never the unsophisticated beauty of the milkmaid type – fair she certainly was, but a radiant more ~~brittle fairness~~ manicured and pedicured fairness, and she knew so well how to use her hands when she talked, eloquently without over-gesticulation, ~~she still moved beautifully – Altogether the beauty of Flo Lancaster was a polished shining thing~~.

In the published text, Florence is described on her first entrance simply as 'brilliantly dressed almost to the point of being "outre"' [*sic*], and her face 'still retains the remnants of great beauty' (*PP1*, 173/M1, 79–80).

Notebook 42 is in the smaller quarto format (approx. 10 by 8 inches): the front has a list of characters and scheme of Act 1 and drafts of scenes for Acts 1 and 3. The pages are unnumbered, and there are signs of Coward writing at speed, such as words or phrases cancelled and immediately replaced, scanty punctuation and even at one point the change in mid-flow to a sharper pencil. The cast list in Notebook 42 includes a character, Miss Hodge, whose presence was short-lived. Act One begins with a stage direction that refers to Florence Lancaster by the first name of the actress originally cast in the role. (It is also corrected in the notebook's cast list.)

> ~~Kate's~~ Florence's flat in London – Miss Hodge is shown in – she carries a little bag – when she is left alone she goes swiftly and furtively to the ~~desk~~ Bureau and glances through the loose letters in the blotter – she is disturbed by the sound of ~~voices~~ someone coming – she seats herself demurely on the sofa – ~~Helen Saville and Pauncefort Quentin come in~~ —

The absence of a first name and her carrying a small bag suggests that Miss Hodge is more likely to be an inquisitive and potentially treacherous manicurist rather than an intimate friend. Any intrigue that might have been developed from this was not pursued, and the superficiality and cynicism of other characters probably seemed sufficient to establish the fragility of Florence's world. After this initial direction, Coward apparently decided to write down a list of eight scenes for the act. From an early stage he was careful to build a succession of scenes that would raise questions the succeeding acts would be expected to answer: Florence's milieu and her friends, including Pawnie, Alice and Helen; the problem of Nicky's failure to commit to his chosen work; Tom's relationship with Florence and Nicky's attitude to him; the status in the household of his father, David; the response of Florence to Bunty; and, at the end of the act, the revelation of Bunty's relationship with Tom. The list includes two that would have included Miss Hodge, the first of which is deleted:

> ~~Scene between Helen Pawnie and Miss Hodge~~
> Scene between Miss Hodge and Florence
> Scene between Florence, Nicky, Helen, Pawnie and Bunty
> Scene between Bunty Nicky and Florence
> Scene between Florence and Bunty
> Scene between Bunty and Nicky

Scene between Tom and Nicky
Scene between Florence, Tom and Nicky

At the bottom of the page is a note that 'during Act I David [Lancaster] enters for a moment'. As well as omitting the appearance of Miss Hodge, in the first act Coward added Clara Hibbert; decided not to have a scene between Tom and Nicky alone together; and removed Florence from the stage before the final scene between Bunty, Nicky and Tom. In the earlier scheme, the act would have ended with a confrontation between Nicky and Tom, followed by some sort of crisis involving them and Florence. Coward chose to end with a less potentially melodramatic sequence in which Nicky shows his distaste for Tom. After Nicky has left the stage, Bunty and Tom discuss Nicky and anticipate the planned country weekend as a revival of the 'old times' they shared together. This lays the foundations for the coming conflict, and leaves the form it will take as a question to be carried by the audience into the second act.

After the outline for the first act, Notebook 42 has two scenes. The first is a 'scene between Florence and Nicky, Act I', and the second is for the third act. Both appear to be first drafts, written quickly, with only a few corrections made in the flow of the writing. As often in his early drafts, Coward uses dashes to stand in for more precise punctuation and omits the apostrophe in such contractions as 'won't'. An example is Florence's account in the Act I scene of the photographer's waiving payment for her work: 'It *is* good – she's so sweet Madame Henderson – she wont dream of my paying for these – she says it's such wonde quite sufficient payment to be allowed to [?illegible] exhibit my photograph them in the window.' (*PP1*, 185/M1, 88). The scene is incorporated with only a handful of changes in the 'complete' draft in Notebook 41: there is no indication that Helen is on stage and about to take her farewell during the opening moments. The entrance of David while Nicky and Florence are dancing is included (*PP1*, 187/M1, 87, 90).

Coward developed the amateur singer Clara's role in the first act after the completion of the full draft, adding dialogue for her with Helen in which she complains of a headache and asks for the popular pick-me-up, a *cachet faivre* (*PP1*, 78–9/M1, 78–9), and with Florence in which she asks to borrow her 'green fan' for her imminent performance. She is described in the direction for her entrance in Act One as 'affected, but quite well dressed', and in Act

Two as 'an emaciated soprano' (*PP1*, 199/M1, 78,100). Similarly, after the early drafts, Pawnie's characterization as 'an elderly maiden gentleman' (*PP1*, 167/M1, 76), with decided views on interior decoration, was developed in Notebook 42's 'revisions' to the first scene ('This whole room is typical of Florence. . .') and the expository dialogue in which he and Helen discuss Florence and Nicky was added (*PP1*, 170/M1, 77–8). This includes one of his notable forays into camp: Florence is of course 'two hundred years too late – she ought to have been a flaunting intriguing King's mistress, with black page boys and jade baths and things too divine'. As in Arlen's *The Green Hat* and Evelyn Waugh's novels of the late 1920s, 'divine' (whose frequency in the play at first annoyed the *Daily Sketch*'s reviewer) recurs as a vogue word predominantly employed by society women, either the 'bright young people' themselves, those like Florence who imitate them, or effeminate men like Pawnie.

In addition to a shorter version of the opening scene's conversation between Helen and Pawnie and the less fully developed scene with Clara noted above, the first act of the 'complete' Notebook 41 script differs from the final version in lacking eleven speeches of the dialogue with David, Florence and Nicky (*PP1*, 187–8/M1, 90). Also absent are the exchanges between Florence and Nicky (*PP1*, 191/M1, 92–3) in which she asks her son 'not to take one of [his] tiresome prejudices' against Tom, setting him up as the antithesis of Nicky (Tom 'adores music', dances 'divinely' and is 'so good at games'). Act Two does not include the long passage between Helen and Nicky in which she quizzes him about his life in Paris and his relationship with Bunty, and which leads up to her telling him 'All the same, I should give up drugs if I were you' (*PP1*, 209–12/M1, 108–10). Without this, the advice comes with too little of the preparation present in the final script. Among the drafted 'revisions' is the final version of David's conversation with Nicky (*PP1*, 214–15/M1, 111–13) in which he tells his son he looks as though he 'needed a rest' and suggests he should spend time in the country, and Nicky explains that his engagement is 'only a sort of try-out, you know'. In the 'complete' Notebook 41 script the crucial scene between Nicky and Bunty follows directly from the 'goodnights' of Clara, Florence, Pawnie, Bruce Fairlight and Helen (*PP1*, 227/M1, 118–19) rather than preceding them. In this version exchanges between Nicky and Bunty in which she explains her reasons for deciding they are 'not very suited to one another' (*PP1*, 216–17/ M1, 114) are absent, so that the dialogue moves directly from her 'I've only just realised it' to his question 'I suppose you've taken a hatred to mother' (*PP1*, 217/M1, 115: the passage is among the 'revisions' in Notebook 41). In Nicky's explanation that his mother is 'terribly silly about being "young"' and can't get used to the absence of 'admiration and flattery', the MS includes and then deletes lines present in the published version (the deletions are marked):

> she feels she sort of can't give it up – you do see that, don't you? ~~And she hasn't really anything in the least comforting to fall back upon, she's not clever – real kind of brain cleverness – and father's no good,~~ and I'm no good, and all the time she's wanting life to be as it was instead of as it is.
>
> *PP1*, 218/M1, 115

Moving the scene between Bunty and Nicky to its earlier position allows an interval between the rapprochement of Tom and Bunty ('So you've broken it off already?'), and the act finale in which Florence finds them together, tells him to get out of the house, and then – realizing what she has done – runs upstairs after him, while Nicky, who has come in on the scene, 'goes to the piano and plays jazz' and 'never stops playing for a moment', until, left alone on stage he 'at last stops playing and lets his hands fall from the keys' (*PP1*, 227/M1, 123). A deleted direction and line of dialogue in the manuscript make Nicky's entrance more dramatic: 'realising the situation and running downstairs', he exclaims 'Come on! – [deleted word] dance a bit before bed – it makes you sleep like tops'. In the 'complete' manuscript a version of this is present but is deleted: after telling Bunty to 'control herself' he calls out to Helen and Pawnie (who have left the stage) and urges Bunty and his mother to 'stop that silly game – Come on Bunty – One more dance before bed'. He also makes two more attempts to intervene as he continues to play. The wisdom of cutting Nicky's lines is reflected in the description of the scene's effect in a review by Ashley Dukes:

> The notes that were at first a well-bred attempt to preserve the proprieties become a desperate protest – an expression of tragedy

and horror. Forte, fortissimo, there is no drowning this woman's voice. 'Get out of my house this moment!' it cries to the younger rival. The player attempts a crescendo as the curtain falls.[21]

Dukes, himself a successful playwright, identified this as evidence of indebtedness to Maugham: 'It is even more effective, from the standpoint of pure theatre, than the scene in *Our Betters* [i.e., the end of the second act], which it inevitably recalls. But the younger writer has greater depth. It is the sensitive interpretation of the spirit of youth that lends real force to *The Vortex*'. Coward had 'written something better than the Frenchman's well-made play because the quality of character – a moral quality, if you like – underlies the dramatic movement'.

In the short final act – James Agate, oddly enough, thought it too long – a crucial moment is Nicky's admission that he is addicted to cocaine. (As in the Act Two scene with Helen, the substance is not identified explicitly.) After Florence's line 'how could you possibly help me?' (*PP1*, 243/M1, 136) the 'complete' Notebook 41 version continues as follows:

> **Florence**   Don't be so cruel.
>
> **Nicky**   Cruel – I dont want to be cruel – it's the truth –
>
> **Florence** (*pulling herself together and rising*)   Nicky – listen – you go to bed ~~now~~ – we'll talk that all over to morrow.
>
> **Nicky**   No now – *now*!
>
> **Florence**   Nicky, – I implore you –

As they struggle for control of the scene, Nicky tries to make her see herself as she really is: 'I'm seeing for the first time how old you are – ~~youre an old woman~~ – it's horrible – horrible'. In the final version a long speech beginning 'Mother – don't go on like that' has been moved to follow Florence's claim that David 'knows nothing – he doesn't understand me any more than you do', Nicky's insistence that 'it's between us alone', and her 'I tell you I don't know what you're talking about' (*PP1*, 239/M1, 129). In the second of the exchanges drafted for the third act in Notebook 42 (8–9) but not present in the 'complete' manuscript, Nicky's revelation that he has become a cocaine addict is treated more obliquely than in the play as published. After a line subsequently moved earlier in the scene – Nicky's 'We're utterly rotten – both of us' (*PP1*, 239/M1, 132) – and a rapid exchange in which she tries to resist his insistence that she 'see things as they really are', he shows her a small box of cocaine:

> **Nicky**   Look mother – we lead awfully petty lives you and I – look
>
> **Florence** (*collapsing*)   What is it[?]
>
> **Nicky**   You know well enough
>
> **Florence**   Oh Nicky
>
> **Nicky**   Why do you look so shocked[?]
>
> **Florence** (*hopelessly*)   Oh Nicky –
>
> **Nicky**   I thought it might interest you – its really your fault –
>
> **Florence**   What can I say to you – what can I say to you –
>
> **Nicky**   Nothing – it would be ridiculous in the face of things
>
> ***Florence*** *suddenly seizes the box out of his hand and hurls it out of the window*

In the published version Nicky tells Florence he has a 'slight confession to make' and produces the 'small gold box'. She takes it '*with trembling fingers*', and opens it, then '*stares at it for a moment. When she speaks again her voice is quite dead*':

> **Florence**   Nicky, it isn't – you haven't –?
>
> **Nicky**   Why do you look so shocked?
>
> **Florence** (*dully*)   Oh, my God!
>
> **Nicky**   What does it matter? (**Florence** *suddenly rises and hurls the box out of the window*) That doesn't make it any better.
>
> *PP1*, 242–3/M1, 135

(In Notebook 41, after Florence's 'Oh, my God', and before she throws the box away, Nicky says 'We lead awfully petty lives – you and I'.)

So far as the third act is concerned, the grounds of Kate Cutler's objections may lie in the longer version of this revelation – if it was included in the rehearsal script – together with the original position of Nicky's speech beginning 'Mother, don't go on like that – it's useless'. In this hypothesis, Coward would have written the 'complete' script represented in Notebook 41, and then inserted the speeches from Notebook 42, which seem to have been drafted more roughly, to adjust the 'balance' of the scene. In *Present Indicative* he describes Cutler as objecting to his revisions in the final act, but added passages in the second act, notably dialogue between Nicky and Helen and Nicky and Bunty also increase the emphasis on his role, and it is possible that it was these, as much as the changes to the third act, that contributed to the dispute.

In the introduction to *Three Plays* (1925) Coward wrote that he was 'only just beginning to discover imperfections' in *The Vortex*, as it was 'comparatively new': 'strange as it may seem, they are not those which some of the critics pointed out'.[22] In the introduction to the first *Play Parade* (1934), he declared that his 'original motive was to write a good play with a whacking good part in it for myself', and he was 'thankful to say' that 'with a few modest reservations' he had succeeded (*PP1*, xi). Unfortunately, he did not give any further account of what these 'imperfections' and 'reservations' might be.

Fallen Angels (1923, produced 1925): Boulevard comedy, anglicized

Although *Hay Fever* and *Easy Virtue* were written in the autumn of 1924, the latter did not reach the stage until November 1925 (in the United States) and had its first British performances in Manchester and London in May and June 1926. It was preceded by *Fallen Angels*, written in 1923, and (as noted above) offered to managements at the same time as *The Vortex*. *Fallen Angels* differs from the other plays in the frank adoption – noticed by several critics – of elements of French boulevard comedy and its moral ambiguities. Although like several other plays submitted for licensing at the time, it aroused anxiety on account of its potentially incendiary depiction of immorality in the upper classes it was passed for performance on condition of some cutting, including the excision of such expressions as 'sex', 'illicit' and 'illegitimate'.[23]

As with *The Vortex*, Coward's development of the script can be documented from manuscripts in the archive.[24] It seems that, with his habitual generosity of spirit, Arnold Bennett had not been offended by the mimicry of him as the serious playwright Bruce Fairlight in the second act of *The Vortex*. On Tuesday 28 April he lunched with Coward who answered all his 'arguments in criticism of *Fallen Angels*. He said that he wrote it in five days, and *The Vortex* in four days (or three). When he once began, he worked straight through. He showed much intelligence'.[25] Unfortunately, his published *Journals* do not disclose the nature of Bennett's criticisms.

The first act's exposition is simple, establishing that Jane Banbury and Julia Sterroll, whose husbands are setting out for an overnight golfing trip, expect a visit from a Frenchman, Maurice Duclos, with whom they both had brief affairs before they married. He has sent each of them a postcard announcing that he will arrive in London 'this week' – it is now Saturday. It is established that for both of them a shared song, 'Même les anges succombent à l'amour', had been a significant element of their relationship: 'succombent' – 'yield' – is ironically appropriate to 'fallen' angels. At the end of the act, as they prepare to leave London to avoid him, they hear a loud knock and ring at the front door: 'Curtain'.

Early in the second act it is revealed that it was the plumber who had arrived at the end of Act One. It is now early evening, and the women have arranged to have dinner together, convinced that Maurice will turn up in the course of the evening and will find them 'quietly dining together in charming domestic surroundings'. They decide not to wait for him, and embark on their dinner, preceded by cocktails and accompanied by champagne and followed by liqueurs. What follows is effectively a long two-actor bravura scene with occasional brief appearances by the maid, Saunders, who serves the meal. (For a later production Coward filled out Saunders' role with comic business and additional lines, including an extended version of exchanges at the beginning of Act Three about a hair in the marmalade.)[26] After false alarms in the shape of a person mistaking their flat for that of another tenant, and a phone call that turns out to be wrong number, the women, who have drunk a good deal before, during and after the meal, quarrel bitterly. Jane flounces out, declaring (falsely, it turns out) that she knows where Maurice is staying and is going to meet him.

It is in the third act that Coward develops the play's farcical confusions. The next morning Willy arrives earlier than expected. He and Fred have quarrelled and he has returned to find Jane absent. Julia tells him about last night's drunken quarrel, and that Jane has gone off with a Frenchman who had been the lover of both of them. After Julia and Willy have left at his insistence in search of Jane, Saunders takes a telephone call from Maurice. Fred enters, and sends the maid to Jane's flat to find his wife, but Jane enters, much the worse for wear after her night alone in an hotel. Saunders now returns, and tells them that Julia has just left with 'a dark man'. Assuming this must be Maurice, Jane tells Fred about her quarrel with Julia, and its cause: their previous involvement with Maurice and the rush to be the first to find him. Fred is insisting that they must set out together to find the guilty couple, but Julia and Willy arrive. The women have decided to take a common stand against their indignant husbands, when Maurice is shown in. He kisses the hands of both women and asks to be introduced to their husbands. Seeing the situation at once, he explains that Julia and Jane had arranged the apparent betrayal to make their husbands understand that they were not being paid sufficient attention. Maurice turns out to have taken a flat upstairs, and he asks the two women to come upstairs to help him choose curtain material. They leave, and although Fred is more inclined to accept the explanation, Willy still thinks something 'very queer' has been going on and that Maurice was 'bluffing' them: 'The whole damned thing's true from beginning to end – I'm sure of it'. Fred is protesting that he cannot be serious, until Willy points out that the women have gone upstairs 'alone' to Maurice's flat, and they hear the strains of 'Même les anges succombent à l'amour' from above. In the published edition's final direction, as Maurice is heard singing the refrain, '*with great feeling*' – 'Je t'aime, – je t'aime – je t'aime' – Fred and Willy '*gaze at one another with stricken faces*', and the curtain falls. (PP2, 494/M1, 190–1)

In the manuscript the play's incidents and revelations are developed exactly as in the final version, with no major alterations, which suggests that Coward was working from a scene-by-scene outline of the kind he had prepared for *The Vortex*. Nevertheless, in addition to many incidental variants in individual speeches, the draft differs from the published text in four major scenes: the exchanges between Fred and Julia in Act One (*PP2*, 431–2/M1, 142–3); the quarrel between Julia and Jane in Act Two (*PP2*, 465–6/M1, 168–70); the Willy/Julia dialogue in Act Three; and the final moments of the play. The first page has a list of characters, a description of the setting, and a draft of the French song. Revising the opening stage direction, Coward was at pains to emphasize that nothing extraordinary should be expected to happen: 'The rest of the furniture can be left to the Producer's discrimination if he has any. At all costs the whole scene must give an impression of good taste and perfect married comfort'. (The final version lacks the reference to the room's decoration.) Coward insists that Julia should be 'dressed plainly and appropriately for an ordinary London day in which nothing particular may be expected to happen', and that there must not be the faintest suggestion of the usual elegant silks and satins so beloved by the theatrical dressmaker'. The manuscript's note that '**Fred** *is going to play golf and his clothes are naturally picturesque*' is later replaced with '**Fred** *is in golfing clothes*' (*PP2*, 329/ M1, 141).

The published text omits a passage early in Act One after Julia remarks that Fred has been 'rather taciturn and important this morning' (*PP2*, 243/M1, 142):

> **Fred** I'm only living up to being married – happily married – if you had any instincts at all you'd play up and make a fuss of me – and send me off to my golf in a good humour having managed me as only a true woman can manage a true man – not worry me with your tiresome presentiments.
>
> **Julia** I've already tried reading the paper aloud and offering you coffee.
>
> **Fred** (*suddenly kissing her lightly*) I think it's awfully silly of people to lead unhappy lives dont you?
>
> **Julia** (*with her arm round his neck*) I suppose so –
>
> **Fred** Are you happy?
>
> **Julia** Perfectly.
>
> **Fred** Sure?
>
> **Julia** Positive.

Fred Good.

Julia We shall both know the first minute we go off one another – because we analyse such a lot.

At this point, as in the published text, Fred says 'We've been married five years', and Julia's response, 'A divine five years', is followed by the argument about their current state and being 'in love', and 'violent passion' (*PP2*, 432/M1, 143). The omitted passage shows an easier, more physically relaxed and affectionate relationship between the couple. In a later exchange, after Fred accuses Julia and Jane of being 'psycho-analytical neurotics' and Julia's 'That sounds lovely, Fred', he and Julia seem able to tease one another:

Fred I'm exceedingly glad I'm playing golf today with Willy. We shall be in the open air and –

Julia Do you find the atmosphere of this house choking you?

Fred Yes

Julia Do you sometimes long for wide open spaces and the tang of salt water on your cheek [?]

Fred Frequently –

Julia (*twining her arms round him*) Do you writhe vainly in the effort to extricate yourself from the [slimy?] decadent embraces of your neurotic wife [?]

Fred Yes – yes (*he rises*)

She tells him that in his plus-fours he looks from behind like the famous clown Grock.

The manuscript continues with Fred's line 'Do you always discuss everything with Jane?' from which point it corresponds to the published text up to the arrival of Willy. Again, physical expressions of affection have been removed, while in his earlier incarnation Fred seems less stuffy in his responses.

The most important alteration in the second act is the addition in the *Play Parade* edition of a series of exchanges, beginning with Jane's 'I should like to shake you Julia, shake you and shake you and shake you until your eyes dropped out!' (*PP2*, 468/M1, 168).

This follows Julia's drawing herself up and becoming 'the outraged hostess', and her 'disdainful' response to Jane asking where her shoes are: 'I really don't know – they can't have gone far'. The new lines suggest an underlying tension between the two women that informs their uneasy truce over the claim on Maurice's affections:

> **Jane**   Yes, when you're superior and grand like that you rouse the worst in me.
>
> **Julia**   Obviously.
>
> **Jane**   You make me feel like a French Revolution virago. I'd like to rush up and down Bond Street with your head on a pole!
>
> **Julia**   You'd better pull yourself together and I'll ask Saunders to help you up to your flat.
>
> **Jane**   If she comes near me I'll throttle her.
>
> **Julia**   I've never seen you so violent before – it's very interesting psychologically.
>
> *PP2*, 468/M1, 170–1

The quarrel continues with Jane pursuing the 'psychological' line of thought: 'I must have realised subconsciously all the time that you were going to turn out false and beastly'.

In the manuscript of Act Three, when Julia is trying to explain Jane's absence to Willy, she tells him in plain terms that his wife has left him. Exasperated by Willy's 'smug complacency' and his belief that 'no woman could ever bear to leave [him]', she insists that she has done just that, and has gone out 'to look for him'. After this, Willy seems even more obtuse when, as in the published play, he says 'I'm trying hard to understand' and insists that 'there's something awfully silly behind this – it doesn't seem to ring true' (*PP2*, 476/M1, 176–7). There is indeed 'something awfully silly' in the situation, but it is the farcical comedy of the wives' complicated situation rather than their readiness to elope with Maurice. Willy's refusal to accept this, even as a possibility, has been sufficiently established without the extra beat in the manuscript's version: there will be enough bafflement to go round in the plot's resolution. In his adjustment of details in the manuscript's final act, Coward is particularly attentive to such matters of timing and rhythm, but the final moments have not yet been achieved. The curtain falls on this point of suspension, with Fred less sceptical than Willy about the story of the innocent stratagem, and the play ends with Willy's line: 'I've never seen Jane hysterical like that before – she must have been upset over something'. As a 'tag line' this is not very impressive: Coward had yet to find the final version's more effective conclusion.

Hay Fever, 1924 (produced 1925): Symmetry and comic re-coupling

In *The Vortex*, Coward had shifted the temper of the play from the social comedy of the opening scene to absolute seriousness, addressing Nicky's predicament and the decadence of his mother's circle and culminating in a final scene that may or may not hold promise for the future. This kind of 'serious' treatment involved the distancing of both playwright and protagonist from the superficiality (or 'flippancy') of the play's comic characters. The careful crafting of the 'scenes' that have to be made or avoided had taken it a stage further than his previous variations on the theme. *Hay Fever*, equally precisely crafted, turns for comic effect on the blithe inability of its principal characters, male and female, to take matters seriously. Both here and in *Fallen Angels* Coward deploys strategies associated with farce, but *Hay Fever* is more sophisticated. The by now familiar – possibly already over-familiar – generational issues figure in unequivocally comic form, with parents as 'artistic' as their children, and the play parodies situations that would conventionally precipitate serious 'scenes'.

Coward remembered that *Hay Fever*, billed simply as 'a new comedy', had been 'written and conceived in three days'.[27] It marks a further departure in his craft as a playwright, as the first of his comedies of re-coupling, structured round the interchangeability of partners. It also has a greater degree of theatrical self-consciousness than his earlier work. A pattern of misunderstandings derives from failures on the part of their house guests to perceive the play-acting of the Bliss family rather than from the usual accidents of popular farce. Characters are paired off in couples that are then rearranged, only to be dismissed altogether in the final act. What follows is a series of misunderstandings in which situations that seem like sexual intrigue bewilder the outsiders, each invited by one of the family without the others' knowledge. Judith has invited Sandy Tyrell, a 'fresh-looking man' with 'an unspoilt, youthful sense of honour and rather big hands, owing to a misplaced enthusiasm for amateur boxing', whose adulation she relishes; Sorel has invited Richard Greatham, a 'diplomatist' she has recently met; Simon's guest is Myra Arundel, a sophisticate who (as Judith remarks), is 'far too old' for him and 'goes about using Sex as a sort of shrimping net'; and David Bliss, as part of the research for his latest novel, *The Sinful Woman*, has invited Jackie Coryton, a 'flapper' described by Coward as 'small and shingled' – that is, with fashionably short, waved hair – with 'an ingenuous manner which will lose its charm as she grows older' (*PP1*, 287/M1, 25).

By the end of the second act there seems to have been a general redistribution. Sandy has been paired with Sorel, Richard with Judith, Myra with David and Jackie with Simon. But what does that 'with' mean? Behind the comedy is the ghost of a more serious drama in which these revised pairings would be 'real'. Simon and Sorel make clear to (respectively) Jackie and Sandy that they were only flirting, but it is not clear how the Richard/Judith and Myra/David pairings might have played out. The shifts into parody and Judith's inveterate play-acting prevent any development, but in the last pages of the second act the shift into performance is not so clearly defined. In any case, the interruptions have been decisive: The opening of the third act makes it clear that all the guests spent the night in their allotted bedrooms. The play's structure of temporarily redistributed couples does not call for the kind of resolution required even in Coward's earlier plays where the 'well-made' formulas were adjusted and challenged, let alone in hackneyed melodramas like Judith's great vehicle, *Love's Whirlwind*.

The opening minutes introduce Sorel and Simon, whose combination of artistic pursuits and casualness recalls the younger generation of *I'll Leave It to You*. Sorel, more given to reflection than her brother, explains to him that they can never keep servants – except for Judith's dresser Clara – because they are 'slap-dash' and 'awfully bad-mannered'. The people they like put up with this 'because they like *us*', and the lack of manners consists not so much in (as Simon suggests) their 'lack of social tricks and small-talk', as in a failure to look after their guests. Using a word more commonly applied in the 1920s to sexual rather than merely social aberration,

Sorel insists that they are 'abnormal': 'People stare in astonishment when we say what we consider perfectly ordinary things'. Simon is dismissive: 'we see things differently, I suppose, and if people don't like it they must lump it' (*PP1*, 254–5/M1, 7). Sorel later explains to one of the guests that she and her brother are 'devastatingly lacking in restraint' because their parents are 'so vague – they've spent their lives cultivating their Arts and not devoting any time to ordinary conventions and manners and things. I'm the only one who sees that, so I'm trying to be better' (*PP1*, 284/M1, 29–30). The stage is prepared for the entrance of Judith Bliss, who has been in the garden learning the names of flowers as part of her performance as the mistress of a country house. Her readiness to move into a scene from *Love's Whirlwind* will in due course mystify those who do not understand that, as Sorel later explains, 'One always plays up to Mother in this house; it's a sort of unwritten law' (*PP1*, 307/M1, 47). In Coward's earlier plays, the upholders of conventional values are misguided at best and, most likely, consciously or unconsciously hypocritical. Here, the guests are unprepared for a whole household pervaded by performance.

Sandy, Richard and Myra have their own standards, nurtured by experience of their particular sphere, while Jackie is totally out of her depth, a factor used to great comic effect in the game played at the beginning of the second act. This is a version of 'clumps' (also known as 'adverbs'), in which one person leaves the room while the rest of the company decide on an adverb: when she or he returns, they ask each of the others to perform an action in the manner of the word. Judith is in her element with this kind of performance (she even gives notes, like a director). After the game descends into confusion, the act now proceeds to a series of encounters between Judith and Richard, Sandy and Sorel (in the library), and David and Myra. When Richard misreads the signals and assumes he is beginning a flirtation with Judith and kisses her, she skips a few pages ahead in the play she is performing in her mind and tells him they must tell David about their affair. He is to wait in the summer house:

> *She pushes him into the garden and waves to him bravely with her handkerchief; then she comes back into the room and powders her nose before the glass and pats her hair into place. Then, assuming an expression of restrained tragedy, she opens*

the library door, screams and recoils genuinely shocked to C[entre.

PP1, 304/M1, 44–5

Sandy and Sorel emerge from the library, and Judith performs what Sorel describes as her 'renunciation scene'.

Sandy (*moving down* R.)   I feel a fearful cad.

Judith   Why should you? You've answered the only call that really counts – the call of Love, and Romance, and Spring. I forgive you, Sandy, completely. There!

She goes to him and pats his shoulder.

Sorel   Well, that's all right then

She sits on the sofa.

Judith   I resent your tone, Sorel; you seem to be taking things too much for granted. Perhaps you don't realize that I am making a great sacrifice (*pointing to* **Sandy**).

Sorel   Sorry, darling.

Judith (*starting to act*)   It's far from easy, at my time of life, to –

Sorel (*playing up*)   Mother – Mother, say you understand and forgive!

PP1, 306/M1, 46

After a display of magnanimity, Judith makes a slow and pathetic exit up the staircase. Sorel explains to Sandy that he kissed her because he was 'awfully nice' and she was 'awfully nice and we both liked kissing very much. It was inevitable. Then Mother found us and got dramatic – her sense of theatre is always fatal'. Sandy does not know the code by which kissing may not be serious, let alone the signs that Judith is transforming everything into the terms of an old-fashioned theatrical tradition.

In the later 'scene' where Judith discovers David kissing Myra, it is not easy for the uninitiated to recognize the moment when fact – allowing for Judith's propensity for 'theatrics' – turns into the much-rehearsed fiction of *Love's Whirlwind*. David insists that

'There isn't any real necessity for a scene' (*PP1*, 315/M1, 52) but it soon develops into another full-scale melodramatic episode, leaving Myra bewildered and indignant. Simon comes in and announces to Jackie's dismay that they are engaged to be married, prompting Judith to cry 'picturesquely' that all her 'little chicks' are leaving the nest. This is too much for Myra:

> You're the most maddening set of hypocrites I've ever seen. This house is a complete feather-bed of false emotions – you're posing, self-centred egotists, and I'm sick to death of you . . . Don't speak to me – I've been working up for this, only every time I opened my mouth I've been mowed down by theatrical effects.
>
> PP1, 319/M1, 56

When Richard enters from the garden to find them all speaking at once and asks what has happened – 'Is this a game?' –

> **Judith's** *face gives a slight twitch; then, with a meaning look at* **Sorel** *and* **Simon**, *she answers him.*
>
> **Judith**   Yes, and a game that must be played to the finish!
>
> *She flings back her arm and knocks* **Richard** *upstage.*

Recognizing 'Dear old *Love's Whirlwind*', Simon and Sorel join in a full-blown rendition of a climactic scene, ending with Sorel (now in a male role) about to strike Simon with 'You cur!' and Judith preventing her by exclaiming 'Don't strike! He is your father!!!' After this approximate quotation from the second act of Wilde's *A Woman of No Importance*, she '*totters and falls in a dead faint*'. As the curtain falls, Myra, Jackie, Richard and Sandy '*look on, dazed and aghast*'. In a prompt copy for the 1933 revival, directed by Coward, Judith (now played by Constance Collier) pulls Richard into the performance rather than pushing him out of the way, and it is him rather than Simon whom Sorel is about to strike. In the revised final direction,

> **Judith** *dramatically falls into the amazed* **Richard's** *arms – he totters to his knees dropping* **Judith** *on the floor. The family applaud vigorously while* **Judith** *still on the floor takes her call.*
>
> **Curtain**'.[28]

The third act's comedy lies in the guests' dismay as they meet over breakfast, and their agreement to leave without any further contact with the family absorbed in David's reading of his new novel as their guests '*creep downstairs with their bags, unperceived by the family*' and '*make for the front door*' (*PP1*, 338/*M1*, 70). At the height of an argument about the geography of Paris, '*the universal pandemonium is suddenly broken by the front door slamming. There is dead silence for a moment, then the noise of a car is heard*'. Sorel reports that they have all gone, and the comedy of bad manners ends with the family's response to this breach of etiquette:

Judith (*sitting down*)   How very rude!

David (*also sitting down*)   People really do behave in the most extraordinary manner these days –

Judith   Come back and finish your breakfast, Sorel.

Sorel   All right.

She sits down.

Judith   Go on, David darling: I'm dying to hear the end –

David (*picks up the MS from the floor – reading*)   'Jane Sefton, in her scarlet Hispano, swept out of the Rue St. Honoré into the Place de la Concorde –'

Curtain

Here, as with the end of Act Two, for the 1933 revival Coward revised the script. After David's insistence on his version of the street map of Paris, Judith looks up, but Sorel, who has her head on his shoulder '*signs to her to let it pass*'.

Judith   Very well, darling (*puts her head on his shoulder*)

David   The blossoms trembled in the high chestnut trees, intermingling their subtle perfumes, which ~~were~~ was spring –

Judith   What was spring?

Curtain

The new versions of both act endings give the curtain line to Constance Collier as Judith, but also present an effective (and triumphant) picture of a family blissfully united in their own 'artistic' world.

Easy Virtue and *Semi-Monde*, 1924: A woman with a past and the international set

Easy Virtue, one of Coward's closest approaches to the fully-fledged well-made play, was written in what he recalled as 'a mood of nostalgic regret' for the outmoded but dramatically productive social values of 'woman-with-past' plays like Pinero's *The Second Mrs Tanqueray* (1895). The effect was not lost on the critics. The *Spectator*, under the headline 'Mrs. Tanqueray's New Clothes', wondered how the heroine 'could fall into the old nineteenth century trap' of seeking to mend her ways by marrying a blameless young man, but admired the skill with which, 'by means of "frightfully" up-to-date dialogue' he had 'managed to conceal his resort to "old fashioned ways."'[29] After making some preliminary notes, including a synopsis of the first act and part of the second, Coward completed a full script between 20 July and 1 August 1924.[30]

John Whittaker, an ingenuous, clean-living young man who has been pursuing a conventional career in India, was expected to marry Sarah, the eminently 'suitable' daughter of a neighbouring family. When the play opens the family is awaiting his arrival with his newly-married wife. Larita (her exotic name in itself enough to provoke anxiety) is a divorced woman he has met in what the *Times* reviewer described as 'one of those French watering-places whence feminine disaster is for ever marching in its emeralds against the stately homes of England'.[31] As a sophisticated woman of the world, Larita is not interested in the healthy outdoor activities or charitable works that engage the women of the family. Rather than watch or play tennis she prefers to stay indoors and read Proust's *Sodom and Gomorrah*. (Published in C.K. Scott Moncrieff's English translation in 1927, this includes the first explicit references to homosexuality in *À la recherche du temps perdu*.) Mrs. Whittaker devotes her energies to supervising the morals of the village. Her elder daughter, Marion, after suffering from the vagaries of an inconstant suitor (now in temporary exile), has adopted a cheery, determinedly Christian approach to life, and has her own way of interfering with the lives of others, usually with a 'straight talk'. The father, Colonel Whittaker, is a man of the world with a record of infidelity that partly accounts for his wife's neurotic obsession with moral turpitude in the village. He does not share her prejudices or those of his elder daughter, and (as Larita explains in Act Two) has 'not allowed himself to be cluttered up with hypocritical moral codes and false sentiments', but 'sees things as they are, and has tried to make the best of them' (PP2, 579/M1, 256). At the end of the first act, Charles Burleigh, who is staying with Susan's family, establishes that he and Larita have friends in common in the Continental set she has forsaken to marry John.

In the second act Larita tries to convince John, with whom she realizes she has little in common, that their marriage was not a good idea, and that her past life will inevitably become known. He refuses to listen: 'I don't want to find out anything.' (PP2, 562/M1, 242). The play's major crisis is provoked by Hilda, the younger of the Whittaker daughters, who has grown envious of Larita and unearths a press cutting revealing her involvement in a relationship that led to a man's suicide. Larita's unsuitability as a daughter-in-law is confirmed, and Mrs Whittaker attempts to banish her to her room, telling the guests at the family's annual dance that she is indisposed. The act ends ambiguously: Larita tries to settle down in her fur cape to reading Proust but, '*acutely conscious of an imperfect statuette of the Venus de Milo which is smirking at her from a pedestal by the drawing-room doors*', she '*hurls the book at it, knocking it to the floor and smashing it*', exclaiming 'I've always hated that damned thing!' The curtain falls but, '*when it rises once, she has buried her face in the sofa cushion and her shoulders are heaving, whether with laughter or tears it is difficult to say*' (PP2, 585/M1, 260). In the final act, to teach the family a lesson, Larita makes a spectacular entrance decked out as the sophisticated and 'painted' hussy they have supposed her to be. She is giving them a 'scene' of the kind they had not bargained for, after what James Agate described as 'two scenes of gathering exasperation and subsequent explosion' in the second act.[32] In the final moments of the play, she wraps herself in her fur cape and departs for London.

In the course of composition, as well as some verbal alterations and corrections, Coward made a few changes in the scenes between Charles Burleigh and Larita, and minor adjustments in the reactions to Larita's entrance in the final act. As corrected, the manuscript corresponds in all but a few details to the published version. The play's organization is clear: exposition establishing the family and their attitudes; the arrival of the son and his wife; encounters evincing her lack of sympathy with her new mother- and sisters-in-law; a crisis precipitated by revelations of her past; further confrontations and frank talk, with Larita in control; and Larita's escape. Two important ingredients that assert the family's isolation in the modern world are the sympathetic good sense of Sarah, the childhood friend who was expected (but not by her, it seems) to be John's 'intended', and the presence of Charles as a representative of sophisticated society. Susan represents a kind of 'modern' open-mindedness, in which Larita's way of life is understood and tolerated without necessarily being shared. In Act Three Charles makes her a tentative offer of marriage, which she rebuffs without indignation, telling him pleasure in each other's company would soon be killed by marriage, unless there were a 'vital spark to keep it going':

Charles Dear, dear. The way you modern girls talk – it's shocking, that's what it is!

Sarah Never mind, Charles dear, you must move with the times.

Charles I didn't know you thought so highly of the vital spark, anyhow.

Sarah Of course I do. It's a fundamental instinct in everybody. Being modern only means twisting things into different shapes.

PP2, 591/M1, 265

Sarah, the clear-sighted and sympathetic childhood friend, would have been wasted on the weak-willed John, who fails to understand why Larita cannot embrace the life of his family, and she and Charles accept that their respective worlds are mutually exclusive.

'Modernity', the 'twisting of things into different shapes', and the world inhabited by Charles and Larita are addressed in *Semi-Monde*, written in 1924. Like *Easy Virtue*, it is not identified as belonging to a specific genre. This is one of Coward's most meticulously planned plays, with its multiple plots deployed over three acts of three scenes each, from January 1924 to June 1925. Although each act takes place within one year, the gaps between scenes vary in length: 'a few days' elapse between the first two scenes of Act One, set in January 1924, with the third taking place in March; the three scenes of Act Two are set in January, February and March respectively; and after the first two scenes of Act Three (January) there is a lapse of some six months, so that the final scene takes place in June. The manuscript of the complete play, corresponding in all but a handful of details to that published in Volume 9 of the Methuen edition, is accompanied by a detailed breakdown of the play's action and chronologically arranged 'stories' for each of the main characters.[33] Although Coward had the public rooms – bar, lounge, men's bar – of the Ritz in mind when the wrote, the Paris hotel's name was removed from the manuscript and the identity of the adjoining streets was carefully revised. The presence of a manuscript 'preface', a polemic against the censorship regime and the repressive attitudes it supports, suggests that Coward was preparing the play for publication. First impressions of the play, with its openly gay and lesbian characters, may have tended to confirm John Lahr's description of it as a series of 'sexually mischievous *tableaux vivants*', in which Coward's 'camp sensibility has a field day'. This may reflect the souped-up decadence of the 1977 Glasgow Citizens Theatre production, which introduced elements of camp excess not indicated in the manuscript, with 'rival schools of butch lesbians and screaming, highly strung young men [who] hit each other with handbags and jumped on tables'.[34] Nevertheless, focusing on this undeniably significant aspect tends to obscure the sophistication of the play's narrative. The multiple plots unfold in a public milieu, with 'extras' coming and going in the background, drinks and meals being served, and the normal business of a hotel taking its course. The episodic structure offers freedom from the need to establish milieu and exposition in the usual manner. Apart from the question of its gay and lesbian characters, the number of speaking parts militated against *Semi-Monde* as a proposition for the commercial or even private theatres in Britain, and plans for a production in Germany were frustrated by the appearance of Vicki Baum's novel *Grand Hotel* (1929) and the 1932 Hollywood film based on it.[35]

There are two sets of interrelated story lines, in both of which couples change places. One set features the play's gay, lesbian and bisexual characters, but begins with a newly-married young couple, Owen and Tanis, who in due course become bored with each other. She has an affair with Jerome, an older man and a successful author (in the first outline, he is a painter); and by the end of Act Two, Owen has begun an affair with Norma, Jerome's daughter. A classic 'obligatory scene' takes place, in which Tanis tries to prevent Jerome from making a declaration that would not have been out of place in a turn-of-the-century drama: 'Why, it's true isn't it? – I'm your lover – Owen is Norma's lover. Owen's your husband – Norma's my daughter – there's real life for you – love – romance – beauty – happy ever after.' (M6, 84). This conventionally heterosexual plot line merges with that concerning Cyril Hardacre, a young man first encountered in Act One as the lover of an older man, Beverley Ford, who is introducing him to the cosmopolitan gay world. Cyril grows disenchanted with him, and has an affair with Inez, a lesbian whose lover, Cynthia, leaves her for another woman, Elise. Thus, by the end of Act Two, both Cyril and Inez have been confirmed as bisexual, but six months later, in January 1926, Inez finds love with a new arrival, Violet Emery, and in the play's final moments it is confirmed that Cyril has followed his heterosexual inclinations, and is married to Norma. Beverley meanwhile has transferred his affections to an American musical comedy star, Luke, who has arrived in the first scene of Act Three with a group of ostentatiously camp men characterized in Coward's outline as the 'queens'. This group of narratives establishes the fluidity not only of sexual relationships, but also of sexual identity itself.

A second strand of the plot follows the careers of Dorothy Price, described in the outline as a 'fully-fledged courtesan', and Beryl Fletcher, 'young, rather over-smart and extremely lovely', who arrives in the first scene with her parents. Dorothy, the mistress of a middle-aged businessman, Mike Craven, has been providing funds to a Russian émigré, Julius Levenovitch. In the first scene of Act Three, Mike bursts into the bar and shoots him. In the final scene, Beryl, having followed Dorothy's example, is being kept by a millionaire, Edgar Darrell, but is playing off two other suitors against one another. Much as Beryl, in the play's first scene, had admired Dorothy's bangles, Phyllis Hancox, yet another newly arrived American ingénue, is impressed by Beryl's pearls.

Although Coward manages all these characters and their affairs adroitly, the cumulative effect is an embarrassment of riches, as though the material for several short stories had been combined. The only evidence of uncertainty in the manuscript occurs in the scene where Jerome declares himself as the lover of Owen's wife, where Coward added the seven exchanges beginning with Owen's 'You don't mean'. Before 'It's all quite natural really', Jerome explains: 'I feel terribly wise and ashamed just for a moment – it won't last, nothing lasts for ever – I shall creep back into the moral refuges of codes and pretences – utter futility.' (MS, facing p. 12; M6, 83). This is the point where Jerome speaks like an observer of hotel life, who sees the situation ironically in terms of conventional fiction:

> There's nothing to be done, you know – nothing at all. We might of course start our lives all over again – that would be interesting – or we might rush into convents and monasteries and repent in religious fashion – hasn't anyone a suggestion to make – I don't want to monopolise the conversation.
>
> M6, 84

As professional singers, Cyril and Inez share the artists' similarly detached perspective on their various affairs, but Jerome is the play's only author, a *raisonneur* in the manner of Maugham's plays and fiction who for once has become entangled in the stories he witnesses. As for Beverley's gay acquaintance Albert, whom Cyril meets when they arrive, and the group of 'queens' who arrive subsequently, their openly camp behaviour is of a kind Coward found distasteful. As Cyril walks ahead of them, Albert asks Beverley 'My dear – where did you find *that*? It's *divine*.' (M6,10: emphases marked only in the manuscript). The lesbian characters are not notable for any affectations: Coward simply presents them as elegant and, in the case of Inez, possessive. His disapproval is reserved for Dorothy and her fellow 'courtesans' and the men on whom they batten.

In many respects, *Semi-Monde* offers an intensely moral view of the kind of 'immoral' world associated with Larita in *Easy Virtue*. Its construction is also 'well-made' in the counterpointing of story-lines. Nevertheless, Coward did not experiment further with this kind of complex plotting. His next West End successes, *Private*

Lives, was radically concise, while the extravagantly 'epic' *Cavalcade* would develop a traditionally linear narrative of the intersecting lives of three groups of characters. (*Post-Mortem*, with its more radical approach to narrative, would remain unproduced.) Although he was habitually associated with the milieu that critics were calling 'cocktail society', as the new decade began it would still be difficult to define a 'typical' Noël Coward play.

2

The 1930s: Old and new designs for living

> **Otto** I read about the play in the train. It's a riot, isn't it?
>
> **Gilda** Capacity – every performance.
>
> **Otto** Is it good?
>
> **Gilda** Yes, I think so.
>
> **Otto** Only think so?
>
> **Gilda** Three scenes are first-rate, especially the last act. The beginning of the second act drags a bit, and most of the first act's too facile – you know what I mean – he flips along with easy swift dialogue, but doesn't go deep enough. It's all very well played.
>
> *Design for Living*, Act Two, Scene Two: *PP1*, 392–3/M3, 52–3

The first scene of the second act of *Design for Living* (1935) had begun with Gilda and Leo reading reviews of his play *Change and Decay*, including a verdict in the *Daily Mirror* of the kind Coward had come to expect: the play is 'gripping throughout', and 'the dialogue is polished and sustains a high level from first to last and is frequently witty, nay even brilliant', but 'on the whole' the play is 'decidedly thin'. (*PP1*, 374–5/M3, 4–5) The metatheatrical moment has been incorporated more subtly than Sheila Keld's observations on her husband's work in *The Rat-Trap*, quoted in Chapter One, and in the second scene, Gilda's account of the play to Otto, which seems to share the paper's view, has now become a reflection on Leo himself. Theatrical self-consciousness has moved onto a new level, as an integral part of characterization and the shared sensibility of a group of outsiders. They are 'abnormal' in the sense of Sorel Bliss's use of the adjective, but closer to the commonplace view of those whose sexual, as well as social, lives are outside convention.

By *Easy Virtue*, it might have seemed to Coward that he had exhausted the potential of the 'bitter generation conflict' and 'woman with a past' for shaping the action of a play, even though he would return to the latter in *Operette* (1938) and *Pacific 1860* (1946–7). Nevertheless, although they do not provide the motive power of the plots, generational differences are present in *Bitter-Sweet* (with its doubly romantic flashback from 1890s London to 1870s Vienna) and in a chronicle context in *Cavalcade* (1931) and *This Happy Breed* (1939). The related 'misalliance' theme returns incidentally in *Cavalcade* and in *Pacific 1860* and *Relative Values*. In *Private Lives* and *Design for Living* the central characters all have a 'past' and have left anxieties about an older generation far behind them. Coupling and recoupling govern their lives and the structure of the plays. In both – as later in *Present Laughter* – the presence of separate off-stage bedrooms kept them the windy side of the censors' law. The sense of a revision of the farce genre, in which the characters are now aware of themselves as performing roles, is taken a stage further than in *Hay Fever*. In 1958, when he was struggling to adapt Feydeau's *Occupe-toi d'Amélie* (as *Look After Lulu*), Coward declared 'Personally I loathe farce anyway'.[1] Nevertheless, the genre's patterns of comic deception and suspense proved effective for sophisticated plays that celebrate the fluidity of sexual and emotional alliances, the re-coupling shadowed in *Hay Fever*.

Private Lives, 1929–30: Farce on the 'high comedy plane'

The account of *Private Lives* in *Present Indicative* (1937) is one of Coward's most detailed descriptions of the genesis of a play, and his report of an exchange of telegrams with Gertrude Lawrence is a memorable example of an occasion when brevity was the soul of his wit. The romantic nature of his moment of inspiration is reflected in a play where (as Faye Hamill observes) 'sophistication proves unexpectedly compatible with sentiment and romance'.[2] Although in this case evidence from early drafts is not available, an unpublished letter to Gertrude Lawrence gives a remarkable insight into Coward's conception of the 'shrewd and witty comedy' and the kind of performance it called for.

In November 1929 Coward left New York, where *Bitter Sweet* had been produced successfully, to begin a journey to the Far East. Lawrence had given him 'a little gold book from Cartier's which when opened and placed on the writing-table in my cabin disclosed a clock, calendar and thermometer on one side, and an extremely pensive photograph on the other'. It 'served as a delicate reminder' that he had promised to write a play for them both, but he was not able to find 'some inspiring echo, some slight thread of plot that might suitably unite us in either, comedy, tragedy or sentiment'. Waiting at the Imperial Hotel in Tokyo to be joined by his travelling companion, Jeffrey Amherst, he was suddenly struck with the sought-for inspiration: 'the moment I switched out the lights, Gertie appeared in a white Molyneux dress on a terrace in the South of France, and refused to go again until four a.m., by which time *Private Lives*, title and all, had constructed itself'. In 1923 he might have written and typed it within a few days, but since then he 'had learned the wisdom of not welcoming a new idea too ardently'. He 'forced it into the back of [his] mind, trusting to its own integrity to emerge again later on, when it had become sufficiently set and matured'.[3] Later, as he convalesced in Shanghai from a bout of influenza, he returned to it:

> The idea by now seemed ripe enough to have a shot at it, so I started it, propped up in bed with a writing-block and an Eversharp pencil, and completed it, roughly, in four days. It came easily and with the exception of a few of the usual 'blood and tears' moments, I enjoyed writing it. I thought it a shrewd and witty comedy, well constructed on the whole, but psychologically unstable; however, its entertainment value seemed obvious enough, and its acting opportunities for Gertie and me admirable, so I cabled to her immediately in New York telling her to keep herself free for the autumn, and put the whole thing aside for a few weeks before typing and revising it.[4]

After a week in Hong Kong, most of which was spent 'typing and revising the play', on 7 January 1930 he sent copies to Lawrence and John C. Wilson (Coward's business partner in the United States), asking them to cable him in Singapore to tell him what they thought about it.[5]

The letter that accompanied Lawrence's copy reflects his sense that *Private Lives* was a challenging proposition for them both. She should 'read it slowly' as though she were playing it, because 'it will sound awfully scrappy read quickly, owing to the shortness of most of the sentences'. Not only does the letter reflect Coward's sense of the demands of the dialogue, it also confirms the strong erotic intention of the protracted physical struggle that forms the climax of the second act.

> I've worked very hard on it, and I think it is good, but God knows it's going to be hard to play. The situation is obviously farcical, and our difficulty will be to keep it on the high comedy plane. I'm sure this is necessary, and we shall have to watch one another like lynxes to see that we don't overdo it. In order to sustain it, we shall have to use every subtlty [*sic*] and change of mood we are capable of, and the only place we can really let go and enjoy ourselves will be the big quarrel at the end of the [second] act. I do think that will be fun, although probably slightly painful! I'm all for being really abandoned in the love scenes, and doing a few things that will give the old ladies a treat at matinees! Copulation has been the basis of the dear old British Drama for so long, we might just as well salute it. As far as the music is concerned, I've tried not to be too serious about it. I shall write a sort of theme song, the one that brings us together in Act One, and for the rest, I think we might do any of the popular old songs that we feel like singing, changing every now and again when we get tired of them.
>
> I am terribly anxious to keep the performance on such a level, that however lightly we may be playing, we can always switch to complete seriousness without too much of a jerk. But of course we can fix all that when we're working on it.

There were suggestions regarding their respective financial stakes in the production, the assurance that Edward Molyneux would create her first-act gown, and playful suggestions about her shoes and stockings and dressing room arrangements. He ended with an invitation to be frank in her response: 'I seem to be taking it rather for granted in this letter, that you are going to be delighted with the play! Perhaps you'll simply hate it, if so, send me a tactful subtle cable saying 'Think Play Bloody terrible' or something like that, and I shall understand'.[6]

Between 9 and 18 March, Lawrence strove to extricate herself from a contractual commitment that would keep her in New York and another to André Charlot for a revue in London.[7] In an undated cable from Palm Beach, Wilson acknowledged receipt of the script: 'ADORE PLAY MARVELOUS PARTS AND BRILLIANT DIALOGUE'. He would see Lawrence when he arrived in New York ('RETURNING NEW YORK NINETEENTH'.) A cable from Lawrence was received on 25 March in Hong Kong: 'HELLO DUCKIE READ PLAY TWICE AND ADORE. NOTHING WRONG THAT CAN'T BE FIXED AFTER THAT ALL DEPENDS ON ACTORS WOULD BE GREAT ADVENTURE'. She was 'SAILING TO LONDON APRIL THE THIRTEENTH TO OPEN NEW THEATRE FOR [ANDRÉ] CHARLOT'.[8] In *Present Indicative*, Coward remembered this message as being received in Singapore at the beginning of 'a tremendous telegraphic bickering': 'She had cabled me [. . .], rather casually I thought, saying that she had read *Private Lives* and that there was nothing wrong in it that couldn't be fixed. I had wired back that the only thing that was going to be fixed was her performance'.[9] Wilson reported, probably on 26 March, that she was 'hedging a little' and suggested Ina Claire as a possible substitute, and on 27 March Coward cabled him from Singapore, asking for Lawrence's cable address. Another undated cable from Wilson broached the problem of the contract that would preclude her appearing in *Private Lives* until 1931: 'GERTIE LIKES PLAY BUT NOT LAST ACT HOWEVER SHE WANTS TO DO IT BUT WANTS TO OPEN WITH CHARLOT LONDON MAY AND FEARS CONFLICT SUGGESTS OPENING PLAY FOLLOWING SPRING FRANKLY AM BEING SUPER AMIABLE AND SUBTLE BUT PRIVATELY ANNOYED HER ADDRESS MAJESTIC THEATRE'.

It was presumably on 27 or 28 March, after receiving her address from Wilson, that Coward sent the cable paraphrased in *Present Indicative* as 'The only thing that was going to be fixed was her performance'.[10] In the following weeks there was further discussion of the contractual problem, with Lawrence airing the suggestion that Coward might appear in the Charlot revue, and (as Wilson reported)

'NOW WILLING FORGO CHARLOT BUT TALKS OF GOING AWAY WITH YOU FOR TWO MONTHS TO WORK OVER PLAY MEANING PRESUMABLY REWRITE SOME NERVE'. Coward cabled to Wilson: 'CONSIDER FATAL MISTAKE GERTIE APPEAR LONDON BEFORE MY PLAY HAVE CABLED GERTIE EVASIVELY. WILL NATURALLY WAIT OCTOBER FOR HER IF ALL ELSE FAILS BUT DON'T TELL HER UNLESS CHARLOT REALLY ADAMANT'. On 8 May, Charlot sent Coward copies of the cables between him and Lawrence, as evidence of her contractual obligation. On 21 May, C.B. Cochran wrote to Coward, acknowledging receipt of a 'terrific' play. Lawrence negotiated her release from the contract with Charlot, whose revue, *Charlot's Masquerade*, now starring Beatrice Lillie, opened London's new Cambridge Theatre on 4 September. *Private Lives*, financed (as Coward had suggested in his letter to Lawrence) jointly by Cochran and the two stars with each putting up £1,000, was the first production at the Phoenix Theatre – also newly built – on 24 September. Cochran recalled that in fact they 'paid off all expenses and made a profit during the preliminary canter out of town, and the capital was really superfluous. It could have been produced on the proverbial "shoe-string"'.[11]

Private Lives is streamlined, constructed with elegant symmetry and limited to two couples, plus a servant in Act Three. Christopher Innes reads these limitations as an affirmation that 'society has no hold on the individual'.[12] (They also help to make it a good financial proposition for producers.) In the first act, two sets of alternating scenes between the couples, who occupy balconies of adjacent suites in their hotel, frame the inevitable encounter between Coward as Elyot Chase and Lawrence as Amanda, formerly 'Chase' and now 'Prynne'. Their newly-acquired second partners embody the 'normal' social and amatory attitudes that Elyot and Amanda refuse on principle to take seriously. They are a *couple* with a past, members of a younger generation that has matured: divorced five years ago, they would have married in 1924 or 1925, and would be the same age as Coward (born 1900) and Lawrence (born 1898). All four characters have no visible means of material support, but are evidently wealthy. The act can be divided into 'scenes' in the manner of Coward's preliminary plans for *The Vortex* and other plays:

1. Sybil and Elyot
2. Amanda and Victor

3. Elyot and Amanda
4. Sybil and Elyot
5. Victor and Amanda
6. Elyot and Sibyl
7. Elyot and Amanda
8. Victor and Sibyl

The sixth is a very brief exchange, in which Sybil tells Elyot 'I wish to heaven I'd never seen you in my life' and goes down to have dinner on her own; in the seventh, the longest in the act, Amanda and Elyot realize that they cannot suppress their feelings for each other and resolve to go away together. They decide that they will need 'some phrase or catchword, which when either of us says it, automatically cuts off all conversation for five minutes'. They settle for 'Solomon Isaacs', abbreviated to 'Sollocks'.

As well as marking a new approach to construction, being even more tightly focused than *Fallen Angels*, this is the first play in which Coward is writing a role for himself in the by now distinctive personal voice – familiar by 1930 from his performances in revue – and in partnership with Lawrence as Amanda. The notice in *The Times* (probably by Charles Morgan) was echoed in many other reviews:

> Amanda and Elyot are the fine, flippant flower of Mr Coward's talent [...] Miss Gertrude Lawrence has a brilliant sparkle and extraordinary skill in embellishing speech with silence. Mr Coward's wayward mannerisms have here their most fitting background, and the dialogue which might seem in print a trickle of inanities becomes in the theatre a perfectly timed and directed interplay of nonsense.[13]

The *Era* noted that the dialogue consisted 'mainly of passages of a few words each, there were few very witty lines, and the writing is an excellent example of the clipped, naturalistic talk that passes for conversation in these days'. Coward's skill had 'brought out every shade of meaning in each syllable. There is a remark about a hairbrush – "the nastiest" that the hero had ever seen. Nobody could claim that the phrase is witty, yet in its context and because of the way it was said, the line received the biggest laugh of the evening'.[14]

The nimbleness of Elyot and Amanda's responses, complementing their moral independence, distinguishes them from Victor and Sybil, who are far slower on the uptake and inhabit happily (in his case, belligerently) the commonplaces of society. For them, kissing is what they ought to do at appropriate moments of endearment or consolation, while for Elyot and Amanda it is something passionate and pleasurable that they can't resist. Moreover, attitudes to kissing correspond to the couples' divergent notions of when aggression might be called for. When Victor confesses to Amanda in their first scene that he is 'rather scared of [her] at close quarters', he seems not to understand or even hear her comment that this 'promises to be very embarrassing' (*PP1*, 479/M2, 59). Elyot would never have missed such a cue: like Coward and Lawrence, he and Amanda are a perfect double act, part of the play's metatheatrical quality. Even for the very first audiences, in theory innocent of the knowledge of the plot, casting made the subsequent development both inevitable and desirable. The development of the second act is predicated on this, prepared for by their realization that they need a code word to stop any quarrels. When and how will those 'two violent acids' react to one another? The possibility that Victor and Sybil will turn up is not only sensed as inevitable by the audience, but occurs to the fugitives.

As if this were not enough, Sybil and Victor have been marked from the outset as unsuitable partners by addressing Elyot and Amanda as 'Ellie' and 'Mandy'. In his first scene with his new wife, Elyot makes a brave attempt to convince not only Sybil but himself that 'Love is no use unless it's wise, and kind, and undramatic.' (*PP1*, 471/ M2, 7). The fullest explanation of the play's title, and clue to the play's 'psychology', is saved for Amanda in her first scene with Victor. (As well as being generous in allowing his co-star this important exposition, Coward may well have wanted to make sure it was not missed by any latecomers.) Having explained that she is 'not so sure I'm normal', Amanda is at pains to explain to Victor that 'very few people are completely normal, deep down in their private lives'. Her explanation of 'circumstances' and 'various cosmic thingummys', and comparison of herself and Elyot with 'two violent acids bubbling about in a nasty little matrimonial bottle', passes over Victor's head. He insists that she isn't 'nearly as complex' as she thinks she is, and is alarmed when she insists that she may not be 'particularly complex' but knows she is 'unreliable'.

In what way is she unreliable? – 'I'm so apt to see things the wrong way round'. He simply doesn't understand:

> **Victor** What sort of things?
>
> **Amanda** Morals. What one should do and what one shouldn't.
>
> **Victor** (*fondly*) Darling, you're so sweet.
>
> **Amanda** Thank you, Victor, that's most encouraging. You really must have your bath now. Come along.
>
> **Victor** Kiss me.
>
> **Amanda** (*doing so*) There, dear, hurry now; I've only got to slip my dress on and then I shall be ready.
>
> PP1, 481/M2, 17

The sense of symmetry is augmented by the running joke of references to the Duke of Westminster's yacht, and by contrasting attitudes to acquiring a suntan – conventionally acceptable for men but not women – and the discovery of a pair of champagne cocktails when Victor and Sybil emerge to discover that their respective spouses are missing. The act ends with them unaware of the true situation, with them toasting absent friends '*with rather forced gaiety*', laughing '*mirthlessly*' and then sitting on the balustrade '*pensively sipping their cocktails and looking at the view*':

> **Sybil** [. . .] It's awfully pretty isn't it? The moonlight, and the lights of that yacht reflected in the water –
>
> **Victor** I wonder who it belongs to.

This is the limit of their conversational ability: the curtain 'slowly falls' on silence.

Act Two, in Amanda's flat in Paris (in the fashionable Avenue Montaigne) opens with an amusingly inconsequential conversation about the maid Louise, whom Amanda and Elyot have 'let go' for the evening. This moves seamlessly from comment on her 'grunting and snorting all the evening like a whole herd of Bison', to wondering about the collective noun for the animals, and Amanda's suggestion that 'school' would be 'lovely'– 'The Royal London School of

Bisons'. Speculation on Louise's home life follows, which segues into a few lines on foreign travel, reminiscent of the conversation in Act One about Elyot's 'travelling about' (*PP1*, 497–8/M2, 33–4), in their brief and vain attempt not to talk about each other. (The topic recurs later in the act when Elyot starts talking about his 'damned trip round the world', but has to admit that the 'breathlessly lovely' things he saw were 'completely unexciting' because she was not there' [*PP1*, 516/M2, 52].) As well as being a prelude to their 'serious' consideration of the situation, these opening pages of Act Two establish (if more evidence were needed) that they relish absurdity. When they find themselves talking about promiscuity ('Don't be cross, Elyot, I haven't been so dreadfully loose actually'), the code word 'Sollocks' brings them back from the brink, and a similar exchange of surreal humour clears the air. Subsequently, sharing a duet at the piano will serve the same purpose, but in a different and more sentimental mode.

The act is structured round moments of danger and the couple's shared sense of humour, as a technique for evading 'seriousness'. The most significant (indeed, serious) discussion of this occurs when Elyot elaborates on the idea that 'things that ought to matter dreadfully, don't matter at all when one is happy'. Amanda insists, 'Don't laugh at me, I'm serious', and he responds, '*seriously*', with 'You mustn't be serious, my dear one, it's just what they want'. Amanda asks who 'they' are, and his reply is another of the play's declarations of faith, comparable to her first act speech about 'private lives': 'All the futile moralists who try to make life unbearable. Laugh at them. Be flippant. Laugh at everything, all their sacred shibboleths. Flippancy brings out the acid in their damned sweetness and light'. (*PP1*, 520/M2, 56) When Amanda's thoughts turn to death, he insists it is 'very laughable, such a cunning little mystery. All done with mirrors'.

Amanda   Darling, I believe you're talking nonsense.

Elyot   So is everyone else in the long run. Let's be superficial and pity the poor Philosophers. Let's blow trumpets and squeakers, and enjoy the party as much as we can, like very small, quite idiotic school-children. Let's savour the delight of the moment. Come and kiss me, darling, before your body rots, and worms pop in and out of your eye-sockets.

Amanda steers the talk away from this macabre *memento mori* with the quick-witted flippancy that serves them both as a defence against the censorious world:

Amanda Elyot, worms don't pop.

Elyot (*kissing her*) I don't mind what you do, see? You can paint yourself bright green all over, and dance naked in the Place Vendôme, and rush off madly with all the men in the world, and I shan't say a word, as long as you love me best.

PP1, 521/M2, 57

From this point the act builds towards the climactic physical struggle, progressing from reminiscence about a quarrel in Venice, to the vexed subject of her affair with Peter Burden, Amanda's disapproval of Elyot's drinking, another argument about Peter Burden, to the dispute about the gramophone and – as if inevitably – her breaking a record over his head. What Maria Aitken, in a brilliant analysis of the acting opportunities of the scene, has labelled 'the war of consonants' has turned into the physical conflict the audience has been led to expect.[15] The arrival of Victor and Sybil, just as the fight reaches its climax, fulfils the expectation that sooner or later they will turn up. It has been suggested that the scene they have barged in on is the equivalent of passionate sex, reached after the excitement of bouts of bickering. (Coward had after all pointed out to Lawrence in the letter accompanying the script that 'Copulation has been the basis of the dear old British Drama for so long' that they 'might just as well salute it'.) As Elyot and Amanda take refuge in respective bedrooms, Victor and Sybil *'advance apprehensively into the room and sink on to the sofa'*, and the curtain falls.

Several reviewers felt that the final act was anti-climactic, but it corresponds to Act Two in being structured on conflicts that verge on combat, and ends with the spectacle of Victor and Sybil squaring up for a fight that parallels those of Elyot and Amanda, but without any of their wit – and they are not even married to each other. The defence of flippancy recurs in another key, with Elyot's refusal to accept the 'traditional' values represented by Victor:

Victor If you don't stop your damned flippancy, I'll knock your head off.

> **Elyot** (*raising his eyebrows*) Has it ever struck you that flippancy might cover a very real embarrassment?
>
> **Victor** In a situation such as this, it's extremely bad taste.
>
> **Elyot** No worse than bluster, and invective. As a matter of fact, as far as I know, this situation is entirely without precedent. We have no prescribed etiquette to fall back on. I shall continue to be flippant.
>
> PP1, 534/M2, 50

Elyot's most flippant (and potentially offensive) response comes when he and Amanda seem to be building up to another fight:

> **Amanda** I've been brought up to believe that it's beyond the pale, for a man to strike a woman.
>
> **Elyot** A very poor tradition. Certain women should be struck regularly, like gongs.
>
> **Amanda** You're an unmitigated cad, and a bully.
>
> **Elyot** And you're an ill mannered, bad tempered slattern.

Victor's attempted intervention – 'Keep your mouth shut, you swine' – prompts Elyot's 'Mind your own damned business', and what looks like the beginning of a fight. When Sybil appeals to Amanda to prevent the men fighting her advice is 'Let them fight if they want to, it will probably clear the air anyhow.' (*PP1*, 536/M2, 72). Together with the scene that follows, with Elyot insisting that the women simply want them to fight each other out of 'primitive feminine instinct', this clears the air by challenging the terms on which the situation would be 'serious' enough to call for a manly set-to. Victor wants the traditional 'scene' in which an upright man punishes a 'cad', which would divert the play away from its true genre. He has seen too many old-fashioned plays. Elyot's line about women and gongs, tasteless as it may be, is extreme enough to fire up Amanda's response, and in the headlong rhythm of the exchanges it is, so to speak, the last straw.

At the end of the play, over the breakfast table, Victor and Sybil begin to bicker while Elyot and Amanda have been reunited by their sense of the absurd. They make their escape from the apartment as the quarrel between the 'respectable' but profoundly unimaginative pair develops. Sybil slaps Victor's face 'hard' and he *'takes her by the shoulders and shakes her like a rat, as* **Amanda** *and* **Elyot** *go smilingly out of the door, with their suitcases – and* **The Curtain Falls'**. The argument had begun with Amanda choking with laughter over Elyot adding to her aria in praise of foreign travel: 'arriving at strange places, and seeing strange people, and eating strange things' – 'And making strange noises afterwards.' (*PP1*, 550 /M2, 86). Once again inspired flippancy and a sense of the absurd have triumphed. Victor and Sybil are quarrelling, but they have none of the wit that fuelled the arguments between Elyot and Amanda. Nor is it likely that they will find themselves on the verge of the sexual release that was in prospect for their sophisticated (soon to be former) partners when they were interrupted at the end of Act Two.

Post Mortem and *Cavalcade*, 1931: Two approaches to social upheaval

Post Mortem was published in 1931 but not performed: introducing it five years later in the first *Play Parade* volume, Coward insisted it 'was not actually written for the theatre' but was 'put into play form, for the simple reason that [he] felt more at home in that than in any other' (*PP1*, xv). Written on a 'P. and O. ship returning from the East', it was 'primarily [...] a gesture to [him]self', and with 'certain moments of genuine passion [...] which redeem it from bathos'. It was the expression of 'violent' emotions, and 'an experiment' that 'undoubtedly did [him] a power of good'. 'It opened a lot of windows in my brain and allowed me to let off a great deal of steam which might have remained sizzling inside me, and combusted later on, to the considerable detriment of *Cavalcade* and *Design for Living*.' In Singapore he had appeared for three performances as Stanhope in a touring company's production of R.C. Sherriff's *Journey's End*, and this had fed into his dark mood. Although in this account he appears to regard the play as an 'experiment' in its expression of pent-up emotion, *Post-Mortem* is more immediately experimental in its formal organization, and in the nature of some of the writing.

Post-Mortem is a 'ghost story' in reverse, in which the central narrative turns out to be an illusion, with the hero anticipating his experiences as a revenant rather than recalling his past. Its opening scene in a dugout immediately evokes Sherriff's play. A soldier, John Cavan, is mortally wounded in the first scene, and in his dying moments imagines his supposed future rather than his recalling past. He is dismayed to discover that the values he has been fighting for have been betrayed. In the final scene, which returns to the dugout, his death is confirmed. The familiar theme of a soldier's return is treated, especially in the penultimate scene, with satire stylized beyond Coward's habitual realism. John arrives in the office of his father, the proprietor of the '*Daily Mercury*'. He discovers that his miraculous return will be turned into a jingoistic and sentimental front-page story. His friend Perry Lomas has written a bitter anti-war book which those in power are seeking to suppress, and John's father has convened a committee of grotesquely reactionary figures to discuss tactics for dealing with 'the rising tide of Sedition, Blasphemy and Immoral Thought which, under the guise of "War Literature," is threatening to undermine the youth of our generation' (*PP1*, 621/M2, 343). (The previous scene has shown Lomas preparing to commit suicide.)

Although *Post-Mortem* remained unperformed, some of its bitterness made its way into the expressionistic First World War episode of *Cavalcade* (1931), where it qualifies the patriotic pride that predominates in a saga of two families, the Marryots and the Bridges, played out against a musical and pictorial panorama of major historical events from the turn of the century to the eve of the 1930s. In the first of the four parts Ellen is the Marryots' maid and Alfred Bridges their butler. The stagecraft corresponds to the resources of Drury Lane, with alternating shallow and full-stage sets, and domestic scenes are interspersed with spectacular representations of public events. The more elaborate include the embarkation of troops for South Africa; the announcement during the performance of a musical comedy of the relief of Mafeking; and a final sequence that represents the state of the world in 1930. The death of Queen Victoria is represented by a mute scene with figures in mourning dress meeting in front of a backcloth of the Green Park seen from Birdcage Walk, and her offstage funeral procession is watched by the Maryott household from the windows of their drawing room. In one of the shortest scenes, on the deck of an Atlantic liner, a newly married couple, the Maryott's son Edward and his childhood sweetheart Edith Harris look forward to their life together. As they leave the stage, she comes back to pick her up her cloak, which has been hanging over the rail, to reveal a lifebelt with 'S.S. Titanic' in black lettering: *'The lights fade into complete darkness, but the letters remain glowing as / The orchestra plays very softly and tragically "Nearer my God to Thee"'*.

In *Present Indicative* Coward describes the play's origins in conversations with Cochran during the London run of *Private Lives*. He felt 'an urge to test [his] producing powers on a large scale', with a 'big spectacular production at the Coliseum'. After mulling over various historical themes and 'grand and portentous' events, he had reached an impasse when he came across a series of illustrations in old volumes of the *Illustrated London News* and *Black and White*. The play's 'emotional basis' was 'undoubtedly music', with 'the whole story threaded onto a string of popular melodies'.[16] The 'original story' lacked the working-class element, and focused entirely on the 'bright young people of the nineties' and their children, ending with 'the same eager emptiness but a different jargon'. He then realized that he had 'flogged the bright young people enough' with his 'Poor Little Rich Girls' and 'Dance Little Ladies' in revue numbers, and that 'thirty years of English life seen through their eyes would be uninspired, to say the least of it'.[17]

Coward cabled Cochran from mid-Atlantic with a summary of the principal incidents as he then conceived them, including references to the technical demands and his plans for rehearsal time and casting, with the stipulation that no details of this synopsis, which was 'more or less accurate but liable to revision', should 'reach private or particularly press ears'.[18] Writing began in earnest, working closely with the designer Gladys Calthrop, when he returned from the New York run of *Private Lives*. Although the preliminary account of the scheme features the 'White City' (the Empire Exhibition of 1925) and the General Strike of 1926, in the final version these were discarded in favour of a more impressionistic representation of the post-war decade. (Both would figure in the account of the inter-war period in *This Happy Breed*.) In the event, the Coliseum was no longer available, being taken by Erik Charell's spectacular production of the romantic musical comedy *White*

Horse Inn, and the plans were revised for Drury Lane, which lacked a revolve but had five hydraulic lifts. At last, after a 'rigid daily routine' the dialogue was 'all written and typed, the sets designed and coloured, the changes approximately timed, the dresses and uniforms sketched, individually for the principals, in blocks for the crowd'.[19]

As well as the cable sent to Cochran before Coward's arrival in England, the archive holds an almost complete and very neat pencil draft, possibly a fair copy prepared between any earlier drafts and the typing of a script for performance and publication. There are only a handful of differences between this and the version published in 1932, the most notable being the omission of lyrics for musical numbers – for example, in the musical comedy 'Mirabelle' (Part One, scene four) – and of the final 'Chaos' sequence (Part Three, scene two), in which 'The Twentieth Century Blues' is sung by the Bridges' daughter Fanny, now starring in the floor show of a night club.[20] This accompanies what Ivor Brown in the *Observer* described as 'a nightmare vision', in which 'the lightning of expressionism plays on a moving stage heaped with a jumbled panorama of the follies and fanaticisms and gallantries of today'.[21] After the first rendition of her number, Fanny's night-club audience rise from their tables and dance 'without apparently any particular enjoyment', then the lights 'fade away from anything but the dancers, who appear to be rising in the air'. The ensuing visions included 'six incurables [i.e., blind ex-servicemen] in blue hospital uniform [...] sitting making baskets', and a communist addressing a small group, presumably at 'Speaker's Corner' in Hyde Park. He is not provided with dialogue in the 1932 Heinemann edition, and is represented only by a photograph with the caption 'The world's gone broke!' (The programme cast list also includes a 'religious fanatic'.) In the culmination of the performance

> *The visions are repeated quicker and quicker, while across the darkness runs a Riley light sign spelling out news. Noise grows louder and louder. Steam rivets, loud speakers, jazz bands, aeroplane propellers, etc., until the general effect is complete chaos. Suddenly it all fades into darkness and silence and away at the back a Union Jack glows through the blackness. The lights slowly come up and the whole stage is composed of massive tiers,*

upon which stand the entire company. The Union Jack flies over their head as they sing 'God Save the King'.

PP1, 75/M3, 199

The play's pervasive nostalgic patriotism is summed up in Jane Maryott's defiantly optimistic toast to the New Year of 1930. The future of England and the past are coupled: 'Let's drink to the spirit of gallantry and courage that made a strange Heaven out of unbelievable Hell, and let's drink to the hope that one day this country of ours, which we love so much, will find dignity and greatness and peace again'. (*PP1*, 73/M3, 197: the manuscript omits 'dignity and greatness'.)

Cavalcade's mixture of short dramatic scenes, tableaux, music and montage suggests a degree of kinship with the revue format, transmuted into stage-filling spectacle. A review in the *Illustrated London News* referred to Coward as 'the English [Max] Reinhardt', treating him as producer (that is, director) rather than author: 'He has set out to write a picture rather than write a play, and the most effective scenes are those that are presented in mime'.[22] In the midst of a political and social crisis, when the economy was entering the 'Slump' and Britain had come off the Gold Standard, the message of Jane Maryott's final speech and the literally flag-waving conclusion outweighed any negativity in what Richard Jennings in the *Spectator* described as 'twenty-two episodes from a short history of England's miseries'.[23] The *Stage* admitted there was 'a very frail thread of story on which to hang a series of spectacular scenes as fine in their setting and the handling of masses of people as any theatre has ever seen'.[24] The dialogue scenes tracing the tribulations of the Maryotts and the fall and rise in the fortunes of the Bridges family are effective but often melodramatic, achieving laboured poignancy rather than tragic force. (Arguably, though, this is achieved in the 'Titanic' scene.) The ex-butler Bridges, now a publican, is removed from the picture conveniently by his offstage death, and the entanglement of Joe Maryott with Fanny Bridges occasions an acrimonious scene between Jane and Ellen that is ended by the telegram announcing the young man's death in action. Jane has a near-breakdown just before the relief of Mafeking, another when war is declared in 1914, and a third when she wanders, crazed with grief, among the jubilant crowds on Armistice Night in 1918. She thus earns the right to her concluding stoical declaration of faith, which is contrasted with the behaviour of her friend Margaret, who embraces the post-war world by making herself up and dressing in an attempt to reclaim her youth – behaving, in fact, like Florence Lancaster in *The Vortex*.

Although Coward makes no reference in *Present Indicative* to his intervention, in a newspaper article published in March 1932 Cochran described how, in the face of the difficulties encountered in lighting the 'Chaos' sequence at the dress rehearsal, Coward was prepared to cut it and suggested that 'a slight transposition' would allow the play to be 'finished in two parts'. (Exactly how this might be achieved is unclear.) Cochran insisted that it should not be cut:

> This, I felt, was a bad move. I argued that his change of mind was due to fatigue and the technical difficulties of the scene had got him down. He did not think so. He believed the scene was unnecessary and perhaps a little pretentious. 'You thought the scene was good when you planned it', I told him, 'and you have thought it good up to now. Before we cut it out we will see it done perfectly'.[25]

Writing at the end of the decade, Robert Graves and Alan Hodge recalled that 'conservative playgoers' who had been 'accustomed to look upon Coward as a degenerate', were 'delighted to find their feelings so pleasantly stirred'.[26] In both his *Play Parade* introduction and *Present Indicative*, Coward was anxious to disclaim any political intentions. His nerves were on edge after technical problems that had almost stopped the performance, and when he was called on stage after the final curtain he 'managed to make a rather incoherent little speech which finished with the phrase: "I hope that this play has made you feel that, in spite of the troublous times we are living in, it is still pretty exciting to be English."'[27] Among the 'deluge' of congratulations he received 'on all sides', he was astonished to be commended for his 'uncanny shrewdness in slapping on a strong patriotic play two weeks before a general election which was bound to result in a sweeping Conservative majority'. This was particularly embarrassing for a playwright who was 'so bleakly uninterested in politics' during the arduous rehearsal process that he had 'not the remotest idea, until a few days before production' that there was going to be a general election (*PP1*, ix).

Design for Living, 1932–3: 'Love among the artists' and a retriangulated triangle

In *Past Conditional*, the unfinished draft of the volume of autobiography that would cover the period between 1931 and 1939, Coward described the composition in January 1932 of *Design for Living* as the fulfilment of a pact made with Alfred Lunt and Lynn Fontanne in 1921 that 'when [they] had all three achieved individual stardom in [their] own rights', he would write a play they could all star in.[28] The moment had now arrived. Coward had embarked on a long voyage from San Francisco to South America, returning by way of Panama. Among the mail awaiting him in Santiago was a cable from the Lunts reminding him of the promise: 'CONTRACT WITH THEATRE GUILD UP IN JUNE. WE SHALL BE FREE. WHAT ABOUT IT?'[29] Inspiration did not come immediately, but he was not 'unduly haunted or worried':

> I knew from experience that once I could snatch out of the air the right idea for a play, the actual writing of it would not take long. Once the basic theme of a play has been worked out in my mind I have always written quickly. It's getting the basic theme that takes the time. And of course as I was so intent on getting a plot for the three of us, my own eagerness defeated itself.

In the last stage of his journey, ten days on a small cargo ship 'creeping slowly' up the Pacific coast of America, Coward had no distractions. He had a suitcase full of books and his typewriter, 'on which, with no urgency, no consciousness of Time's winged chariot at [his] back, [he] began and completed' the play: 'The idea slipped into my mind, with neither prayer nor supplication, on the first evening out of Panama. I wrote it morning after morning, effortlessly, with none of the routine moments of unbalanced exultance or black despair'. He 'finished it tidily two days before we were due to dock in Los Angeles and celebrated the occasion by having a royal piss-up with the crew'.[30] Given the terms of the original pact with the Lunts, it is likely that one aspect of this idea that slipped into Coward's mind was the theme of success and its effect on personal relationships. Another was his response to the demand for 'depth' or 'substance' in addition to the wit of his dialogue, which is addressed humorously when Gilda and Leo (played by Coward) discuss the reviews of his new play at the beginning of Act Two.

The essential apartness from society's conventions of those gifted with artistic temperament, and their mutual solidarity, are treated more radically than their equivalent in *Private Lives*. The principal accomplishment of Elyot and Amanda is simply being who they are, on a higher level than Victor and Sybil but without any evident occupation in life. A sidelong glance at the moral assumptions that govern the well-made plays of an earlier generation is common to both comedies, as to many of Coward's plays since the 1920s. In *Design for Living* the amatory relationships go beyond those of the classic 'eternal triangle'. The 'triangle' in the first two acts consists of three lovers, two male and one female, with an onlooker, Ernest Friedman, who in the final act finds himself unwillingly part of a not-so-eternal quartet. John Lahr suggests that '[T]he homosexual dream of sexual abundance comes true' in 'Coward's antic version of love conquers all', with Ernest lacking 'the charm or the wit to outpoint [the threesome] in this prize fight'.[31]

Not only is *Design for Living* more sophisticated and less equivocal in its erotic implications than *Private Lives*, it is also technically more sophisticated. It encompasses farce and a strong element of theatrical self-consciousness that, as often in Coward's plays, is present in two senses: as something the playwright must devise, and as an element of the series of emotional crises or 'scenes' created intentionally by the characters. The play uses the familiar method of construction by means of a progression from scene to scene (or indeed, beat to beat) of questions and answers, but now in a more complex form. Some of the questions are voiced by the characters themselves – how will Leo, Otto, Gilda or Ernest rise to a situation? Others are part of the mechanism by which the audience's expectations are managed, while in some cases both are combined. The third act is briefer and simpler than the first two, but repeats the pattern of revelations, questions to be answered, surprising entrances and (at the end of the first scene) enigmatic exits, until it reaches its equivocal conclusion. Given the personalities involved, it promises not a conventional resolution, but rather the continuation of their lives with the same pattern – or design.

Archival evidence for Coward's work on *Design for Living* reflects important decisions made at an early stage – perhaps even before he reached Panama, and certainly before he laid hand to typewriter on the voyage up the West Coast towards California. A complete manuscript (or early typescript) has yet to come to light, but as well as an outline for the acts and scenes, discussed below, the archive includes two pencil drafts of parts of the first act, and additions to a draft (no longer extant) of the third act. In the following account, these partial drafts are discussed in their apparent order of composition. A typescript at Yale, in the John C. Wilson Collection, seems to reflect the play as originally performed, and corresponds except for a few details to the first edition, published in 1933.[32] The authority of its many pen and pencil markings, principally substantial cuts, is unclear, but the typescript itself would most likely have been made near the date of the New York performances, either for touring or as a basis for an 'acting edition'. (In the event none was published, probably because the play was not yet being released for amateur performance.)

Mar del Plata is in Argentina, far down the coast from the entrance to the Panama Canal. If the inscription 'Mar del Plata January 7th 1932' on the manuscript outline of the play is correct, in *Past Conditional* Coward would appear to have misremembered the place and time when the idea 'slipped into [his] mind'. Nevertheless, this document suggests that the overall pattern of the play was firmly in place at an early stage. Possible titles are jotted down: *Three Bags Full*, *Equal Parts*, *Fun in the Long Grass*, *The Random Elephant*, *Tryptique*, *Change and Decay*, *Life is for Living* and, finally, *Design for Living*. (*Tryptique* is also written above the cast list, but has been crossed out.) *Change and Decay* (from the hymn 'Abide with Me') occurs in Act Two as the title of Leo's successful play.

The principal characters are listed, and the locations of the scenes correspond to those in the finished play. Gilda is given a surname, Langani, not mentioned in the play, and there are some variations among minor characters. 'Jeanne' (probably a French maid or housekeeper) does not appear in the final version and there are names for two servants at the New York apartment. The outline charts the dynamics of the shifting relationships of Otto, Leo and Gilda, and Ernest's status as a concerned but ultimately excluded participant. Although Coward was aware that 'big scenes' between two or more of the characters were needed, he had not yet arrived at a definitive pattern for them.

Act I, Otto's studio in Paris
Jeanne preparing breakfast. Ernest enters with 'Matisse'. scene between Gilda and Ernest. Ernest goes – Enter Leo – big scene Gilda and Leo – Enter Otto – big scene between the three finishing with tremendous outburst from Otto and exit.
Act II
Scene I, Two years later. Leo's Flat in London
Scene between Leo and Gilda, press notices, enter Otto having been successful in America – gay scene between the three – telephone rings incessantly, all the trappings of Leo's overnight success
Scene II, A week later
Love scene Otto and Gilda
Scene III, The next morning
Scene between Ernest and Gilda – Ernest goes – enter Otto – scene: Otto and Gilda – Enter Leo – big scene between the three – Gilda loses control, has violent nerve storm and exits. Big scene between Otto and Leo ending in tears
Act III
Scene I, Two years later. Ernest's Penthouse in New York
Dinner scene Gilda Ernest the Carvers and Grace Torrance – Ernest leaves to motor to Long Island. The others settle down to Bridge. Enter Otto and Leo – bridge scene – Gilda faints Otto and Leo carry her off to bed
Scene II, Two days later
Scene Breakfast Otto and Leo in Ernest's dressing gowns – Enter Ernest – scene between three of them – Enter Gilda – Fourfold scene – Furious outburst from Ernest – Exit, tripping over mat – Laughing scene Gilda Otto Leo[33]

The final version's time scheme is tighter, so that Act One is followed by a lapse of eighteen months; the second scene of Act Two is in the evening, two days (rather than a week) later; and the third scene begins at 'about ten-thirty the next morning'. Act Three is still 'two years later', with the final scene taking place the morning after the first rather than 'two days later'.

Comparison with the completed play shows Coward working to achieve a balance between the principal actors and, in terms of construction, to arrange their 'big scenes' across the first two acts. Perhaps the most important development is the creation of the final 'laughing scene'. Rather than tying up loose ends, this confirms Leo, Otto and Gilda in a common cause against philistinism, although, in at least one performed version it did not decisively exclude Ernest. In his outline Coward had envisaged a series of such scenes without specifying their content, but the play's trajectory is implicit in the progression over time and location, and the reference to a final 'laughing' scene for Gilda, Otto and Leo with Ernest's final exit. The structure created consists of a series of questions regarding possible consequences of successive actions and situations, as well as variations on a number of topics. As Leo observes in Act Two, Scene One, 'The whole business of living is a process of readjustments' (*PP1*, 384/M3, 42).

In the play as published and performed, in the opening scene Ernest assumes that Otto is asleep in the bedroom, and is told he is suffering from neuralgia so cannot be woken up to see the painting. Ernest tells Gilda that Leo has returned from New York and is staying at the George V. He is still at the studio when Otto arrives. After the two men go off to meet Leo at the hotel Leo emerges from bedroom and he and Gilda discuss what is to be done. Otto arrives and the 'big scene' then takes place, ending with Otto, furious, exiting and slamming the door.

Otto does not appear in the first scene of Act Two, and there is no 'gay scene between the three'. Leo and Gilda are discovered reading the reviews of his new play, which has been a smash hit, but it becomes apparent that Gilda is not content with their life together and feels that something has been lost. Miss Hodge, a 'daily' servant, is present, a sign, like the flat itself, of growing prosperity. By the end of the scene the 'row' between the couple seems to have been smoothed over, and it has been agreed that Leo will attend a weekend house party alone. A reporter, accompanied by a photographer, arrives to interview Leo. Gilda leaves 'to do a little shopping' and as the curtain falls Leo manages 'just a little smile' for the photographer. Otto now arrives in the second scene, and is told by Gilda that Leo 'went away this afternoon'. At the end the 'curtain slowly falls' as Otto and Gilda have 'gradually subside[d] on to the sofa' in each other's arms. In the third scene there is no 'big scene between the three', and after her conversation with Ernest Gilda does not 'lose control' or have a 'big nerve storm', but decides to leave for New York with him, leaving notes for Otto (who is still asleep) and Leo. When Otto enters from the bedroom, Miss Hodge is outraged by the change of male personnel in the flat. He settles down on the sofa and 'lies on it with his back towards the door, blowing smoke rings into the air'. Leo enters, having just arrived from New York. Otto admits that he has stayed with Gilda. Their 'big scene' is interrupted when Leo notices the two letters. Another 'big scene' of a different kind follows, ending in drinking and – as planned – tears.

In Act Three, Scene One, there is no dinner or bridge game. Gilda does not faint, and is not carried to her bedroom by Otto and Leo, but leaves to stay the night in a hotel. In the final scene, Ernest is met by his servant Matthew when he arrives, and Gilda returns from hotel. By omitting the meal and the card game Coward allows for a smoother unfolding of the dialogue that establishes Gilda's new situation as Ernest's wife and (most important) sets up a milieu that is unlikely, on the evidence of the preceding acts, to prove wholly congenial to her or her old friends. During the intervening two years the alliance between Leo and Otto has been renewed and strengthened, and their arrival as a disruptive force effectively rescues Gilda and confirms Ernest as an outsider: as he makes his indignant exit 'on his way into the hall he falls over the package of canvases' he has brought with him rather than simply (as in the outline) tripping over the mat, thus creating a deft comic echo of his entrance at the beginning of the play.

The earlier of two longer manuscript drafts for the play's opening scene takes the action up to Otto's arrival in the studio, and his departure with Ernest in search of Leo at his hotel. The second includes Leo's emergence from the studio's bedroom and the beginning of the scene between him and Gilda. Both drafts reflect adjustments in the characterization of Ernest and his relationship with Gilda, Otto and Leo. In the published script, when Ernest divulges that Leo has come back to Paris and is staying at a luxury hotel, the George V, Gilda declares that she 'adores' Leo, and Ernest's 'What about Otto?' leads to an elucidation of the relationship between Gilda, Otto and Leo. Gilda declares that 'there's a crisis on. A full-blooded, emotional crisis'. and paints a lurid picture of her relationship with Otto and Leo, urging him to 'look at the whole thing as a side show'. This is the point at which 'the door bursts open' and Otto 'fairly bounds into the room' (*PP1*, 353–6/M3, 13–16).

In this scene, particularly up to the arrival of Otto, Coward had to achieve a number of goals. Ernest's arrival would prompt Gilda's anxiety not to have her secret – having slept with Leo – revealed to either Ernest or Otto, and her perception of the significance of this for her feelings about herself as well as her relationship with all three men. Explanations of her 'temperament' include the lines about 'glands' and hormones 'rushing madly in and out of my organs like messenger boys'; her reasons for not wanting to marry Otto and the explanation that 'It's not just a dashing Bohemian gesture to free love'; her insistence that Ernest should 'leave [them] to grapple with consequences of their behaviour'; her description of her 'standards' as being 'not female standards at all'; and the advice to Ernest that he should treat the three of them as 'a freak show' that immediately precedes Otto's arrival (*PP1*, 348–53/M3, 8–11). With the exception of the speech about 'female standards', these bravura set pieces appear in some form in the drafts, being moved around to varying effect in the process of composition. In the earlier of the two longer drafts, more emphasis is placed on Ernest's feelings towards Gilda, but in each version the overall shape of the scene is dictated by her emotional state, and the playwright's need to relate it to the information the audience will be given (or will intuit) about the men in her life.

In the opening direction of the first (sixteen-page) pencil draft, the knocking at the door is 'violent' and is repeated 'more violently than ever' before Gilda, having closed the bedroom door let in Ernest 'a tubby little man of about forty-five with a glint in his eye and a package under his arm'. Except for the package, these details will not reappear in subsequent versions. He is annoyed about the delay ('No one will ever know Gilda how much I resent being kept waiting') and she explains that she was in the kitchen making coffee. When she asks where he has come from, he tells her that she knows 'perfectly well' that he has been in Berlin. He has the Matisse, which is 'incredible … Its subject, a "still life" quite formal, completely different from anything else' (MS, p.2). Gilda explains why Otto should not be woken up (his neuralgia), and when she insists, Ernest decides to let her see the picture, despite the fact that he knows her 'to be both stupid and unperceptive'. He begins to observe that he is showing it to her 'in the hope that some glimmer of its beauty may penetrate through that...' but she interrupts him with an offer of coffee (MS, p.3). They discuss his transaction and what he intends to do with the picture, and when Gilda remarks that 'it will need a room to itself' he replies with 'None of your decorating schemes – hands off' and admits that he does not think she is a 'particularly' good decorator (MS, p.4). Otto 'will go mad when he sees it', and in response to her question 'You think he's all right don't you – you think he's good?' he suggests the artist is 'coming along, coming along'. Her reaction prompts his remark that she is a 'tigress defending her young', and that Otto is weak and she strong. At this point the dialogue shifts to Gilda's vehemence and her state of mind and her declaration that she is 'sick of this studio', without the exchanges (*PP1*, 346/M3, 36) that develop the animal comparison and his claim to be 'a bitter old family friend'.

This manuscript lacks Gilda's description of the person that she wishes she could be ('a nice-minded British matron', etc.), In its place is what seems to be an admittedly guarded suggestion of a possible relationship with Ernest:

> **Ernest** (*drinking his coffee*)   Perhaps you wish I were somebody quite different too.
>
> **Gilda**   Oh yes sweet I do. – I do indeed. I wish you were eight feet high and bursting with foolish glamour. I wish you were a single tracked, romantic cavalier, with only one desire in the world –
>
> **Ernest**   That being?
>
> **Gilda**   To carry me away on a horse.
>
> MS, p.5

This leads to the question of her being fond of horses:

> **Ernest**   This is very interesting – tell me, when you were a child did you dream that you were riding, riding, riding –
>
> **Gilda**   Yes like anything
>
> **Ernest**   Used you to nuzzle and bite at your nurse with your tiny gums?
>
> **Gilda**   My gums were always enormous.

Told that she used to 'whinny at the breast' Ernest concludes that she has 'a horse fixation'. Playing along in a parody of Freudian analysis, Gilda asks where she should 'lay [her] tortured spirit' and is told to 'have a set religion, something orthodox and excessively formal', but with ritual 'only on feast days' (MS, pp.5–6).

The upshot of these exchanges is that Ernest tells her that although he thinks her 'misguided, obstinate and very badly organized', because he is 'quite impervious to [her] sexually', he would 'still like to marry' her 'someday'. Gilda objects that this would be 'just to grace [his] table and be polite to [his] damned art dealers and buyers'. He admits that 'would be part of the bargain' but when he responds to her vague 'Perhaps, some day' with 'when it's all over' – 'it' being 'all this casual foolishness' – she 'flares up': 'It isn't casual' (MS, p.7). Ernest persists: it is 'all this snatching and grabbing and evading', and she evades 'all responsibilities'.

> **Gilda** Only social responsibilities – and they have nothing to do with me. I'm free and financially independent enough to do as I like.
>
> **Ernest** That's a delusion
>
> **Gilda** Oh no it isn't. It is the truth. If I were dependent on Otto I couldn't live with him, I couldn't love him and help him as I do.

As the conversation continues, Gilda declares that she does not want to marry Otto, or, indeed, anyone. 'Even me?' asks Ernest:

> **Gilda** Even you with your wit and your wisdom and your deep-down yearning for respectability –
>
> **Ernest** Let me out, let me out. I'm being insulted.
>
> **Gilda** Yes you are, you are. You know a lot about pictures and social amenities but you don't know about life.
>
> **Ernest** Laife [*sic*], laife, what is laife. Tell me about it!
>
> **Gilda** Don't just laugh at me. I'm terribly unhappy. (*she suddenly bursts into tears*)
>
> MS, p.8

At this point, after she has told him he must go away and he refuses, she 'controls herself' ('I'm sorry, I suddenly had a come over') and they drink some of the coffee. Gilda says that she was out last night and has a hangover: 'I drink far too much – this is a hang over, that's what this is – a hang over. Oh dear (*she laughs*)' (MS, p.9). Ernest's complaint that this rapid play of emotions is 'getting [him] down' and she will be 'screaming hysteria in a minute' prompts more laughter ('she buries her head in her hands and roars with laughter') and leads to the equivalent of her characterization of him as 'a permanent spectator' (*PP1*, 355/M3, 15).

After claiming she was wrong about the studio – 'it's not squalid it's delightful – it is filled with memories, charming intimate memories and it's going to have a hell of a lot more soon'– Gilda calms down and explains her state of mind as 'just a crise, probably glandular, everything's glandular you know'. (This passage is placed near the beginning of the equivalent long conversation in the final version [*PP1*, 347–8/M3, 7–8].) She admits 'I've discovered lots of things about myself that I didn't know before and I'm horrified', and Ernest asks whether she knows Leo is back in Paris and staying 'at the Lancaster, a reasonably expensive hotel' and has written Ernest a note (Ms, p.13).

An emotional switchback ride has thus run its course, including elements subsequently relocated to precede the news of Leo's return: Gilda's way of life, her relationship with Otto and her refusal to consider marrying him, and Ernest's position *vis-à-vis* all three of them. (The suggestion that Ernest would consider marrying Gilda appears only in this draft.) By moving this material earlier in the scene, having already intimated that Leo is in Paris, Coward enhances the element of suspense for the audience – who will have guessed that Leo rather than Otto is in the bedroom – and increased the tension for Gilda in the face of Ernest's enquiries. He also saved for later a subtextual motivation for Gilda's decision to marry Ernest. This remains a possibility rather than a firm decision at the end of the second scene of Act Two, to be confirmed only at the opening of the third act. Here, it leads to Gilda's account of her relationship with the other two men, the equivalent of the section in the final version of the scene, where Ernest speaks as a 'bitter old family friend' with no explicit hint of any other intentions on his part (*PP1*, 347/M3, 7).

Otto arrives within moments of Ernest's revelation that Leo has returned to Paris, in an effectively managed passage:

Ernest He probably came here last night when you were out.

Gilda (*suddenly animated*) Of course – he must be here – he wanted to surprise us – that's why he didn't leave any message. Otto will be thrilled. I'll tell him the moment he wakes up.

Ernest If Otto isn't awake now after all the noise you've been making he must be dead.

Gilda No, when he does get off he sleeps terribly soundly.

There is a sound of footsteps outside on the landing. The door bursts open and Otto bursts in – He is wearing a travelling coat and carrying a suit case and a large package of painting materials

MS, pp.13–14

The final version builds up to this entrance to even greater effect, with Gilda's invitation to Ernest to 'walk up' and see 'freaks' that 'people pay to see', including 'the three Famous Hermaphrodites!' (*PP1*, 355/M3, 15).

In the final two pages of the sixteen-page manuscript, Otto describes briefly his work on the portrait he has been painting: he finished it 'last night' and made the patron 'sit for hours and hours... She hates the picture but it's good, it's really fine, and better than I hoped'. He did not have time to cable Gilda before he left Bordeaux. Shown the Matisse, he responds without enthusiasm ('It's weak ... It's pretty – no guts') and Ernest tartly remarks that the only thing that convinces him Otto is a good painter is his 'abysmal ignorance of painting'. Ernest huffily refuses to divulge how much he paid for the Matisse, and tells him he's 'just blown out with pride' because he has 'succeeded in making a stupid old woman sit still in Bordeaux' (MS, p.15). Otto is about to show them the portrait, but Gilda tells him to wait, because 'we're not all here, there's one missing'. She explains that Leo is in Paris at the Lancaster, having sailed back on the Mauretania. His play is still running in Chicago, and he has sold the movie rights and 'made thousands'. At this point, with two slightly different versions of Gilda's speech, the draft breaks off at the top of the sixteenth notebook page.

In the second long manuscript Ernest refuses to show Gilda the picture until Otto is awake. Offered coffee, he asks why, if Otto has neuralgia, there are two cups on the table. Gilda explains that this is the result of 'habit'. This exchange is practically identical in all three versions, suggesting that Coward had arrived at it as a simple way of establishing the situation, along with Ernest's perceptiveness and Gilda's talent for improvization. At this point – and only in this draft – it is Gilda who announces Leo's return to Paris, telling Ernest he is staying at the George V. Quizzed on her attitude to Leo's success, Gilda claims she is jealous only for Otto's sake. In the final version, where the revelation of Leo's return is made by Ernest and is placed much later (*PP1*, 351/M3, 11), the issue of jealousy is inflected differently: Gilda remarks that Ernest is 'trying to find out' whether she is jealous of Leo, and insists that this is not the case. In the draft, as in the final version, this is followed immediately by the exchange about Ernest having known them all for 'so long' and the two men first. Gilda's remark that Ernest is 'nothing but a respectable little old woman in a jet bonnet' is placed here rather than earlier in the scene (*PP1*, 349/M3, 9).

Ernest's disapproval of Gilda's 'untidiness' leads to her defence of herself, her apology to him for being so vehement, her explanation that his affection 'is a scared thing', and the assertion that she, Otto and Leo should be looked at 'clearly as human beings, rather peculiar human beings, I grant you'. (The sequence corresponds, with minor differences, to that in the published play.) Ernest now asks why she does not marry Otto and she explains that it is because she loves him, shouting and turning towards the bedroom. She describes the 'only reasons' for her to marry – 'To have children; to have a home. . .' and so on – in a speech that once again corresponds with minor differences to its equivalent in the final text (*PP1*, 350/M3, 10). Her announcement that she is 'sick of the studio', the opening of the window, and the explanation that the cause of her state of nerves is 'glandular' are placed here rather than earlier in the scene. She then admits that she has been 'out too late' the previous night without claiming to have a hangover, and they drink coffee. Neither pencil draft includes Gilda's claim that she 'looks upon [her] own damned femininity with complete nausea' or the outburst that in the final version precedes the coffee-drinking moment:

> It humiliates me to the dust to think I can go so far, clearly and intelligently, keeping faith with my own standards – which are not female standards at all – preserving a certain decent integrity, not using any tricks; then, suddenly, something happens, a spark

is struck and down I go into the mud! Squirming with archness, being aloof and desirable, consciously alluring, snatching and grabbing, evading and surrendering, dressed and painted for victory. An object of strange contempt!

PP1, 354/M3, 14

It is at this point in both drafts that Gilda tells Ernest he is a 'permanent spectator' with a knowledge of paintings rather than life, and urges him to 'take a look at this my darling, measure it with your eyes – Portrait of a Woman in three cardinal colours. Portrait of a too loving spirit tied down to a predatory female carcass'. In this second draft, for the first time, Gilda describes herself, Leo and Otto as 'the Three Famous Hermaphrodites', before Otto is heard on the landing outside before making his entrance.

When Otto enters 'he strikes an attitude' and Gilda responds to his 'I've come home!' with 'You see what happens when I crack the whip!' Otto kisses 'little Ernest' ('how very sweet to see you') and Gilda asks when he left Bordeaux. He explains that he didn't telegraph because he doesn't hold with 'these modern inventions'. Ernest, looking at Gilda, says 'This is all very interesting'. Otto asks what is 'interesting' and Gilda, perhaps to deflect a possible revelation from Ernest that Leo is in the bedroom, tells him there is a 'surprise'. It isn't the contents of the package (the Matisse, which has not been revealed yet), but he must go at once to the George V – Leo has arrived. Otto, 'prancing about the room', has a speech that begins, as in the final script, with 'This is good, good better than good!' but differs in this manuscript by including an account of his completion of the portrait of 'Mrs. Driscoll' (as yet unnamed), ending with a childish proposal for a 'gesture' to celebrate Leo's return:

I've finished the old bitch. I made her sit for hours and hours. She hates it too, by God how cross she was, I wouldn't let her near it until the end. – I brought it away. I don't suppose she'll pay the rest of the money but to hell with her if she doesn't, I shall have the picture. I worked like a dog to get it done, and here I am, two days to the good. Leo's back, Ernest, back and we can all celebrate – let's make a gesture of some sort, something defiant – let's all go and wee wee in the Louvre.

MS, p.11

Ernest 'looks fixedly at Gilda, with meaning' and asks 'What are you going to do'. She replies that she will stay and tidy up while they go to the hotel and fetch Leo: 'You said my mode of life was untidy didn't you – Well I've taken it to heart'. As they are about to leave, Gilda calls Otto back and, 'with a slight strain in her voice' tells him to be careful crossing roads. As Otto leaves, he *blows her a kiss* with 'Be quiet – don't pester me with your attentions', and then tells Ernest as they go out 'She's crazy about me, poor little thing, just crazy about me'.

When they have gone, Gilda and Leo discuss strategy. Almost immediately, Leo suggests they might say he could have 'hurried here and missed them on the way' (MS, p.14). (In the first edition it is Gilda who makes the suggestion, two pages later.) They then discuss whether Ernest will say anything:

Leo   Still Ernest won't say anything He's a loyal old puss.

Gilda   I wonder if he guessed it was you.

Leo   Does it matter?

Gilda   Not a bit. (*she gets up*)

Suddenly Leo kisses her passionately. They stand there clinging to one another.

Leo   (*releasing her*) [Artfully?] arranged aren't they human beings? It's nice being human beings isn't it – I'm sure God's angels must envy us.

MS, p.14

In the published play this version of Leo's speech occurs eight lines after the exit of Otto and Ernest.

Two short drafts, each of two pages on the same lined notepad paper and also in pencil, include further variations on this section of the play's first scene. One carries the scene from Otto's arrival up to the news that Leo has returned. Here, when Gilda tells Otto about the surprise in store for him, his first thought is one not represented in any other version of the scene:

Otto   Surprise. What sort of surprise – you're not – Oh my

Gilda: Who do you think's here? God you're not going to have a baby are you?

Gilda Don't be silly of course I'm not.

Otto What is it then.

Gilda Leo is here.

MS, p.15

The second fragment differs in minor respects from the final version of the rest of the scene, up to Otto's exit with Ernest. A third manuscript is a draft for the confrontation in the play's final scene that leads up to Ernest's departure (*PP1*, 460/M3, 120). It begins with Leo's 'You should see more Ernest you really should' and concludes at Leo's 'We all have our own decencies'. The manuscript includes Gilda's declaration of solidarity with Otto and Leo – 'I'm no different from them. We're all of a piece, the three of us', but it lacks Ernest's equally frank admission of his past disgust at the spectacle of their relationship: 'It was painful to watch her writhing in the throes of her own foolish love for you. . .' The drafted version is simpler: 'You let her down utterly. You threw away everything she gave you. I tried to make her happy and contented, quietly, without fuss'.

When *Design for Living* opened at New York's Ethel Barrymore Theatre on 14 January 1933, the critical response was overwhelmingly enthusiastic, and the performances by the three principals were praised unanimously. They were (wrote Brooks Atkinson in the *New York Times*) 'an incomparable trio of high comedians'.[34] Misgivings regarding the play's morality were largely discounted on account of the 'unreality' of its characters and their way of life. Robert Benchley's *New Yorker* review opens with the suggestion that Coward's design for living, 'as set forth in his play of that name, is an extremely freehand drawing of delightful line and aspect, regardless of its practicability as a blueprint'.[35] Benchley's reflections on the situation at the end of the third act are unusual in hinting at the possibility of a liaison between the two men: 'Stranger things have happened than that it should be the young lady who was out of luck'. For all his urbanity, consonant with the tone of the magazine, Benchley admits to feeling 'vaguely uncomfortable' at the final curtain, 'as if three people whom we had learned to like very much had suddenly gone slightly bad on us'.

Reviewers were intrigued as much by the unconventional ending as by the moral uncertainty that some found unpalatable or disturbing. Burns Mantle, in the *New York News*, while admiring the manner in which the play 'develops an entirely new kind of triangle, exposes it boldly, plays with it brilliantly, and leaves it dangling', found the ending 'more casual than life and hardly defensible', and concluded more conventionally than Benchley that it offered 'a situation' conceivably plausible [. . .] in the lives of some artists', but 'not exactly tenable in human nature'.[36] Atkinson proposed that Coward's way with 'the familiar triangle' was 'decadent [. . .] if you feel obliged to pull a long moral face over this breezy fandango', but in 'an audacious and hilarious way if you relish the attack and retreat of artificial comedy that bristles with wit'. In a long article, effectively a version of his introduction to the first *Play Parade* collection published the following year, Coward insisted that his title was 'ironic rather than dogmatic', and that he never intended for a moment that the design for living suggested in the play should apply to anyone outside its three principal characters. The play was 'equivocal', and 'different minds found different meanings' in their laughter at the end: 'Some considered it to be directed against Ernest. [. . .] If so, it was certainly cruel, and in the worst possible taste. Some saw in it a lascivious anticipation of a sort of triangular carnal frolic. Others, with less ribald imaginations, regarded it as a meaningless and slightly inept excuse to bring the curtain down'. As author, he preferred to think that Gilda and Otto and Leo were laughing at themselves.[37]

Although it would not be played in Britain until January 1939, *Design for Living* was published in London in May 1933. St. John Ervine hailed it in the *Observer* as 'easily its author's best comedy'. It was 'primarily a plea for personal freedom, and the fact that it appear[ed] also to be a plea for polyandry' was 'comparatively of minor importance'.[38] Although some subsequent accounts have suggested it was initially banned for production, it was not submitted to the Lord Chamberlain's office until the autumn of 1938, when Beaumont and Coward 'pulled strings' to obtain the licence.[39] It was passed for production in the light of a reader's report acknowledging the 'immorality' of its theme but (like a number of reviewers) pointing out that it was as much an 'artificial comedy of manners' as *The Country Wife*. There were the usual complaints from self-appointed guardians of public morality, who received a letter of reply to the effect that Coward had 'taken the old theme of "The Eternal Triangle,"' and 'solved the problem in a new way which [was], of course, entirely unsuitable for the majority of people in a reasonable world'. *Design for Living* was hardly likely to convert anyone to the characters' way of life.[40] The play opened in London at the Haymarket in January 1939, with Diana Wynyard as Gilda, Rex Harrison as Otto and Anton Walbrook as Leo. In September, during the temporary closure of London theatres, the production was taken out on tour, returning on 23 December, this time to the Savoy Theatre. As performed in London and on tour in Britain in 1939–40, the final moments differed from those of the New York production. Reporting on the performances in Brighton on the pre-London tour, the *Stage* described Ernest as exiting 'ignominiously, falling over a bundle of Gilda's clothing at the doorway' – the evening cloak she had brought back after changing into 'a dark day coat and hat' (*PP1*, 455/ M3, 113).[41] The reviewer in *Punch* recalled the New York version, where 'the curtain fell on poor Ernest going out from his own flat with the callous laughter of the others ringing in his ear; now he is made to trip up on the stairs and join in the laughter himself. But it is friendly laughter. Not even he really cares, and so the ending is meaningless'.[42] Coward did not oversee this production, so the decision that Ernest should join in the laughter might have been that of the director, Harold French. However, Ernest's exit 'upstairs' rather than towards the door of the apartment is also indicated in Wilson's typescript copy, where Ernest's final speech ('This is ludicrous . . .') is preceded by the direction '*As he climbs staircase*'. The final page of the script is missing, but a pencil note at the bottom of the page adds '*As he goes up start laughter then Curtain*'. There is no suggestion, either typed or in the annotations, that Ernest joins in the laughter.[43]

In the *Sunday Times*, James Agate complained that Coward's English cast let him down 'by its very niceness', with Otto and Leo 'both decent fellows'. As for Wynyard, given that 'the note of Gilda, however you try to disguise it, is, in the last resort, an elegant sluttishness', she 'achieved only elegance'.[44] The play's alleged immorality was disturbing enough for Archie de Bear in the *Daily Sketch* to refrain from describing the plot 'in a family newspaper', even though he admitted to enjoying the play, and Philip Page in the *Daily Mail* took against this 'rather unhealthy piece of impertinence, all too rarely amusing', objecting to 'the quaint manner in which [Coward] imagines men and women behave who are alleged to be in love with each other'.[45] Some critics invoked Restoration Comedy in a spirit of condemnation, and A.E. Wilson in the *Star* complained of 'the squalid theme at the morality of which Wycherley himself might have blushed'.[46] But in a more sophisticated spirit, Ivor Brown's *Observer* review identified the 'couplings and uncouplings' as being 'in the manner of 1670' while the dialogue was 'pure 1930'.[47] Lionel Hale in the *News Chronicle* seems to have been the only British reviewer to have speculated publicly about what has since become an accepted element of the play's subtext: 'Minds more earnest than Mr. Coward's have even discovered homosexuality [sic] in one corner of the triangle'.[48]

Tonight at 8.30, 1935–6: An experiment in presentation

In a programme note to the first production of the nine plays that make up *Tonight at 8.30*, Coward explained that the short play had been relegated to the status of 'curtain raisers', but had 'a great advantage over a long one in that it can sustain a mood without technical creaking or overpadding'. If he could 'do a little towards reinstating it in its rightful pride' he should have achieved one of his 'more sentimental ambitions'. They were also a shrewd commercial proposition, and he admitted in the introduction to the fourth *Play Parade* volume that 'upheld by [his] stubborn faith in the "star system"', he had written them for Gertrude Lawrence and himself 'as acting, singing and dancing vehicles' (*PP4*, x). Two of them were experimental in dramaturgical terms, and one, *Still Life*, is adventurous in its presentation of near-tragedy in the context of comedy. It would be the basis for one of the most successful films of the next decade, *Brief Encounter*, in which the use of flashbacks and voice-over narration would go beyond anything Coward attempted in his theatrical work.

After an extensive provincial tour in various combinations, seven of the nine plays were performed at the Phoenix Theatre in January, 1936, with another two added to the repertoire in May. (A tenth, *Star Chamber*, was given only one performance, at a matinee on 21 March.) Of the nine, *Family Album*, *Red Peppers*, *Fumed Oak* are effectively extended revue sketches, while *Hands Across the Sea*, *We Were Dancing* and *Ways and Means* are short comedies. The

Astonished Heart, *Shadow Play* and *Still Life*, billed simply as 'plays', are unconventional in form. The second scene of *The Astonished Heart* takes place a year earlier than the first ('November, 1935'), in which an eminent psychiatrist is dying offstage, and is followed by two more showing the development of the affair that precipitated the suicide that results in his death (still offstage) in the fifth and final scene. For Coward, this was in itself 'experimental' in technical terms, but an additional unconventional element was the decision of the psychiatrist's wife in the second scene to condone his liaison in order to cure his nervous condition, sending the lovers off on a tour abroad with her blessing. *Shadow Play* is in an even more adventurous, quasi-expressionistic mode: a woman facing the ordeal of a divorce takes an overdose of a sleeping draught, and as she hovers between life and death episodes from the past, including song and dance, revisit the early love she shared with her husband. At the end she revives, and he tells her he no longer wants a divorce. (The numbers, notably 'Play, Orchestra, Play', went on to a life independent of the dramatic context.) Peter Fleming, in the *Spectator*, thought that the series of dream-like episodes made the play 'a suggestive failure', and that 'rather more obvious treatment – a sharper definition of the boundaries between past and present, illusion and reality – might have made it a notable innovation in dramatic technique'. As it stood, it was 'a puzzling, pleasing chiaroscuro, charmingly illuminated by the grace and beauty of Miss Lawrence'.[49] *The Times* found this 'the least successful and the most interesting of the six pieces' in which, 'feeling like the rest of us, that the naturalistic convention is often inadequate to the emotion of love', Coward had 'applied his own remedy'.[50]

This was to be the last time they appeared together on stage in London. In New York, after its Boston opening on 26 October 1936, the nine plays of *Tonight at 8.30* ran for 118 performances at the National Theatre. The *New York Times* suggested that 'no student of drama [would] ever grind out his doctor's thesis on Mr Coward's contribution to thought on the basis of the current one-act panels'. But no-one 'save Mr Coward and Miss Lawrence [would] give them such vibrancy on the stage'. They were 'personal vehicles'.[51]

3

The 1940s: Wartime entertainment, post-war discontent

Roland (*heatedly*)   [. . .] Every play you appear in is exactly the same, superficial, frivolous and without the slightest intellectual significance. You have a great following and a strong personality, and all you do is prostitute yourself every night of your life. All you do with your talent is to wear dressing-gowns and make witty remarks when you might really be helping people, making them think! Making them feel!

Garry   There can be no two opinions about it. I am having a most discouraging morning.

Present Laughter, PP4, 352/M4, 172

Coward spent much of the Second World War 'helping people', gathering information in Paris, raising international support for Britain abroad, entertaining troops and workers, and making one of the most applauded films to come out of the conflict, *In Which We Serve*. In the theatre his contribution to the war effort included two of his most successful comedies, one of which featured a comic alter ego, Garry Essendine, vain and self-centred but thoroughly professional – and written to be played by Coward himself.

At the outbreak of war in September 1939, *Design for Living*, which had opened in January at the Haymarket, was still running at the Savoy Theatre. With the temporary closure of the London theatres the company went on tour, returning to the Savoy in

December. The two plays Coward had written in the spring, *Present Laughter* and *This Happy Breed*, were in rehearsal for a tour that would have begun in Manchester. Coward started on the first phase of his war work, and the plays were not staged until 1942. In the meantime, on his way back from Australia, he wrote *Salute to the Brave* to fulfil a promise to John C. Wilson. This bitter attack on the selfishness of rich British expatriates who had taken refuge in the United States was not produced. On his return to the United Kingdom *Blithe Spirit* was written during a break of five days at Portmeirion, the exotic seaside village created by the architect Clough Williams-Ellis in North Wales. It opened in Manchester on 16 June 1941, and began its initial London run at the Piccadilly Theatre on 2 July, transferring subsequently to the St. James's and the Duchess and reaching a total of 1,977 performances. With Coward in the leading male roles, *Blithe Spirit* (with a touring cast), *This Happy Breed* and *Present Laughter* were presented together under the title 'Play Parade' in a twenty-five-week tour, beginning in Blackpool on 21 September 1942. *This Happy Breed* and *Present Laughter* played, again alternately, at the Haymarket in London for a season beginning in April 1943.[1]

The two comedies unfold in a world of peace, plenty and – in *Present Laughter* – unrestricted international travel. Their escapism was in itself a contribution to the war effort, and in each of them the central character has no graver responsibility than to entertain his public and please himself and those close to him. In *Blithe Spirit*, Charles Condomine – the author who engages a medium in order to obtain material for a novel about spiritualists and gets much more than he bargained for – recalls the romantic novelist David Bliss in *Hay Fever*. He inhabits a cosily upper middle-class milieu, while in *Present Laughter*, Garry Essendine, a star actor surrounded and protected by a faithful 'family' of confederates and prey to the incursions of outsiders and his own sexual opportunism, leads a life of glamour and gratification for his well-developed ego, his career serviced by dedicated professional associates. Paradoxically, Charles's respectable life is turned into a parody of the 'eternal triangle' by the arrival of the ghost of his first wife, while the philandering Garry's professional 'family' is defended and his security confirmed by the return in the final moments of the wife who separated from him 'years ago' but somehow 'never got round' to a divorce (*PP4*, 336/*M4*, 156). This is not quite the freewheeling convention-defying life of the leading characters in *Private Lives* or *Design for Living*, but in both the later plays a sense of freedom from earnestness is as much a feature (and attraction) of their pre-war world as the availability of fuel, food and opportunities for travel. Unlike *This Happy Breed* they are not products of the desire to be taken as a serious dramatist. Seriousness, though, marked the project that had preoccupied Coward between the writing of *Present Laughter* and *Blithe Spirit*. This was *Salute to the Brave*, but the work proved frustrating and, ultimately, unsuccessful.

After the war, Coward's mood was darkened by the treatment he had received at the hands of the authorities, particularly over his financial affairs, and the failure of *Pacific 1860*, the 'operette' (his chosen term) with which Drury Lane reopened in 1946. *"Peace in Our Time"*, was informed by his experience of France in the aftermath of the Occupation and the revelations of collaboration – at various levels – on the part of members of the fashionable and artistic worlds. Further disappointments were to follow in the ensuing eighteen months, including the tortuous saga of the musical *Ace of Clubs* and the frustrations surrounding the 'Samolan' comedy *Home and Colonial*, begun in 1949 but not produced in the United Kingdom until 1956 in its revised form as *South Sea Bubble*.

The Coward films, 1941–1945

The experience of work on the script of *In Which We Serve* (1942) in the late summer and autumn informed the decision that his collaborators on the film, David Lean, Ronald Neame and Anthony Havelock-Allan ('the boys') would do most of the scripting for subsequent film projects. In a letter to Wilson in April 1943 he noted that they had 'made an excellent script' for *This Happy Breed*, 'under father's supervision'.[2] Nevertheless, in January 1945 he told Wilson that he had 'finished an extremely good film script of "Still Life" which is called "Brief Encounter"'. His 'film boys' would start work on it at the end of the month. He would be 'hardly involved at all'. Meanwhile he was already at work on the 'operette' that would become *Pacific 1860*.[3] *This Happy Breed* and *Blithe Spirit* were filmed in 1943 and 1944–5 respectively, both directed by Lean, with minimal involvement on Coward's part. In the context of this study, *Brief Encounter* is the most significant, on account of Coward's involvement in revising a short, episodic stage play whose time scheme implies a longer encounter than that shown on screen.

Three notable aspects of the making of all the films are apparent from the diary: the collaborative nature of the scripting; the rapidity with which the writing had to be done; and Coward's openness to ideas that engaged his lifelong obsession with construction. In their subsequent accounts his collaborators tended to minimize Coward's participation in the scripting of *In Which We Serve* and *Brief Encounter*, but his diary and letters suggest otherwise. The first film required a new narrative and dialogue, while the second called for expansion and radical restructuring to concentrate into a short fictional time span a story that in its stage version developed over almost a year. In the process ownership of the story was given to one of the protagonists, Laura Jesson. Because almost everything is shown through her eyes, nothing is shown of her lover Alec's life when he is away from her. Richard Dyer has observed that in this film 'made almost entirely by men, most of whose story is told by a woman', there are moments when the voice-over may seem redundant as she is seen doing things she describes, and the effect is 'to insist that this long flashback is not just a device for telling one story in the context of another, but is specifically Laura's telling of it'.[4]

In *Future Indefinite* Coward deals with the film's genesis in a few sentences: 'I adapted *Still Life* [...] into a film script, rechristened it *Brief Encounter* and persuaded David Lean and Ronnie Neame to put it into production. [...] This, after some argument, they proceeded to do, which was lucky from all points of view, for it turned out to be a very good picture'.[5] Nevertheless, his diary shows that, as with *In Which We Serve*, a good deal of work on his part and several conferences were needed before this 'very good picture' was ready for production. In their accounts of the film 'the boys' later insisted that Coward did not write the script, and Neame suggested that they proposed episodes that would need to be added and that Coward then wrote the necessary dialogue. Sometimes they would provide 'stand-in dialogue' until they were able to meet with him: 'We would go to his studio and give him an outline of what the scene should convey. "Get out your little pencils," he would say. He would then pace up and down the room, pouring out the dialogue. He worked very quickly.'

On one occasion, after reading the 'stand in' text he asked 'Which of my little darlings wrote this brilliant Noël Coward dialogue?'[6] Coward's diary entries indicate an intensive period of 'work' that seems to indicate his own writing of scenes, which follow on from meetings and 'conferences'. Nevertheless, the film retains much of the play's dialogue in the station buffet, including the passage fraught with subtextual meaning in which Laura asks Alec to tell her about the diseases of the lung (*PP4*, 252–3/M3, 350–1). On 3 October Coward spent the whole day 'working with the boys. [...] Did revising and cutting and changed the title to "Brief Encounter."'[7]

As well as being more inviting to cinema audiences than the enigmatic 'Still Life', the new title is appropriate because the action of the film unfolds over no more than seven successive Thursdays, in what the scripts specify as the winter of 1938–9.[8] (The chronology is made clear in the dialogue between Laura and Alec and her voice-over commentary.) By contrast, the play's five scenes, confined to the refreshment room, span the period from April to the following March, an affair that was extended and real rather than merely potential. At the end of the play's third scene (October), after a conflicted debate about their continuing as lovers, Laura makes her sudden decision to pick up the piece of paper on which Alec has written the address of his friend Stephen Lynn's flat: '*she puts the paper in her bag and goes quietly out as the lights fade*' (*PP4*, 261–5/M3, 364). The lapse of time between this and Scene Four (December) indicates that Alec and Laura have been making use of the flat for at least two months, which suggests that they have had a physical relationship for at least that time. Stephen has come back unexpectedly, and Laura has 'crept out and down stairs – feeling like a prostitute' (*PP4*, 269/M3, 367). It is now that Alec tells her he has decided to take up a position in Johannesburg. The play's final scene takes place in the following March. For the film's presumed target audience (and the censors) the suggestion of a consummated – let alone protracted – affair would have been out of the question. Even so, the possibility of a more serious affair between Laura and Alec disturbed some reviewers. The *Sunday Dispatch* opined that 'a momentary and tearful embrace at the end [...] just saves it from being the Most Immoral Film of 1945', on account of a 'sympathy with reckless romance rather than dull domesticity' that looked like 'immoral propaganda, especially in these days of rather excessive domestic dissolution'.[9]

Sweet Sorrow becomes *Present Laughter*, 1939–1943

Present Laughter begins like a farce, with a young woman emerging from a bedroom – not her own – where she has spent the night after claiming to have lost the key to her front door. But the relationships clustered around Garry Essendine are not the genre's conventional ones: he is, after all, an actor. Liz, his wife, lives apart from him, but they are not divorced; his most intimate relationships are with his personal assistant, Monica, and his manservant, Fred; and his entanglements are with Daphne, an aspiring actress, and (more seriously) Joanna, the wife of Henry Lyppiatt, his best friend. Garry's agent, Morris Dixon, is having an affair with Joanna. There is also an eccentric Swedish maid, Miss Erikson, and he is plagued by Roland Maule, an ambitious young 'advanced' playwright who despises the kind of plays he appears in but is fixated on Garry. The world of *Present Laughter* is that of the theatre, conventionally unconventional in its amatory relationships. In the play these are implicitly heterosexual but, it has been noted, Garry has 'a homosexual's self-conscious anxiety about the maintenance of his public persona and reputation'.[10] His first name, like 'Noël', is disyllabic, his penchant for dressing gowns and the assembly of the 'family' around him, indicate that this is a version of Coward's milieu. The structure is a series of imbroglios successfully negotiated by Garry, with the appropriate moments of suspense and a conclusion in which he and Liz, apparently reconciled, sneak out of the flat, leaving the threats to their equilibrium safely confined in rooms on opposite sides of the stage, Roland Maule in the spare bedroom and the would-be actress Daphne Stillington in the office. Garry has executed a triumph of dramatic organization, appropriate to his kinship with the play's author.

As published by Heinemann in 1943, *Present Laughter* corresponds in all but a few minor details to an undated typescript in the archive that bears its original title, *Sweet Sorrow*, and appears to have been used by or prepared for Joyce Carey, who played Liz Essendine.[11] The first edition provided copy for the text in the fourth volume of *Play Parade* (PP4: 1954), while French's acting edition (1949) includes alterations to dialogue and stage business likely to reflect the 1947 Haymarket revival. In a letter to John C. Wilson, Coward described the play as 'not so much a play as a series of autobiographical pyrotechnics' that needed 'over and above everything else, abundant physical vitality [. . .] I played it more violently than I have ever played anything, and swept everything and everybody along with me at breakneck speed'.[12] Coward directed and played Garry Essendine in both 1943 and 1947, and the alterations recorded in French's edition, many of which relate to his own part, were probably the result of his experience of performance. For example, in Act One, when Garry embraces Daphne Stillington as he gives his performance of romantic parting – '*Au revoir*, my sweet – not good-bye – just *au revoir*', he '*closes his R. arm round her, then looks at his wrist-watch on the other, and kisses her*' (Fr. 14). Roland Maule has been given a '*wrist-breaking*' handshake that he inflicts on each new person he meets, and Garry looks in the mirror each time he goes to answer the door. Other additions include his explanation of a move in which he goes over to the window and waves his handkerchief when Morris claims that he and Joanna love each other: '**Garry** *rises, looks at* **Liz**, *puts a handkerchief to his face, turns and crosses above the settee to the window, at which he waves the handkerchief* [. . .] Just a horse I happen to know.' (Fr. 62). 'Her Majesty's' replaces 'the Haymarket' as a potential venue for the planned production (Fr. 38), and in the final, passionate lines of Act Two, Scene One, Joanna declares her love for Covent Garden rather than the Queen's Hall, which had been destroyed by incendiary bombs in 1941 (Fr. 51).

The acting edition's most elaborate alteration is in Garry's outburst in the play's closing scene, when, as he prepares to leave for a tour of Africa, he declares that he is the victim of exploitation. The first edition and the *Play Parade* text read as follows:

> **Garry** (*brokenly*) Go away – go away all of you – I can't bear any more. I have to face that dreadful sea-voyage tomorrow and then those agonizing months of drudgery across the length and breadth of what is admitted to be the most sinister continent there is. Go away from me – please go –
>
> **Liz** Go on, both of you, I'll talk to him.
>
> PP4, 425–6/M4, 245–6

French's edition gives Garry a more fully developed histrionic outburst:

Garry Go away – go away all of you – I can bear no more. (*He turns his back on them.* **Henry** *moves up* L *and sits on the settee.*) I have to face that dreadful sea-voyage tomorrow (*he turns and faces them*) and then those agonizing months of drudgery across the length and breadth of what is admitted to be the most sinister continent there is. (*He turns his back on them again.*) Please, please all of you go. (*He turns and faces them*) Parasites! Parasites! Vultures waiting to claw the flesh from my bones. For twenty years I've given you everything. I gave you my youth (*He rushes to* **Morris**) Where is my youth today? Sent whistling down the wind. I gave you my vitality (*He turns and rushes up* L. *to* **Henry.**) Where is my vitality? Drained out of me. (*He moves* C.) And now, when I'm nothing but a husk, and empty shell, I'm to be sent out to die in the white man's grave. Oh! Oh!

(*He throws himself on the floor, lies face down, with his head up stage on his arms, and drums with his feet.*)

Liz (*rising and putting her cigarette out*) Go on, both of you, I'll talk to him.

Fr. 92

As the scene moves to its close, in a stage direction included in neither the first Edition nor *Play Parade*, when Liz asks 'What's the matter?' before making gestures towards the office and the spare room, Garry motions her to silence, then '*humming a few bars of some "Hurry Music," he tears off his dressing gown and runs to his jacket, which is on the chair up* L'. He moves down to and asks 'You've got a sofa in your flat, haven't you?' and when she answers 'Of course. What are you talking about?' he speaks the final line, 'You're not coming back to me dear, I'm coming back to you.' (Fr. 93). In the first edition's final direction Liz responds to his mimed indication of the two doors: she '*looks bewildered for a minute and then begins to laugh*' before Garry '*quickly slips off his dressing gown and puts on his jacket and they tiptoe out together*' as the curtain falls. In French's edition the final moment is owned more decisively by Garry – and of course by the actor who plays him.

In early April 1943, when *Present Laughter* opened in Manchester at the beginning of the 'Play Parade' tour, Coward made a curtain speech, repeated at the other venues, with a simple message: 'We want to make you laugh'.[13] (After *This Happy Breed*, according to the *Liverpool Post*, 'Mr. Coward added to his thanks a well-phrased homily on the text "Careless Talk Costs Lives."') With the acting company cast across all three plays, each of which needed only one set, the programme was well adapted for touring in wartime. Because the original production of *Blithe Spirit* was still running in London, only *Present Laughter* and *This Happy Breed* opened at the Haymarket, on 29 and 30 April respectively.

Notions of both farce and 'high comedy' figured in the critical reception. Anxieties regarding possible 'bad taste' of the kind subsequently raised in reviews of *Blithe Spirit* were absent from most reviews of what *The Times* greeted as a 'wittily impudent and extremely well-invented French farce', and the *Daily Herald* welcomed as 'an ideal, sophisticated escape from the reality of our wartime theatre, nimbly witty, and most ably put over'.[14] After the twenty-five-week provincial tour of the 'Play Parade', it ran for 38 performances at the Haymarket, and in the 1947 revival at the same theatre it achieved 528 performances.[15] The defiance of conventional morality, though, remained a problem. W.A. Darlington in the *Daily Telegraph* declared: 'Let us be clear about it. There is no edification in this play, but there is any amount of fun'. Coward presented a 'mad little world with a topsy-turvy code of its own'.[16] Ivor Brown, in the *Observer*, cast the play's success in terms of the triumph of dialogue over plot: 'The story just lasts the distance, but what matters with Coward to-day, as with Congreve of old, is not the complication of events but the commentary upon them. It is the snip-snap of the dialogue, the febrile absurdity of the chatterbox types, that animates the play'. The *Stage*, commenting on this 'leap into the atmosphere of pre-war London', claimed that, as in the earlier comedies, '[b]ehind a façade of smartness nearly all the subsidiary characters in *Present Laughter* have also the morals and manners more or less of the farmyard'. Coward's own performance as Garry Essendine was praised for 'bringing out the man's essential charm in the course of his entirely disgraceful behaviour'.[17] Accusations that he is an 'unmitigated cad' gained credence from Garry's reply to Henry's direct question, 'Have you or have you not been Joanna's lover?' – 'Yes I have' – and his declaration that sex is 'vastly over-rated' but he 'enjoy[s] it for what it's worth' and 'fully intend[s] to go on doing so for as long as anybody's interested' (*PP4*, 420/M4, 422).

This Happy Breed: A 'Clapham Cavalcade'

Of the three plays produced on tour and in London, *This Happy Breed*, following the fortunes of a lower middle-class family in a London suburb from June 1919 to June 1939, is the only one to reflect the social and political situation of September 1939. The episodic structure, with the family's history paralleling national and international events, inevitably drew comparisons with *Cavalcade*. Although other models for a family story had recently proved successful, notably J.B. Priestley's reshuffling of chronology in *Time and the Conways* (1937) and the use of a middle-class family reunion in Dodie Smith's *Dear Octopus* (1938; revived 1940), Coward stayed with the structure that had served him well in *Cavalcade*, progressing in a similar manner through a series of family crises. Comparisons with the earlier play were reinforced by the final scene, in which Frank Gibbons addresses a speech to his baby grandson as the family prepare to leave for a new home. The *Stage* noted the technical significance of this 'break with the realistic art of the play as a whole', which was 'obviously designed as a compliment [sic] to the toast to England that brought down the curtain in *Cavalcade*'.[18]

The patriotic message of the play, expressed most eloquently by Frank's remonstrance to Reg, the son who is straying towards Bolshevism, at the end of Act One, was reflected in the *Liverpool Post*'s brief summary: 'Through weal and woe the Gibbons keep their simple pattern of life intact and its colours are the red, white and blue of the Union Jack'. *This Happy Breed* received less critical attention than the two other plays in the repertoire, but the reviews anticipate the reception of the film version in focusing on matters of class. The valiant efforts of a cast obliged to play outside the class conventions of the other two plays did not convince every reviewer. *What's On* commented that 'many of the cast [were] inclined to make the Clapham Common people a little too common, with the result that there [were] faint signs of burlesque at times'. The severest disapproval came from the *Daily Worker*, which complained that the family was 'no more than a burlesque from an early Coward [. . .] a most extraordinary and vulgar collection of stock vaudeville types'.[19] Given the enthusiastic strike-breaking activities of Frank Gibbons and his next-door neighbour during the 1926 crisis, the Communist paper's response is hardly surprising. Nor would there be much to approve of in Frank's fatherly talk with Reg, and his insistence that the ills of the world are due to 'good old human nature' rather than economic and political conditions (*PP4*, 478–80/*M4*, 296–8). Wry acceptance of the way of the world and underlying decency and patriotism are more or less the sum total of the Gibbons outlook. His speech to his grandson, in the final scene, set in June 1939, is not included in the film version. The shooting script includes a version that, as in the play, includes bitter reflections on the pre-war government's policy of appeasement – put down to the influence of 'people who have let themselves get soft and afraid' – but adds a warning about the conflict that Frank considers inevitable: 'It's no good just fighting for our own security and happiness; we've got to fight for the security and happiness of every living being in the whole wide world'. A handwritten note in the margin warns that 'This final speech awaits the author's final revisions and draft'.[20] The version eventually prepared for the film includes more comment than that in the play on 'the silly old politicians' who have brought the country to this pass, and develops further the idea of fighting for the rights of others:

> In the future, it's other people we've got to fight for as well as ourselves. We've got to fight as we've never fought before, not only with guns and ships and bombs and aeroplanes – and we're going to need a hell of a lot of them – we've got to fight with our minds. If you remember that, there's a hope – just a hope that one day this world will be fit to live in and to die for.

Apart from other considerations, this would have been a singularly 'wordy' note with which to end the film – it might not have struck the right note in early 1944, when the outcome of the conflict could still not be predicted with certainty.[21]

Salute to the Brave and *Time Remembered*, 1941–1943: The British abroad

In January 1941, after his exhausting tour of Australia and New Zealand, where he had been entertaining troops and promoting support for the British war effort, Coward found himself on Canton

Island, an atoll in the South Pacific. He was enjoying swimming ('Sharks rare, so am rising above them'), tennis and relaxed conversation in good company: 'Absolutely enchanting life. This month will stand out in three horrible years with a halo round it'. On the evening of Friday 3 January, he 'began racking [his] brains to think of a play to write for Jack [Wilson]'. The initial motivation was simple: 'I must make some money this year'. Then, just as he was going to sleep an idea struck him, 'an attack on the rich international set migrating to America during the last summer'.

> The title dropped into my mind 'Salute to the Brave'. Heroine, sort of smart English woman coming over to stay with rich people, with her two children. Period of one month passes and bad London bombing begins. She is disgusted with behaviour of house party, particularly English writer in house who is doing nothing but slam England. Final row in last act. She leaves having (a) completely conquered her fear of bombing, discomforts, etc. and (b) having seen how idiotic her life had been for the last fifteen years with all these worthless people.[22]

The next day he 'started work laboriously on characters' and 'doped them all out'. But on Sunday, a 'beastly day' with 'pouring rain', he seemed to have reached an impasse: 'Constructed first act, then stuck. Bad headache. Finally gave up. Went to bed miserable. It's no use, I cannot write a play until the war is over. If only I had time – just a few months really free. There is so much I could write. God damn everything.'

On Monday he at first felt 'relieved' that he had given up the idea of the play, but the moment he thought this, he 'began puzzling at it again', and 'worked like a dog the whole morning and constructed the whole play'. He started the 'first descriptive page' on Thursday 6 February, and began 'the whole play in earnest' the following morning, but by Saturday, despite 'getting through first act', he was finding the characters 'sticky' and had not yet 'got the flow', and cautioned himself to 'have patience and not get into a state'. Despite progress over the next few days, by 13 February his patience was wearing thin: 'Bitterly miserable about play. On the verge of scrapping it. I hate the characters too much, even to write amusingly against them. A few years ago I might have written this play easily, but now it does not seem worth while'.[23] He worked 'laboriously' on the morning of 14 February, but after lunch he read through what he had written and 'made final decision to scrap it'. Nevertheless, he persevered, and by 5 March the work was done: 'Started and finished third scene of second act. Play now finished. Feel exhausted. Not sure whether it is good enough but anyhow it is done and I have never worked so hard on a play in my life'.[24] Ten days later, having arrived in California, he read the play to Jack and Natasha Wilson, who both 'liked it', and in New York on 28 March he recorded that Katharine Cornell and Guthrie McClintic were both 'mad about the part' (that is, the heroine) and she might take it on. After his return to London, though, he read the play again and 'hated it'. Gladys Calthrop and the other members of his inner circle were 'attentive and interested, not violently impressed', and he knew 'it's no good for England anyway'.[25]

He put *Salute to the Brave* aside until April 1943, when he told Wilson that he was rewriting it and explained the new title, a quotation from Swinburne's 'Atalanta in Calydon': 'Time remembered is grief forgotten'. A bout of influenza, followed by jaundice, had forced him to take a period of convalescence in Tintagel at a hotel 'filled with prosperous escapists in evening dress'. The situation gave fresh impetus to his writing, and he had 'ruthlessly cut and rewritten' the play: '[I]t is now I think a very good script . . . The play now goes much more in a straight line and there is not so much talk and not so much bitchiness. It really does look better in perspective. You shall have a script as soon as it is typed.'[26] The plot in both versions is more or less as outlined in the diary entry of 3 January, but in the revised script Coward removed the second scene of the second act. In the first version Lelia is on the verge of starting an affair with Chuck Morris, a Canadian airman in love with her American journalist friend Lindsay Hobart, but pulls back from the temptation. Material from the omitted scene is transferred in the revisions to a later conversation in which Lelia asks Lindsay about the gossip regarding her past *affaires*, and expresses her sense of finding a new perspective on the self-indulgent life she has led until now (M9, 61). In a speech moved verbatim from the original scene, she looks at the room they are in, with its 'monotonous, anaesthetic luxury':

> For years I seem to have been doing nothing but move through a succession of rooms exactly like this, and suddenly, when they

proved to be vulnerable, when I saw that outside pressure could cave them in and break them to bits, I got scared and ran here, because they still exist, they're still important, they're still a bulwark against reality. And, oh God, what a fool I was.

Salute, 2-2-44/M9, 62

She apologizes for 'using, quite unscrupulously, that instinctive mutual liking' she and Lindsay have taken to each other and 'unloading [her] personal dilemmas' onto her: in the deleted scene she uses the same terms in cautioning Chuck against falling in love with her. This affirms a bond between the two women that will support Lelia in the final scene when she tells her hostess Norma about her decision to leave and lets her know exactly what she thinks of her and her way of life. Her declaration of newly-acquired self-awareness would have come too early in the play: 'The whole shape of my life, in the light of all that is happening now, suddenly seems to have been fatuous beyond belief. Not wicked or cruel or bad, but just abysmally fatuous.' (*Salute*, 2-2-13). Placed towards the end, it gives a different trajectory to her development. The change also removes a suggestion of susceptibility to amorous intrigue on Lelia's part, as her solidarity with Lindsay is necessary for the denouement. (Coming earlier, it would also have disclosed that Lelia had already decided to return to London.)

Replacing the patriotic fanfare of *Salute to the Brave* with the new title, *Time Remembered*, emphasized the centrality of retrospection in the development of Lelia, and the manner in which it is distinct from the sentimental and ultimately pointless nostalgia voiced but not deeply felt by some of the other characters. Minor changes in *Time Remembered* include the modification of details of the reported effects of the Blitz, including a reference to there being 'not much left' of Covent Garden and Lelia's account of a friend's death in a taxi during a daylight raid. From the latter Coward removed her explanation that this was 'the only serious casualty so far among people we know', but that there are 'lots of casualties among the people we don't know' in the East End and the suburbs:

> Thousands and thousands of people struggle out every morning from their homes or the air raid shelters, grumbling a bit because they haven't slept very well or making jokes because the trains

aren't quite on time, and a great many of them never get back again.

Salute, 2-1-7

As Barry Day suggests, this may have seemed to be 'laying on the "Britain Can Take It!" message too strongly for his audience to accept' (M9, 3). It also raises the question of which audience – British or American – the revised play was aimed at. By late 1943, as he was still hoping that Wilson would stage the play in New York, it made sense to remove or tone down some references more directly relevant to the situation in the spring of 1941, when the United States had not yet entered the war. In the final moments of Act Two, Scene One and Scene Two respectively in both the earlier and later typescript versions, Lelia, after an argument with Norma and their temporary reconciliation, is apparently on the brink of decision, when she turns on the radio and we hear

'the kind of emotionally charged broadcast report we associate with American radio: The news is a description of the "latest airraid" on London infused with all the extra vocal drama of which the announcer is capable. The voice seems to grow louder and louder and [Lelia] is still striding up and down the room as –
THE CURTAIN FALLS'.

Salute, 2-1-32

The Methuen edition, prepared with performance in mind, substitutes a more measured report, with a recording of an excerpt from the peroration of Churchill's speech in the House of Commons on 4 June 1940: 'We shall not flag or fail...'

Salute to the Brave and its revision show Coward working against the grain, and making changes that included a major alteration in the presentation of his central character. Nevertheless, although *Time Remembered* is more economical in telling the story of Lelia's arrival at a decision based on clear-sightedness, neither version is fully satisfactory. The single plot line seems meagre, and too much time is spent with the characters Coward knew he could not 'write amusingly'. Once they have condemned themselves out of their own mouths, an effect achieved in the first act, there is little to be done with Norma and her less sympathetic houseguests. *Time Remembered* remained unproduced: it was not published until

2018, and, as with *Volcano* in 1957, no references to it were included in the published *Diaries*.

Blithe Spirit, 1941: An 'improbable farce'

Coward's next play was far removed from the bitterness of *Salute to the Brave*, and the experience of writing it was altogether different. On 21 April 1941 he told Binkie Beaumont that he 'had an idea for a play and would try to get away and write it for him', and in the course of discussing financial matters the next day he and Lorn Loraine considered a possible solution: 'Title "Blithe Spirit." Very gay, superficial comedy about a ghost. Feel it may be good'.[27] On 2 May he and Joyce Carey were on their way to Portmeirion, both with plays to write. (Hers, on John Keats, did not reach the stage.) 'Really', he wrote in his diary on 3 May, 'Portmeirion is a lovely place. One of the loveliest I have ever seen in the British Isles'. He had 'spent the morning in the sun constructing play', Joyce was, as ever, 'very helpful'. In *Future Indefinite* he recalled that they 'sat on the beach with our backs against the sea wall and discussed my idea exclusively for several hours'.[28] A daily routine was established: 'Up 7.30. Breakfast 8. Started work 9. Break for Lunch 1 to 2. Worked 2 to 7'. This continued for the next five days, and, despite an 'agonising moment' on the penultimate day when his typewriter 'went wrong', *Blithe Spirit* was completed by Friday 9 May. On Saturday he 'revised a small amount', mainly typographical errors. On Sunday, he read the play through to Joyce: 'Really feel I have done a rousing good comedy'. The grimness of war reasserted itself on their arrival in London after a pleasant journey from Bangor to Euston. He was 'pretty horrified to see what the streets looked like'. The previous night had apparently been 'the worst yet. [. . .] Dirt and dust and smell of burning' were 'everywhere'.[29]

In *Future Indefinite* Coward recalled the rapidity with which the comedy had been written. He had known 'from the first morning's work' that he was on the right track and that 'it would be difficult, with that situation and those characters, to go far wrong'. Other plays had been written at speed, notably *Private Lives* (four days) and *Present Laughter* (six days):

Blithe Spirit was exceptional from these two [. . .] only because its conception was followed immediately by the actual writing of it. *Private Lives* lived in my mind several months before it emerged. *Present Laughter* had waited about, half formulated, for nearly three years before I finally wrote it.[30]

A one-page list of acts and scenes in the archive confirms that at an early stage – probably on 3 May – Coward had planned most of the play's incidents and characters. There were two notable exceptions: the second act would include a scene in which Madame Arcati would be left in tears after a dressing down from 'Mr Emsworth', her superior in the Society for Psychical Research, who would also be present in third act; and the third-act ritual to 'dematerialise' the two ghosts had not yet been worked out – although at the top of the page Coward noted the rhyme to be used in it, 'Ghostly spectre ghoul or fiend'.

The play as it stood at the end of the week in Portmeirion is represented by a typescript endorsed by its author as 'Original Typescript / Port Meirion [*sic*] / May 1941'.[31] 'Mr. Emsworth' does not appear, and in almost every respect this script corresponds to the play as performed and published. Among the lines absent from the first edition, the most interesting occurs in Act Two, Scene Two, when Ruth responds to Madame Arcati's suggestion that she should 'try to look on the bright side' by asking how she would feel if her husband's first wife should 'suddenly appear from the grave' and came to live in the house with her. Does she suppose she would 'be able to look on the bright side'? (*PP5*, 569/M4, 75).

> **Mme. Arcati** I have never had a husband Mrs Condomine. Madame Arcati is merely a nom de plume as you might say. My real name is Gladys Stephens.
>
> **Ruth** I am sure that's very interesting but I am sure you will agree that at the moment it is irrelevant.

Coward evidently decided that this information was indeed irrelevant: it might have detracted a little from the seriousness with which he felt the character should be treated, a point on which Madame Arcati herself insists and which, as soon became apparent, Coward was at pains to emphasize in rehearsal.

He 'felt peculiar' when he read in the *Daily Mail* that Shelagh Leggatt, Lord Monkton's secretary had been killed in a plane crash on Whit Monday. He immediately altered a reference to the death of 'old Mrs. Leggatt' on that day to that of 'old Mrs. Plummet'. (The alteration is made by hand in the typescript.)[32] There is one odd misprint in the first edition (1941) in the first scene, when Charles asks Ruth whether she remembers where he got the inspiration for his novel *The Light Goes Out*. Her response is preceded by a mysterious stage direction that would severely tax any actor and is in fact the first part of Ruth's line: '(*suddenly seeing that haggard, raddled old woman in the hotel at Biarritz*) Of course I remember – we sat up half the night talking about it'. This found its way into the *Play Parade* and Methuen editions, despite being corrected in French's acting edition.[33]

Cole Lesley points out that one model for Madame Arcati was Winifred Ashton (the novelist Clemence Dane), with her formidable vitality, 'gowns – one cannot call them dresses – to the floor', and a penchant for schoolgirl slang.[34] A diary entry from the weeks on Canton Island suggests another possible but less sympathetic inspiration. At dinner on 20 February Coward encountered 'an elderly, tubby, made-up old girl who is a spiritual medium'. 'She talked incessantly about her contacts with the spirit world. Her sole companions seem to be those who have passed on. Poor old thing. She has written three psychic books and is going to lecture in Australia. Think she is mad as a hatter'.[35] Far from being a 'poor old thing', Madame Arcati, arguably the play's most sympathetic character, is described on her first entrance as 'a striking woman, dressed not too extravagantly but with a decided bias towards the barbaric' who 'might be any age between forty-five and sixty-five' (*PP4*, 510/ M4, 16). Nevertheless, his fellow traveller's easy familiarity with those who have 'passed on' may have lingered in Coward's mind, even if the notion of 'a gay, superficial comedy about a ghost' came a while later.

In due course the play was read to Beaumont, Gladys Calthrop, Lorn Loraine and other intimate friends. 'Wild enthusiasm' was qualified by a 'casting argument' with Beaumont, who was 'rather damping about not being able to get anyone'.[36] After a false start with Leslie Howard, 'who was amiable and sweet as usual, but completely uninterested in anything but his film', he approached Cecil Parker and Kay Hammond for Charles and Elvira, and decided to offer Ruth to Fay Compton. Edward Molyneux said he could make the dress for Elvira but not that for Ruth, pointing out that he hadn't the staff or time for both but, in any case, it was not necessary for Ruth's clothes to have 'the Molyneux touch'.[37] Rehearsals began on 26 May and on 3 June 'Margaret Rutherford came for the first time. Word-perfect in the first act and absolutely perfect'. After an afternoon rehearsal that was 'rather tiresome', with 'everyone sleepy', in the evening Coward wrote the lyric for a new song he had 'started composing' the day before, 'London Pride': 'Finally got it. Think it's good'. The next day brought one of the frequent reminders of the paradoxical situation of leading an almost 'normal' theatrical life in wartime: 'Morning rehearsal all right, but I have an awful sense of personal effort as though my mind was not quite on the job. I do wish England realised a little more that there is a war on. Lunched with Binkie and Evelyn [Laye] w[ith] Ivy absolutely crammed and very theatrically gay'.[38] On 12 June – after a first dress rehearsal the previous day – he observed once again the isolating effect of theatre work: 'In theatre most of the day, oblivious of the fact that the Germans were massing troops on the Russian frontier. Occupied only with whether or not Margaret Rutherford remembered her lines'. The dress rehearsal was 'very good, considering'.[39] In Manchester on 16 June for the beginning of the tour, after a day of 'chaos' caused by the stage manager having left the prompt script on the train (it was retrieved from Blackpool before the evening's rehearsal), and further dress rehearsals through the morning and afternoon of the next day, *Blithe Spirit* was ready for its first public performance.

Coward's diary reflects a perennial paradox of theatre work, the contrast between the author and director's point of view and that of the audience: 'Audience marvellous. Performance pretty bad. Fay too slow. Margaret awful. Completely lost her head and dried up all over the place. Play went marvellously, roars and scream of applause'. In his curtain speech, Coward told the audience that 'in spite of the exigencies of war' his 'truest happiness' was and always would be 'to feel that something [he had] written or composed or acted' would have given them pleasure: 'I wrote this light play from entirely selfish motives, not to cheer you up, the people of England don't need cheering up, but to recapture for myself, however lonely, the personal happiness of life in my own true home again, the theatre, for during these last two difficult years I have missed it sadly'.[40] The next morning's notices were all 'enthusiastic, but mostly irritating' but the evening's performance was 'better but still a bit untidy', and on 18 June, after seeing the matinée ('Margaret better, but still fluffy') Coward returned to London.[41]

Over the next few days, he turned to another project, having done a 'rough verse' for 'London Pride', on arrival at the Savoy. Up in Leeds on 26 June he saw two performances of the play, and recognized that Rutherford 'undoubtedly ha[d] a strange, original quality', but was 'technically inexperienced and incapable of taking direction'.[42] After the first night in London – 'Got great ovation on entrance into box. Play went very well. Audience excellent' – he noted that she was 'not good but [would] obviously make a success'. At the curtain there were 'one or two boos' amid the cheers: W.A. Darlington, in the *Telegraph*, thought, like Coward, that they came 'from disgruntled spiritualists'. On 18 July Coward wrote to Wilson with a fuller account:

> The notices were marvellous on the whole and the business terrific even through heat waves. The performance is excellent. Fay is better than she has ever been and was lovely and easy to direct. I've cured her of all her bad mannerisms and she looks charming. Cecil is really first rate and very charming too in a pompous hen's bottom sort of way. The best performance is Kay Hammond who is absolutely bewitching and a much finer actress than I suspected she was with a wonderful sense of timing. Edward has made her as simple and lovely a dress as I have ever seen and she looks a vision.

Coward describes Elvira's 'ghost' effect, achieved with a green follow spot and the actress's 'dead white make-up with a little green in it, green powder on face, hair and arms, scarlet lips and nails and ordinary green eye make-up'. Unfortunately, the 'great disappointment' was Margaret Rutherford. She was 'indistinct, fussy', and 'beyond her personality' lacked technical resources: 'She merely fumbles and gasps and drops things and throws many of my best lines down the drain. [. . .] I need hardly say she got marvellous notices. So much for that'.[43]

In September he offered advice for the New York production, with Clifton Webb as Charles and Mildred Natwick as Madame Arcati. Wilson had been sent a copy of the London promptbook, and Coward offered a few additional notes:

> In our production Fay, with her head down in the dark, does the Little Tommy Tucker verse [from Madame Arcati's 'control', Daphne] in a very high adenoidal child's voice. [. . .] Clifton ought to have a wine-coloured smoking jacket or a blue one – whichever he prefers – as long as it shows the two black arm bands in the last act which is a tremendous laugh.

(The two armbands, one on each arm, specified in French's acting edition and mentioned in reviews, are absent in the first edition's stage direction.) He felt that Natwick would be a more appropriate interpreter of her part than Rutherford:

> The great thing I have been trying to impress, vainly, on Margret Rutherford is that as the part is rather extravagant it must be played with great matter-of-factness. [. . .] The most successful scenes in the play from the point of view of tumultuous laughter are the breakfast scene at the beginning of the second act and the scene between Elvira and Charles – the first scene of the last act. Tempo, of course, all through the play, is essential.[44]

Coward's description of the London reviews as 'marvellous on the whole' in his letter to Wilson was accurate. There was praise for the actors, especially Rutherford and Hammond, and, in the main, for the play itself, albeit with reservations. These were of two kinds: technical questions arising partly from its claim to be a farce, and anxieties about the propriety of its treatment of bereavement and the 'spirit world'. Serious works of the interwar decades grouped together by Rebecca D'Monté as 'ghost plays' – including Coward's own unproduced *Post-Mortem* (1931) – are described by her as having 'underpinned the era's desperate need to make sense of the unfolding tragedy and compensate for the loss of what would amount to a generation' in the 1914–18 war.[45] *Blithe Spirit* was another kind of response altogether to the tragedy that had now arrived, and one that made some reviewers uneasy.

The *Manchester Guardian*'s notice of the premiere reflects both considerations: 'It is a good deal more than farce; it is a sort of chess pattern in psychical research where every move is strictly according to rule'. Even the 'farcical and, theatrically, not very fortunate ending' might be 'justified on that understanding'. After noting 'moments when this very unusual farce trembles on the edge of accomplished tragedy' – notably at the end of Act Two, when Elvira realizes that she has caused the death of Ruth rather than Charles in the car crash – the reviewer makes an interesting point about the matter of genre: 'it provides nearly three hours of extremely diverting stagecraft and dialogue, punctuated by surprises which are often so completely unexpected and yet so completely logical that one has all the satisfaction which arises from following a thoroughly well-constructed thriller'.[46] The same issues were raised in several reviews of the London opening. On farce, A.E. Wilson in the *Star* placed Coward firmly outside the familiar territory dominated by Ben Travers, author of *Thark* (1927), *Rookery Nook* (1928) and *Plunder* (1928). Coward had achieved 'something which is not only entertaining, but also extremely original', by showing 'that it is possible to write a farce which is neither about the debagging of a comedian, the concealment of some inconvenient intruder in a bedroom, nor any of the threadbare tricks'. Elspeth Grant in the *Daily Sketch* ('Coward's Great Farce'), reporting on 'a theatrical occasion of almost pre-war brilliance', hedged her bets: this was 'a theme which might have been hideously macabre, and could even now be considered in quite execrable taste'.[47]

No doubt to the author's chagrin, in the *Observer* Ivor Brown praised Rutherford's Mme. Arcati as 'the saving of this farce about the dead because it keeps it from fact and feeling'.[48] James Agate, in the *Sunday Times*, identified one of the 'tenths of seconds when we held our breaths' as the play ventured into dangerous territory. At Charles's response to Ruth's comment that Elvira 'was of the earth, earthy' – 'Well she is now' – 'you could hear the audience sit up in horror as great as that of a golf crowd when the champion fluffs his ball into a bunker', but in the next four speeches Coward showed himself 'the Hagen of witty retrieval'. (Agate assumes his readers will recognize a reference to the American golfer Walter Hagen, 1892–1969.)[49] The mild misgivings expressed and for the most part dismissed by other reviewers, pale beside Graham Greene's comprehensive attack in the *Spectator*.[50] After pointing out the precedent set by James Thorne Smith in his 'Topper' novels and the films made from them, Greene claims that all Coward has added to his themes 'is crammed into an admirable and witty first act', while 'the rest is all words and repetition and a bad taste of which Thorne Smith was never guilty'.[51] Greene takes issue with Coward over the appearance of Charles in the final act wearing two black armbands, as perhaps his 'most meaningless exhibition of bad taste – a bad taste which springs from an ability to produce the appearances of ordinary human relationships – of man and wife – and an inability to feel them'. (This is a barely disguised reference to Coward's sexuality.) The bad taste, Greene wrote, was all the more evident 'now when sudden death is common and dissolves more marriages than the divorce courts'. His most spiteful comment was reserved for last:

> It would be charitable to suppose that Mr. Coward conceived the play in the crude peaceful sunlight of Australia, between his patriotic broadcasts, and that when he has been longer in this country he will be less blithe about this spirit world of his where dead women behave like characters in *Private Lives* and a saint [Joan of Arc, as reported by Elvira] is 'good fun'.

This can hardly have improved Coward's feelings about Greene, who had made slighting references to him in passing in his cinema journalism.[52]

Most of work on the film of *Blithe Spirit* had been left to 'the boys', but Coward was unequivocal in his response to the result. One report – 'Well, dears, you've just fucked up the best thing I ever wrote' – may be apocryphal, but it reflects other less forthright expressions of his disappointment.[53] In his diary he noted that the notices for the film were 'all raves' which was 'very silly, as it is not good'.[54] This may have stemmed in part from the film's alteration to the story's ending: after his departure from the now haunted house, Charles is killed in a car crash and is seen with his two wives as a trio of semi-transparent ghosts sitting on the wall of a bridge at the site of the accident. There was also the problem of casting: Kay Hammond as Elvira was not as persuasive on film as she had been on stage, and Rex Harrison was too young for the successful novelist Charles and, to the mind of some reviewers, too sophisticated and self-conscious in technique. Among the sequences 'opening out' the film from the confines of the Condomine house, reviews singled out the set for Madame Arcati's eccentric home, and the episode in which Charles allows Elvira to take the wheel of his car, astonishing an Automobile Association patrol man with the sight of an apparently driverless vehicle.

Peace in Our Time and *Home Sweet Home*, 1947: Trying to catch the post-war mood

On 26 July 1945, with the Labour government 'sweeping in on an overwhelming majority', Coward wrote that he 'always felt that England would be bloody uncomfortable during the immediate post-war period, and it now almost a certainty that it will be so'.[55] In the spring of 1945, he had begun work on *Pacific 1860*. After a false start as a musical with a modern setting, the revised 'operette' was completed in the autumn.[56] By now, euphoria following the cessation of the European war had been qualified by increasingly harsh economic conditions at home. On 28 February 1946 he recorded the decision to stage the 'operette' at Drury Lane.[57] This was clearly envisaged as a brightly celebratory event to respond to the bleak post-war situation, but the outcome was not what he anticipated: this was one of the worst winters on record, and the bomb-damaged theatre was in a poor state of repair and barely heated, a situation only partially remedied by opening night. After the opening on 19 December the headlines told the story: 'Coward Show has Colour but Lacks Pep' (*Daily Mirror*), 'Noel Coward is Lost in the Pacific' (*Evening News*), 'Mr. Coward Misses the Pacific Boat' (*News Chronicle*), 'Dead Calm in the Pacific' (*John O'London's Weekly*). Anthony Cookman's verdict in the *Tatler and Bystander* was representative: 'The tender scenes are never more than operetta at its easiest, and the wit of the Coward of comedy and of revue scarcely flickers'[58] *Pacific 1860* managed 129 performances, before being replaced at Drury Lane on 30 April 1947 by *Oklahoma!*, which ran for 1,543 performances.

On 3 November 1946, with *Pacific 1860* still in rehearsal, Coward was contemplating a play based on what might have happened if German forces had invaded and occupied England in 1940. *Might Have Been* would be set in 'a public house somewhere between Knightsbridge and Sloane Square'.

> The whole horrible anticlimax of occupation and demoralization for five years culminating in the invasion of England from France by free English, Americans and French. The family conflict is conflict arising from Resistance movements, etc. Lovely last scene as the publican, with his wife, daughter and son killed,

listens to the secret radio turned on full, announcing the successful invasion from Dover Castle and finishing with 'God Save the King', while the Germans are battering the door down.[59]

Writing began in Palm Beach on 16 February 1947, and on 13 May he thought of the title, *'Peace in Our Time'*. The ironic quotation (hence the quotation marks) of Neville Chamberlain's famous announcement of the 'Munich Agreement' might 'get [them] into trouble, but to hell with that'.[60]

The entire action takes place in the saloon bar of the 'Shy Gazelle' and follows the events in the lives of the publican, his family and their customers from November 1940, in the aftermath of a successful German invasion, to the liberation in May 1945. The publican, Fred Shattock, has much in common with Frank Gibbons, and in one speech he even echoes his Clapham counterpart's opinion of Neville Chamberlain and Appeasement: 'As I see it, it's like this. We were the finest people in the world – see . . . but we were getting too pleased with ourselves. [. . .] Even as late as 1938 we were dancing in the streets because a silly old man promised us "Peace in Our Time."' (*PP5*, 142–3/M7, 142–3). His wife Nora is more timorous but equally steadfast in contempt for the invaders. Their son Steve, an airman shot down in the Battle of Britain, has escaped from a prisoner of war camp and made his way to England to fight with the resistance movement. The Shattocks' daughter Doris, a receptionist at the Savoy Hotel, which has been commandeered by the Germans, is also an active member. In the course of the play the bar is frequented by a suave but 'steely' Gestapo officer, Albrecht Richter and Chorley Bannister, an 'intellectual' author and editor who collaborates with the regime. The various London types include a nightclub singer and her boyfriend, a couple whose son is presumed missing in action but who turns up after escaping from an internment camp on the Isle of Wight, and a prostitute whose clientele includes German soldiers. Janet Braid, an author who specializes in sly digs at Richter, confronts Bannister's self-serving claim to be a realist by announcing that her slogan is John of Gaunt's evocation of 'this sceptred isle' from *Richard II*: 'This blessed plot, this Earth, this realm, this England – This land of such dear souls, this dear, dear land', provoking the response from Bannister that he 'would be the first to agree that Shakespeare was second to none in commercialising patriotism' (*PP5*, 210/M7,

211–12). After several more lengthy exchanges on this theme, she gives him 'two ringing slaps on the face' and walks out.

Materials from the preparation of the play (with its working title *Might Have Been*) include detailed biographies of Fred Shattock and Bannister, whose career as camp follower has included left- as well as right-wing causes. (In this respect, though not in his attitude to the war, the critic Cyril Connolly was a probable model.)[61] There are also notes on the possible scenario for an invasion to rescue Britain from its occupiers and other necessary historical information. A one-page scene-by-scene synopsis differs from the final script in two especially important respects: the Shattocks' son Stephen is 'betrayed by the intellectual' and shot at the end of the Act Two. In the final scene, as indicated in the diary entry from 3 November, Fred dies heroically as the 'Secret radio' broadcasts the liberated BBC's announcement of the invasion: 'German police at door. Radio turned louder. Shots through door and windows. Radio full blast. God save the King. Fred stands to attention'. In the completed script, the wife, son and daughter are not killed, and Stephen's survival to play a part in the rescue mission is part of Coward's elaboration of the 'resistance' movement and its members. These now include Venning, a local doctor, and a visiting lady who is the leader of its Cornwall branch. The synopsis refers to a 'night club singer [who has] been sleeping with Gestapo agent' and 'suffered the brutality under his charming manners'. She has 'tried to murder him and has injured him very badly', and 'never reappears – understood to have been shot'. Possibly feeling that this was a needless complication, Coward saved the idea of 'horizontal collaboration' (as it was known in France) for the expulsion from the pub of the unfortunate Gladys Mott, who appears only in the final scene. Fred's heroic stand is replaced with a satisfyingly melodramatic climax in which the Gestapo official Albrecht Richter is tied to a chair facing the door and is killed by the bullets of his own men as they storm the pub. (According to a report in the magazine *Illustrated*, which published rehearsal photographs from Brighton, until two days before the London opening the chosen victim was Chorley Bannister, but it was decided that his death would not have the same impact as that of Richter.)[62]

After an enthusiastic reception in its pre-London run in Brighton, and on the opening night at the Lyric (22 July), Coward celebrated 'a cosy little triumph' for a 'bloody good play', but the next day's press followed a familiar pattern.[63] The warmest praise came from W.A. Darlington in the *Telegraph*: 'This play cannot possibly fail. It is too moving, too exciting, too deft – and too timely. We need to be reminded, just now, that we are people of spirit'.[64] Some reviewers expressed respect for his technique, with the *New Statesman* finding him 'not only brilliant in his management of an episodic play, but finished and faithful in his Cockney sketches', and the *Spectator* applauding 'an unrivalled, if conventional, understanding of stagecraft', but the general verdict on the treatment of the play's theme was one of disappointment. Alan Dent, in the *News Chronicle*, after complaining about the improbabilities of the plot, homed in on one of Coward's abiding anxieties: 'I should not mind Mr. Coward trying to discover that non-existent (or anyhow non-important) serious side to himself if the process did not do such harm to his wit'. In the *Evening News*, under the headline 'Coward Just Misses Greatness', Stephen Williams wrote that 'the whole thing is good theatre, but I have an idea that Coward wanted it to be great drama'.[65] Harold Hobson in the *Sunday Times* complained that lack of a sense of the true horrors of occupation had produced 'a miniature of Armageddon done in water-colours'.[66] Several reviews compared *Peace in Our Time* unfavourably with Jean-Paul Sartre's *Men Without Shadows*, recently directed by Peter Brook at the Lyric, Hammersmith, with its grim depiction of the torture of captured resistance fighters.

There were a few dismissive references to the play's patriotism, prompted by a first-night speech in which Coward alluded to his words on the first night of *Cavalcade* in 1931. In the *Spectator*, Lewis Ladbroke suggested that sometimes it seemed as though he had 'left his typewriter and unfinished script' to 'a person as sentimental and prejudiced as an Edwardian nursery governess. Or [. . .] to our old friend Colonel Blimp himself'.[67] The *Daily Worker*, whose critic had not been sent seats for the first night, complained that the play 'develop[ed] solidly along the well-tried grooves of the Hollywood Resistance Movement' and that there was no sense of 'Britain struggling in unity with occupied Europe. To be British is enough'. The headline said it all: 'Masterly Piece of Ham'.[68] It was also felt that Coward had gone too far in Janet Baird's impassioned rendition of the lines from *Richard II*. To Beverley Baxter in the *Evening Standard* this suggested that he had 'reached a danger point in his career. Sincerity, patriotism and emotion are not enough. Lack of consciousness is unmaking Coward'.[69]

Another response to the post-war mood, also somewhat jaundiced, is suggested by the plans for *Home Sweet Home*, an undated and incomplete outline for a play, accompanied in the archive with notes on casting that suggest it was written around the time of the *Present Laughter* revival and *Peace in Our Time*.[70] A partial cast list, with the age of each character, indicates that 'N.C'. (born 1899) would himself have played the 47-year-old Nigel Blair, a writer. As a reservist at the start of the war, Blair 'rejoined his old regiment', was evacuated unwounded from Dunkirk and then served in Egypt and India. Transferred to Singapore, he was taken prisoner by the Japanese when they captured the city. After liberation from the prison camp, where he was 'not particularly badly treated', he has returned after two years in comfortable administrative postings. He arrives home unexpectedly early, to find that his wife Jane has been involved with another man, Brigadier George Lumley, R.M. In the second scene the two speak 'man to man', and then there is a scene between all three. The Blair's son Alec (22) is an aspiring actor, but after two failed auditions is already talking of emigrating to Australia, and their daughter Coral (25), after an unsatisfying time in the ATS (the army's Auxiliary Territorial Service), is having an affair with Emeric Hodge (35), who appears from the outline to be a communist. Joyce Carey would play Nigel's 65-year-old aunt, whose main function would appear to be that of a facilitating character, making trenchant comments and providing a link between episodes.

This may not have been the moment for yet another play of bitter reflection on post-war British society, especially one combining an adultery plot with the return of a hero and (one assumes) his disillusion. In any case, by 23 August Coward was in Lake Placid working on the adaptation of his story 'What Mad Pursuit', published in 1939, as a stage comedy, *Long Island Sound*, when he learned from Beaumont that receipts for *Peace in Our Time* were falling off. If the play failed, he would be 'forced to the reluctant and pompous conclusion' that England did not 'deserve [his] work'. It was 'a good play, written with care and heart and guts and beautifully acted and directed'. A month later he had been able to complete the comedy in eleven days.[71] *Peace in Our Time* closed after a mediocre run of 167 performances. On 30 September he wrote to Lorn Loraine that the public's rejection of this 'rattling good melodrama' made him 'bitterly angry' and he did not feel like 'doing any more gestures to England at this moment'.[72] He was not disposed to respond favourably to Beaumont's 'impassioned letters and cables saying that he prays nightly that I will return with a gay comedy for London. [. . .] It looks rather as if he were out of luck unless some hilarious idea knocks me in the kisser between now and the time I get back'. *Long Island Sound* amounts to little more than a series of amusing encounters between an English novelist, newly arrived in New York, with the other guests of a lion-hunter who has promised him a quiet weekend before his lecture tour. For any producer, this would be a hazardous as well as expensive proposition, with twenty-two speaking characters whose New York and Hollywood originals might have been easily recognizable. Lester Gaige, one of Coward's few openly camp gay men, was all too obviously (and amusingly) based on the actor Clifton Webb, and there is even an unequivocally lesbian couple: one can only wonder what the Lord Chamberlain's response would have been. Apart from the fact that it would be difficult to cast without American actors, the satire would be lost (and probably even unwelcome) on audiences in austerity London, and there were no takers on either side of the Atlantic.[73]

4
The 1950s: Keeping a public, losing the critics

> **Crestwell** A coincidence in the best tradition of English high comedy. [. . .] Consider how delightfully Mr. Somerset Maugham would handle the situation!
>
> **Peter** I can think of other writers who wouldn't exactly sneeze at the idea.
>
> **Crestwell** If I may say so, sir, our later playwrights would miss the more subtle nuances. They are all too brittle. Comedies of manners become obsolete when there are no more any manners.
>
> *Relative Values*, Act One, Scene Two: *PP5*, 296/ M5, 38

Maugham continued to haunt the reviews of Coward's plays: he was even present in the audience on the first night of *Relative Values* in November 1951, reported by Alan Dent in the *News Chronicle* to be 'purring amiably' and no doubt relishing this reference to his own comedies of manners.[1] In the butler Crestwell's speech, Coward manages to combine 'brittle', the adjective so frequently applied to his own dialogue, with a barb aimed at the 'later playwrights' whose work he found distasteful or puzzling, and the society with which he was increasingly at odds.

Throughout the 1950s Coward's work on his scripts before and during production reflected the anxiety to strike a balance between the familiar – what was expected of a 'Noël Coward play' – and the element of surprise he always hoped for. Unfortunately, even after diligent reworking, the reception of the four full-length original plays produced during the decade – *Relative Values*, *Quadrille*,

South Sea Bubble and *Nude with Violin* – confirmed the distance between his play-making criteria and those of yet another 'new drama'. Despite their box-office success as star vehicles, the reactionary social and political attitudes of *Relative Values* and *South Sea Bubble* and the disdain for 'modern' (that is, cubist and/or semi-abstract) art in *Nude with Violin* confirmed the sense that he was behind the times, and even his playmaking skills were called into question. Coward's attitude to the 'Welfare State' had hardened. Like many obliged to pay the greatly increased tax rates for high earners introduced by the post-war government, he regarded himself as a victim rather than a beneficiary of changes in healthcare and education that had brought much-needed improvements in the lives of the wider population. His decision in 1956 to take up non-resident tax status by becoming domiciled in Bermuda attracted hostile comment in the press, reflected in many reviews. In some cases, the limited number of days he could spend in Britain prevented him from taking personal charge of rehearsals.

In terms of technique, two plays from the 1950s stand out: *Relative Values* marked a return to the vein of playful theatrical self-consciousness, and *Quadrille* was a carefully designed exercise in the values and methods of Victorian drama and fiction. The revision of *Home and Colonial* as *South Sea Bubble*, while modifying some of the earlier version's more reactionary elements, reflects his nostalgia for an Empire that had been 'lost'. All four plays were conceived with specific star actors in mind, while *Quadrille* was a return to the collaborative relationship Coward had enjoyed with Alfred Lunt and Lynn Fontanne. At the end of the decade, an attempt at a serious drama, *Volcano*, written in 1957, remained unproduced: it was not published until 2018, when Barry Day included it in the ninth volume of the Methuen *Collected Plays*. Like *Point Valaine* (1935), its treatment of passion in the setting of an island colony evokes the world of Somerset Maugham's stories, but both plays veer into melodrama, in which a storm at sea and (in the later play) the eponymous volcano serve as not altogether convincing symbols.

Relative Values, 1950–1951, and *Nude with Violin*, 1950–1956: Country house comedy and satire on modern art

On 12 October 1950, while talking with Cole Lesley, Coward was 'suddenly struck with a really wonderful idea for a light comedy, that 'fell into place easily, which is always a good sign'. On 13 October no title had come to him yet, 'but it really could be a wonderful satire on the dear old art lovers; it will have to be kept at a high artificial pitch throughout'. The next day he 'suddenly thought of a title, *Nude with Violin*, which is really right for the play'.[2] Other projects intervened. On 22 March 1951 he tried to concentrate on *Nude with Violin*, 'but something is holding me back. It really isn't good enough'.[3] This was the point at which the idea for *Relative Values* took over, and the satire on modern art was set aside until early 1954.

Announced as a 'light comedy' and directed by the author, *Relative Values* opened at the Savoy Theatre on 28 November 1951 and ran for 477 performances. This was Coward's first post-war success in the West End after the disappointing runs of *Pacific 1860* in 1946–7 (129 performances), *Peace in Our Time* in 1947 (167) and *Ace of Clubs* in 1950 (211). Although it corresponds to his ambition to write an effectively 'well made' comedy, *Relative Values* can hardly be said to further his engagement with serious contemporary issues. The resolution of the plot returns the characters to their appropriate social positions, and this country house comedy expresses Coward's social conservatism, but there is also a degree of playful theatrical self-consciousness that went unacknowledged at the time. As his first comedy after *Blithe Spirit* in 1943, it occasioned the kind of stock-taking on the part of the critics that would continue for the ensuing decade.

The plot turns on the proposal of the Earl of Marshwood (Nigel) to marry Miranda Frayle, who has risen to Hollywood stardom from the slums of the East End – or so she claims. It turns out that her sister, Mrs. Moxton (Dora, known as 'Moxie'), has been the lady's maid and trusted confidante of Nigel's mother, Felicity Countess of Marshwood, for many years. Under the watchful eye of the family's butler, Crestwell – an Admirable Crichton with a penchant for reading radical social commentary – and with the support of her nephew, the Hon. Peter Ingleton (Peter), Felicity manages to thwart the intended marriage and Miranda is brought back into the arms of her fellow screen idol, Don Lucas, who has followed her from Los Angeles. Moxie admits to Felicity that she is Miranda's sister and insists on leaving, but she is persuaded to disguise herself and accept the temporary status of Lady's Companion while Miranda is still in the house. Because the sisters have not seen each other for twenty years the wearing of appropriate clothing, the loan of some of the family jewellery and the adoption of a pair of glasses, are thought to be sufficient disguise.

Enraged by Miranda's fantasizing account of her 'slum' childhood and the hopeless alcoholism of the sister she has not seen since she decamped to Hollywood, Moxie takes off her spectacles and reveals herself. Don arrives in pursuit of Miranda, who accepts his suit after the humiliation of Moxie's revelations and the news that after the marriage Felicity (and Moxie, her indispensable support) would continue to live with the newly-weds. The play ends with Crestwell and Moxie sharing a glass of sherry and the butler proposing a toast:

> I drink solemnly to you and me in our humble, but on the whole honourable calling. I drink to her Ladyship and his Lordship, groaning beneath the weight of privilege, but managing to keep their peckers up all the same. Above all I drink to the final inglorious disintegration of the most unlikely dream that ever troubled the foolish heart of man – Social Equality!

Moxie replies 'No one's ever going to stop you talking are they?' and Crestwell responds with his habitual mixture of elevated and colloquial language:

> **Crestwell** It would, I admit be a Herculean task, but should you at any time feel disposed to have a whack at it, you have only to say the word.
>
> **Moxie** That'll be the day and no mistake! (*she giggles again*)
>
> **Crestwell** What about another nip at the Amontillado?
>
> **Moxie** I don't mind if I do!

PP5, 371/M5, 113

This finale suggests that underlying the politesse appropriate to the dealings with their employers, Crestwell and Moxie share a sound understanding of the dignity of their own social station as 'Fred' and 'Dora'. In affirming a partnership, it also hints at the possibility of their eventual marriage.

Alan Dent began his *News Chronicle* review by describing Coward as having been 'a present-master of comedy writing when most of our younger playwrights were at school or college' and when 'a past-master like Maugham' was already deciding to write no more plays. The new play had 'the authentic masterly touch' although its plot was 'slight – with hardly more substance than will go to make a passable farce'. It was a comparison Coward had invited. In Act Two, Scene 2, when Moxie tells Felicity that Miranda is her sister, Crestwell admits that he had already guessed as much, 'by simple deduction and putting two and two together'. This is the 'coincidence in the best tradition of English high comedy', that prompts the comments on the state of the drama quoted at the head of this chapter, but the exchange is not the play's only theatrically self-conscious element. The ostentatiously careful plotting provides excellent 'curtains' for each scene; Crestwell, Don Lucas and Moxie evoke conventional comic figures; and Gladys Cooper's presence in the leading role further contributed to the sense of a comedy from earlier decades. Described in Coward's stage direction as 'a well-preserved woman in her fifties', Felicity 'has obviously been a beauty in her day, indeed a vestige of the maligned, foolish Twenties still clings her' (*PP5*, 168/M5, 10).

Composition had been a relatively straightforward process, beginning on Friday 23 March 1951. He finished the first act by 1 April and decided to change the title to *Relative Values*.[4] By 18 April the script was completed and on 24 April he wrote two extra scenes.[5] In London, Coward talked to Beaumont about the play for three hours: the producer wanted it to be given in three rather than two acts 'and strengthened here and there'. Work on the alterations was begun on 27 June, and three days later Coward recorded that he had finished the revisions and thought there was 'great improvement'.[6] He described the changes in a letter to Wilson on 5 July:

> Binkie's criticisms of the play were very intelligent and quite gentle. One was that the characters of Peter and Odo should

either be differentiated or made into one. Another was that the balance of the play would be improved by making it in three acts instead of two and the third criticism was that Moxie was rather indistinct as a character.

'Having digested all this carefully', he had 'lengthened and improved the first act, finishing on the 'She's my sister!' line', and 'turned the two men into one character'.[7]

A typescript dated 20 November 1951 – one week before the London opening – is still in two rather than three acts, with Act One in a single scene, its curtain line corresponding to the final speech of the first scene in the *Play Parade* and French's editions: 'Because, my Lady, Miss Miranda Frayle happens to be my young sister'.[8] In the first scene, exposition is delivered by exchanges between Crestwell and the housemaid Alice – a rather old-fashioned device perhaps designed to alert the audience to the kind of play that is to follow – and the leading lady is brought on only after an appropriate delay, for dialogue that establishes her wit and independence of mind. The scene ends with Moxie's revelation that Miranda Frayle is her sister. In the second scene the strategy is devised of passing Moxie off as an unpaid 'companion' who, after inheriting a competency for life, has elected to stay with her former mistress. The scene ends neatly, as Miranda's car-horn is heard off stage, with Moxie's demonstration of her ability to behave in the appropriate manner.

Theatrical self-consciousness is an element of what is effectively a double role for the actress playing Moxie, together with Miranda's over-acted love of simple, homely pleasures – bringing her needlepoint into the room before dinner – and the recurrent references to her films. In the first scene of Act Two Nigel insists to Felicity that 'She's awfully simple and sweet, really you know. Quite unlike what you'd think she'd be from seeing her on the screen', to which she replies 'I've only seen her as a hospital nurse, a gangster's moll, and Catherine the Great, so it's a little difficult to form an opinion.' (*PP5*, 311/*M5*, 53). Reassuring Don in Act Three that she is sure he will be able to win back Miranda, she admits she is 'disappointed' in him, after having seen him rescue her from a burning village:

Don   That was a movie. Real life doesn't work out like movies.

Felicity   Not as a general rule, I admit, but I see no reason why it shouldn't, just every now and then.

PP5, 352/*M5*, 94

As a butler, Crestwell plays a role with clearly defined guidelines of demeanour and vocabulary. He is not above parodying these in his exchanges with Don in Act Two, Scene Two. Informed by the film star that he and Miranda are 'very old friends', Crestwell responds in a manner that would do credit to P.G. Wodehouse's Jeeves:

Sequestered as we are, sir, in our remote Kentish vacuum, we are not entirely out of touch with the larger world beyond. We have been privileged, thanks to the silver screen and the various periodicals appertaining to it, to follow both your public and private affairs with the keenest interest. You are a very popular figure in these parts, Mr. Lucas.

PP5, 332–3/*M5*, 72–3

'With your fancy dialogue', Don suggests, 'you could make a fortune in Hollywood as a scriptwriter'. In lines dropped before the play's opening, Peter assured Felicity that Crestwell would support any scheme to deal with the problem in hand:

He's been with the family even longer than Moxie, he's worked himself into being a 'character' and a traditional butler at that, the faithful, loveable over-articulate English butler. I should think he would mind Nigel marrying Miranda as much as Moxie, if not more.

1–27

It is Crestwell who, at the beginning of Act Three, tells Peter that, although Moxie is already packing in preparation for her departure, 'it would be premature to abandon hastily all hope of a happy ending' (*PP5*, 348/*M5*, 90).

As reviewers noted, Coward himself might have played Crestwell, but Peter is also given his share of witty comment and a degree of agency in steering the plot. Part of the play's appeal to West End audiences lay in the scattering of comments reflecting familiar upper- and middle-class attitudes to the post-war social and economic situation. The *Bournemouth Daily Echo*, reporting on the pre-London tour performances in that stronghold of Conservatism, applauded Coward for 'refusing to follow the current trend of abstruse, psychological plays' and writing 'a light, down-to-earth comedy of manners satirizing today's social standards, a comedy of the type so badly needed in the theatre today'.[9] The targets of this mild satire include the restriction on the amount of sterling allowed for foreign travel; the nationalization of industries (Felicity remarks that 'by the time they met', one of Nigel's old flames 'was already practically nationalized' [*PP5*, 273/M5, 15]); Kenya and Rhodesia as refuges for disgraced or disaffected British expatriates; the Festival of Britain, a 'tonic for the nation' by no means universally admired; and the parlous situation of the pound sterling. Above all, there is the general sense that the Welfare State has undermined diligence and deference, reflected in Crestwell's observation that 'young Frank', one of the servants, 'like so many of the young people of today [. . .] feels that all menial tasks should be done by someone else' (*PP5*, 294/M5, 36).

Felicity's anxious but stoical attitude to change is dramatized effectively enough in the course of the play's first acts, and it may have seemed unnecessary to make the point as explicitly as in an exchange that appears only in the 20 November typescript (I-1-23):

Felicity   . . . I hate being made to realize that I am out of step with the times I live in. It makes me feel so horribly old.

Peter   Well, you are getting on, you know.

Felicity   At least I'm making an effort, and trying to adjust myself to what's going on all around us. I know it's silly and trivial, in the face of what's happening today, to hang on stubbornly to the beliefs and values of yesterday.

Following 'It's very unkind of you': *PP5*, 279/M5, 21

Crestwell expresses his sceptical social conservatism on several occasions. The 20 November script includes a speech in response to Felicity's question 'What do you think of the idea, Crestwell?' (*PP5*, 295/M5, 37): 'On the basis of reason I can see nothing against it, mylady [*sic*]. As a project it is certainly in tune with the times and theoretically it should work like a charm, but, alas, like so many revolutionary schemes it's [*sic*] practicability has yet to be proved.' (II-1-12).

Auditions were held in August and early September, and rehearsals began on 17 September. After the read-through on 10 September, Coward's diary entry includes a degree of apprehension that would be fully justified in the months to come: 'Gladys Cooper obviously going to be wonderful, although slow in learning.'[10] Over the ensuing weeks this became a serious cause of anxiety. Even after intervention by Beaumont as well as Coward, Cole Lesley recalled that 'as late as the week in Brighton the list of Gladys's mistakes amounted during one performance to no less than twenty-eight, including when, instead of announcing she was going into the study, she announced that she was going into the understudy'.[11]

The premiere was the kind of glamorous occasion Beaumont loved to arrange, and Coward reflected that the play was a success, whatever the press might say. In the event (he wrote) almost all the notices in the daily and Sunday papers were 'raves', the most important being the review by Ivor Brown 'who was a bit pernickety and obviously had not listened to the play very carefully'.[12] The reception was certainly a 'rave' in the sense of promising a long run, but was dominated by praise for Cooper's Felicity, 'a performance of high comedy – incisive, astringent and beautifully timed'.[13] Although Cooper, Judy Campbell (Miranda) and Angela Baddeley (Moxie) were applauded, regarding Coward's own work there were the familiar reservations about limitations of outlook or craftsmanship. Ivor Brown's *Observer* notice, 'Old Worlds for New', focused on the play's detachment from current social and political matters and the apparent freedom of Marshwood from the effects of post-war Austerity, the dearth of servants and the impact of high taxation. On the other hand, for all the talk of 'social equality', Coward's purpose was 'light comedy, not polemic'.[14] Philip Hope-Wallace, in the *Manchester Guardian*, insisted that 'as a social historian' Coward was 'perhaps less on the spot than he imagines'. He allowed nevertheless that this somewhat 'old-fashioned' play, 'with a second act divided by dinner and a final scene on "the morning after" with Sunday church as a pretext for bringing the thing to an end', was a pleasant entertainment: 'nowadays no one does such trifles better than Mr. Coward and few in this generation have done them so well. The skill gives pleasure'.[15] In the *Evening Standard*, Harold Conway characterized the play as 'a Maugham-type sociological comedy written in the Coward style of clipped facetiousness'.[16]

The most interesting comments, given Coward's preoccupation with this aspect of his craft, are those on the play's construction. *The Times* observed that the last act 'merely gives effect to the implications which the penultimate scene makes pretty obvious', and that 'an earlier disclosure' of Moxie as Miranda's sister 'would have given the characters more to discuss' in the first act.[17] J.C. Trewin observed shrewdly that there was 'too much preparation in the first act' and 'too much sorting out in the third'. Coward's dialogue 'flipp[ed] along in the shallows' and was 'unafraid of nonsense, the irrelevant snap-line that is nothing at all in the text but can be funny for a moment in the theatre'. Those who liked 'the Coward of the middles "twenties" would like the new play'.[18] Kenneth Hurren, in his review for *What's On in London*, expressed the view sympathetically, allowing that *Relative Values* only partially supported the theory that 'the changing spirit of the times had changed once too often and finally defeated the brittle, sardonic style which allowed him to chronicle so capably, often in bold and glorious strokes of satire, the confusions of the man-in-the-street and the determined follies of the jazz-age smart set'.[19]

In his weekly journal entry for 21 February 1954, Coward recorded that he had begun work on *Nude with Violin* on Wednesday morning and finished the first act on Saturday. His source for the jargon of art criticism was the work of the art critic and historian R.H. Wilenski, described (in a sentence removed in published diaries) as 'unmitigated bollocks' once the author moved beyond the Impressionists.[20] The first draft was finished on 12 March, and by 19 March he had written 'a short extra scene'.[21] After a number of other actors (and one actress, Yvonne Arnaud) had been considered for the leading role of Sébastien, at Beaumont's suggestion John Gielgud was approached. On 8 November he described the play in a letter to his mother as 'very broad and a bit vulgar, but full of sure-fire situations and brilliant curtains'. He was nervous about playing a role clearly designed for Coward himself, and would 'have to be rather clever at creating a character out of a "type" which doesn't really exist in life'.[22] He overcame these misgivings, and the performance became a notable personal success.

In addition to diary entries and correspondence, four principal sources represent the play's composition and revision: a manuscript draft of the first two acts; a typescript identified as 'First Version', whose first two acts correspond largely to the manuscript; and a typescript of the 'Dublin Version' dated 'September 1956'. This evidently represents the state of the play after rather than before the opening in Dublin and corresponds to the edition published in London by Heinemann in 1957. Doubleday's New York edition (1958) incorporates alterations made for the Broadway production. French's Acting Edition (London: 1956 [for 1957]) is based on the New York prompt script, with additional changes not present in Doubleday's edition. Preparatory materials include a manuscript 'vocabulary' of terms of art criticism and a detailed summary of the background story.[23]

The appropriate discoveries and moments of suspense are parcelled out – somewhat mechanically – across three acts. Sorodin, a famous painter of 'semi-abstract works' that fetch high prices on the international market, has died. His family, from whom he has been estranged for many years, and his dealer Jacob Friedland have assembled in his Paris apartment to hear the will. Sorodin's valet Sébastien meets them and explains that there is no will, and indeed, no money, but the painter has left a letter. From this it emerges that his works were executed by surrogates, each of whom were bound by contract not to reveal the secret. In a series of scenes they arrive, expecting to be able to profit from the situation. These are Anya Pavlikov, a Russian émigrée who was studying in Paris and met Sorodin in 1925; Cherry-May Waterton, the chorus girl who took over when Anya left him; and Obadiah Llewellyn, '*a respectably dressed but very black negro*', who arrives at the end of the second act. (Sébastien exclaims 'My God! The Jamaican Period!' and the curtain falls.) In the first scene of Act Three ('*a few hours later*') Obadiah has turned out to be an 'Eleventh-Hour Immersionist' preacher, bought off with £50 to spend on a stained-glass window for his church. Sébastien deals efficiently with each of them in turn, then reveals that a long-sought-after masterpiece, 'Nude with Violin', has been found. It had allegedly been painted in secret by Sorodin himself; and two experts, the eminent art critic Sir Alaric Craigie and the American museum director Elmore P. Riskin, have been invited to view it. In the final scene it is at last displayed. The 'First Version' of the script describes the painting in a stage-direction absent from the published editions: 'It is a full-length painting of a naked woman of gargantuan proportions; flesh tints are predominantly mauve and the tiny violin she is holding under her chin is bright scarlet. There are some undefinable objects in the background. The anatomical details are, to put it mildly, eccentric.' (III–2–5). In another twist to the plot, Sébastien explains that in fact it was painted by his fourteen-year-old son, Lauderdale. Jacob and the family are persuaded by Sébastien to maintain the deception: otherwise, the reputation of the painter and the market value of his work would be destroyed, and the whole system of art criticism would be discredited. As the play ends, the doors have been thrown open and the curtain falls as the two experts are about to enter. (In at least one performance, after the curtain fell as described in the published script, it rose again for a moment as Lauderdale was seen 'at work in the empty studio industriously adding the final touches' to the painting.)[24]

Coward made a careful selection from the copious background notes assembled for the characters. The most important bear on Sorodin's intimate relationship with Sébastien, not as explicit in the play as in the preparatory summary, where he is described as having found his way 'to his bed and heart', and on Sorodin himself, who is now a man of principle rather than a conscious participant in a mercenary hoax. The emphasis in the play is on the valet's own disreputable career, but Coward is careful to keep him an enigma, gradually adding exotic details of his past and withholding the existence of Lauderdale until the final scene. An exchange added after the manuscript draft contributes to the sense of an emotional rather than merely exploitative relationship between Sébastien and Sorodin. Jane asks 'Were you genuinely fond of my father?' and he replies, '*quietly, after a slight pause*', that he was:

> You may really believe that. [. . .] You would have adored him, and if I may say so, I know that he would have adored you. He was a man of remarkable character. Full of charm, vitality and irrepressible humour. Also he was devoted to pleasure, which in Christian communities is always suspect'.
>
> PP6, 377/M6, 372

Many of the additions made between the manuscript draft of the first two acts and the subsequent versions strengthen the role of Sébastien, notably with additional interventions in the dialogue with the journalist in the opening scene, most of which emphasize Preminger's naivety or undercut his lines. In effect, it is Sébastien who runs the play, organizing the successive revelations and making surprise appearances that indicate he is often listening behind the door.

Coward's vocabulary of critical terms is drawn on in a cancelled ending, present only in the 'First Version' typescript of Act Three, where there is no reference to Lauderdale. The doorbell rings and Sébastien goes to answer it, returning to announce the two experts. When they are shown the painting, Sir Alaric exclaims, 'At long last! [...] Impressive! Profoundly impressive!' and they vie with each other in appreciation:

> **Sir Alaric**   He's reverted to the Futurist-Functional. I always knew he would break away, in the Romantic-Empirical sense.
>
> **Elmore**   Frankly, I can't agree. This is in no way reactionary. It is a perfectly valid evolution from the real-unreal neo-surrealistic technique, but the theoretic system is clear.

Elmore rejects vehemently the suggestion that Sorodin 'only employed the baroque associationist concept as an entertaining pastime', and Sir Alaric accuses 'you Americans' of effrontery in 'lay[ing] down the law on all art forms with a sublime disregard for the flotsam and jetsam of contemporary conditions'. The play ends with a physical confrontation:

> **Elmore**   Effrontery my foot!
>
> **Sir Alaric**   (*mowing him down*) You are incapable of distinguishing between Architectural Aestheticism and the old fashioned crude arabesques of Symbolic Eroticism, but you are more than capable of confusing the early Pseudo-Paranoiac posturings of Surrealists, with the sombre, mature indignation of the later Neo-Purist Functionalists ...
>
> **Elmore** (*wildly*)   Take that back! Take that back!
>
> *He rushes at* **Sir Alaric** *with a snarl of rage and grapples with him violently as*
>
> **The Curtain Slowly Falls**
>
> III-2-18

By all accounts the first-night audience in Dublin on 24 September responded warmly, and the *Evening Herald* assured readers that *Nude with Violin* was 'a sharp, richly amusing and well-sustained criticism of present-day painting with a final parting shot at modern advanced writing'. Unfortunately, none of the other daily papers matched this. The *Irish Times* complained that this was 'average Coward, with a reasonable sprinkling of bright dialogue and laughs planted in deserts of vast monotony where the exposition [was] too repetitive for comedy pace'.[25] Comparison of the 'First' and 'Dublin' versions suggests that most of the alterations were designed to tighten up the dialogue, and in the final scene Sébastien's role is strengthened by having him rather than Jacob report on the offstage negotiations with Obadiah Llewellyn. It is clear from the Dublin reviews that the scene with Sir Alaric and Elmore was not played there, and that after the curtain fell, it rose again to reveal Lauderdale working on the painting. During the pre-London tour further adjustments were made. On 30 October Loraine gave Coward an account of the performances in Newcastle, where Gielgud had 'made it into a two-act instead of a three-act one. He said he thought this advisable because he found the first act only played for 20 minutes'. In a telegram to her on 3 November Coward had written 'STRONGLY DISAPPROVE OF REDIVISION OF PLAY AND HAVE CABLED BINKIE AND JOHN ACCORDINGLY'.[26] (In London the play was presented in two acts, but the published editions reinstate the three-act division.)

In Act Two, Scene One, Jacob expatiates on the critics as 'men of the highest integrity' (*PP6*, 354/M6, 351). In the manuscript, after Jane has declared that 'dramatic critics are well known to be morally impeccable but it's been proved over and over again that as far as the theatre is concerned they haven't got a clue', Jacob replies:

> Dramatic criticism is quite different from art criticism. It is on a more superficial plane. A theatre critic is most probably to be pitied. His life is one long torment. Not only is he forced to sit night after night watching plays that he knows beyond a shadow of a doubt he could have written better himself, but he has to assemble his ideas, or those of his colleagues, with lightning rapidity and get them onto paper in time for the morning edition. Added to this he is infuriated by the applause, bewildered by the acting, and himself aware that he is the only one in the whole row not wearing a dinner jacket.

Coward was undoubtedly wise not to use what would have been a hostage to fortune: the London reviews lived up – or down – to his by now jaundiced expectations. In the *New Statesman*, T.C. Worsley compared three current productions in which the Comic Muse had been 'stalking – or it may be trailing – around London in a variety of disguises, showing off her wares'. *Nude With Violin* had to undergo comparison with Ionesco's *The Bald Prima Donna* and *The New Tenant* at the Arts Theatre, where the muse was 'pony tailed and flat-heeled'. At the Winter Garden she was 'trying to sell us pure period' in *The Devil's Disciple*, but at the Globe she was 'a dowager, giggling and decidedly middle-aged'. The playwright had 'settled for the intellectual level of a Bournemouth hotel television room'.[27] Caryl Brahms suggested in *Plays and Players* that in *The Vortex* Coward, 'the angry young man of the twenties, [...] had something to say and he said it with laughter and tears and a passion of anger'. She wished he would 'lose his temper again', and 'consume his stage with terror and anger', and suggested appropriate topics: 'Hungary, Hanging or the Income Tax – Matrimony, Matriarchy, Juvenile Delinquency'.[28] Responses to the play's construction were summed up in the headline given to W.A. Darlington's notice in the *Daily Telegraph*, 'Plot's Climax too Soon. Weakness of a New Coward Play'.[29]

Nevertheless, the play found its public: in addition to its two weeks in Dublin and a six-week provincial tour starting in Manchester, it ran at the Globe for 511 performances. After Gielgud left to play Prospero in Stratford-upon-Avon, he was succeeded as Sébastien by Michael Wilding (from 24 June) and Robert Helpmann (from 23 November). Coward played the role in the New York production, which opened on 14 November 1957. Script changes made for New York were adopted in the London production when Helpmann took over. The American edition includes two substantial passages of dialogue absent from other published texts, building up the part now played by Coward and catering to American audiences. In Act One, Scene One Sébastien makes one of his sudden entrances, claiming that he heard a bell summoning him, and offers Isobel caviar, explaining that it was left over from a stock 'Professor Vladimir Kashkov used to have [...] flown over [...] regularly from Moscow in the diplomatic pouch'. He was 'a spy in the American embassy, until he was transferred'. Colin is shocked that his father 'was in the habit of accepting presents from a Communist traitor', but Sébastien explains that he 'was in the habit of accepting presents from anyone who chose to give them to him'. In one of

Coward's weakest jokes, Isobel remarks that she does not 'understand what people see in [caviar]. It's so fishy', and Sébastien observes *'charmingly'* that 'almost everything that comes from Russia is likely to be fishy'.[30] There was also an additional entrance for Sébastien to answer the telephone, this time speaking in 'Chinese' to 'the physical training instructor from the Shanghai branch of the Y.M.C.A'.[31]

On 14 September 1957 Coward recorded that he had written a new scene for himself and Preminger – 'and I think it's fairly funny'.[32] This is the long scene – six and a half pages in Doubleday's edition – between Sébastien and Clinton at the beginning of Act Two, Scene Two, preceding the telephone conversation in which the valet tells Jacob that the experts Riskin and Craigie have arrived in Paris and Anya and her accomplice have been paid off (*PP6*, 375/ M6, 370). Sébastien describes Sorodin's likes and dislikes, the latter including the Mona Lisa ('He said she looked as though she had been sick or was about to be'), ballet ('Any form of dancing nauseated him') and Picasso ('What did he think of Picasso?' – 'He tried not to'.) As for what Clinton calls his 'sex pattern', it was 'convulsive'.[33] At the end of the scene, Clinton, who has insisted on being addressed as 'Clint' and to whom Sébastien has clearly taken a shine, reminds him that he has promised a 'dinner date': 'Boy, will we have ourselves a ball! I bet you can show me things in Paris that I never knew existed. So long, Pal'. There is a guarded suggestion of an incipient gay relationship between the two.

After a week out of town and two previews, *Nude with Violin* opened in New York at the Belasco Theatre on 14 November, and ran there for 80 performances. The next day the two most influential reviewers, Walter Kerr in the *Herald Tribune* and Brooks Atkinson in the *Times*, were both dismissive of the play, but praised Coward's performance. In the *New Yorker*, Wolcott Gibbs lamented the absence of the qualities of the earlier plays:

> The neat, exact use of words in odd, hilarious juxtaposition, has nearly disappeared; the sharp definition of character has declined into a roughing in of caricatures; and the abundance of invention, the ability to create a varied sequence of scenes has degenerated into the nagging reiteration of just one – the four-times-repeated disclosure that the hypothetical masterpieces were actually turned out by freaks'.[34]

Quadrille, 1952: Crafting a 'Victorian' play

In the 'Introduction' to his fifth *Play Parade* volume (1958) Coward characterized *Quadrille* as 'a romantic Victorian comedy which the critics detested and the public liked enough to fill the Phoenix Theatre for a year' (*PP5*, xxx). Presented as 'A Romantic Comedy in Three Acts', it owed much of its popular success not only to the acting of Alfred Lunt and Lynn Fontanne, but also to their involvement in its composition. On 18 May 1951, when he was staying at their home in Wisconsin, he had noted that he wanted to write them a 'Victorian comedy'. This was the beginning of what would become a carefully crafted play with a title (arrived at a month later after further discussion) that suggested the pattern of a dance.[35]

Through March and April 1949, he had turned his attention to *Home and Colonial*, and had also been struggling to bring *Ace of Clubs* into a form that would satisfy both him and its potential producers. At this point he resolved he would 'never again embark on so much as a revue sketch that is not carefully and meticulously constructed beforehand'.[36] The formal structure of *Quadrille* and the prospect of another collaboration with the Lunts were all the more attractive. All three of them were commercially bankable, and the elaborate designs of Cecil Beaton made the play the kind of 'quality' product favoured by Beaumont. After an eight-week pre-London tour, it opened at the Phoenix Theatre on 12 September and ran for a respectable 329 performances.

Quadrille is in three acts, with a symmetrical design. In the 'June 14 – 1953' script (but not in the published texts) the opening scene is prefaced with a clear indication of the play as a period piece: 'The curtain rises on a gauze, painted to depict draped Victorian Curtains with a cameo of Queen Victoria in the centre'. Presently, the lights come up revealing the station buffet at Boulogne, and this script (but not the published version) includes dialogue in French for background players to enhance the kind of 'atmosphere' the Lunts had hoped for. The second scene takes place in the London home of Hubert, Marquess of Herondon and his wife, Serena. The central act's three scenes are set in a villa in the South of France, and the third act returns to the London sitting room of Act One, Scene Two, before a brief final scene set once more in the station buffet.

In the play's second scene it becomes clear that Hubert, who was travelling incognito in the first, has run away with a veiled woman he had been seen with at the Zoo by Serena's gossip-mongering friend Lady Harriet Ripley. Shortly after she receives her husband's letter confirming this, Serena is visited by the woman's husband, the American railroad tycoon Axel Diensen. She agrees to accompany him in pursuit of Charlotte Diensen and Hubert, and in Act Two all four find themselves in the same villa, where Charlotte and Hubert are persuaded to return to their respective spouses. In the first scene of Act Three, a year later, Serena is visited once again by Axel, who tells her that Charlotte, now divorced from him, is in her native Boston. Serena knows that her husband, under the pretence of going on an expedition to Africa with a Mr. Mallory, is in fact planning to run away with his wife. The final scene finds Axel and Serena in the buffet at Boulogne, waiting for the train to Paris. In a consummation denied to Alec and Laura in *Brief Encounter*, they set out for a new life together:

> **Serena** If only you and I were younger! If only there were more time –
>
> **Axel** There is time enough, my dear. Time and to spare. Come.
>
> **Serena** *rises from the table.* **Axel** *takes her hand. There are sounds of whistles blowing, steam escaping, and the clanging of bells.*
>
> *The* **Courier** *appears in the doorway.*
>
> **Axel** *offers* **Serena** *his arm; she takes it, and with her other hand gathers up her dress ... There is a flood of sunshine as they go out onto the platform*
>
> **Curtain**
>
> PP5, 490–1/ M7, 118–19

Coward adds a number of characters to facilitate exposition. As well as Lady Harriet Ripley, there are a fussy and intrusive clergyman, the Rev. Edgar Spevin, with his wife and daughter, and Octavia, Countess of Bonnington. Harriet is an attractive role in a vein of 'high comedy' congenial to her first interpreter, Joyce Carey, but distinct from the commanding stylishness given to Fontanne's Serena. Spevin, seen in the play's first and final scenes and in the middle scene of Act Two provides a useful comic means of underlining the awkward social situation of Hubert and Charlotte. Octavia, an elderly lady living in exile, writes scandalous but bestselling romantic novels. She comes to congratulate the lovers who her 'inner voices' tell her have arrived at the villa. Her assumption that these are Axel and Serena, whom she encounters first, is an oblique confirmation of the growing attraction neither of them can express directly at this point. Otherwise, the action is as tightly focused on the central group as it is on their equivalents in *Private Lives* and *Design for Living*, a similarity remarked on by a number of reviewers. The period of the action, 1873–4, allows for reference to a social and moral code more clearly defined and far less fluid than that of the 1930s.

The period and elements of the plot may have been inspired by Coward's reading of Anthony Trollope. On 2 October 1949 he was 'still revelling in "Phineas Finn,"' and reflected that reading Trollope was 're-awakening immortal literary longings'.[37] *Quadrille* offered the opportunity to create situations reminiscent of the political novels, with a heroine who, like Lady Glencora Palliser in *Can You Forgive Her?* (1864), is witty, perceptive and sympathetic but, unlike her, is able to make a successful attempt to decamp with a lover. Unlike Burgo Fitzgerald, Glencora's worthless would-be seducer, Axel Diensen is an admirable and energetic businessman, while Serena's husband, outwardly a pillar of society, is a romanticizing philanderer. Over the middle act of the play hovers the familiar notion that Italy offers the opportunity for convention-breaking relationships or, seen from the perspective of respectable society, a refuge for erring wives and their consorts.

Coward prepared with research into the historical background: lists of events that might be either topics of conversation in the dialogue or germane to the biographies of his principal characters; information on French railway timetables of the 1870s; and a list of books on American railroad history.[38] His preparatory notes on Serena indicate that she has had other romantic episodes, none of them serious, and that there have been two children: a girl who died and a son, Tarquin, who will inherit his father's title. (A draft list of characters suggests that at one point Coward intended Tarquin to appear in the play.) Hubert's indiscretions, to which she has learned to turn a blind eye, are enumerated. An outline of the three acts corresponds broadly to the finished play except in two important respects: there is no equivalent of Lady Bonnington, and in the first scene of the final act both Charlotte and Axel visit Serena in London. The first act was drafted by 20 September, and on 17 January 1952 in Jamaica Coward finished the play. He cabled the Lunts: 'QUADRILLE IS FINISHED I LOVE IT VERY MUCH AND ONLY HOPE THAT YOU WILL'.[39]

They did. On 5 February in New York, when he read them the completed script, they were 'absolutely ecstatic about it and really could not have been more grateful and sweet'. They had some reservations, but these would be addressed in due course.[40] A temporary cloud appeared in April in the form of a letter from Wilson to the effect that the Lunts were not happy with the play and Alfred was demanding cuts to the role of Hubert. Coward was prepared for the processes the Lunts had to go through before (or for that matter, during) the production of a play, and after the New York run of *Design for Living* he had guyed them affectionately in a skit, *Design for Rehearsing*.[41] However, he did not expect what seemed like underhand behaviour from them.[42] In a letter sent on 3 April, Lunt set out his reservations in less confrontational terms than those Wilson had reported: the play was unbalanced by the attention devoted to Hubert, Axel's role in the second act's ensemble scenes needed strengthening, and his 'Trip across America' speech needed lengthening.[43]

Subsequent events, and the consequent revisions to the script, would reflect the strength of this argument. The versions performed in Britain in 1952 and New York in 1954 varied significantly from that published by both Heinemann and Doubleday and reprinted in *Play Parade*. These correspond, with a handful of minor alterations, to a typescript dated 5 June 1952, which seems to be Coward's preferred text but differs in important details from the play as it emerged from work with the Lunts before and during production. In addition to correspondence and diary entries, evidence for this acting script survives in another copy, made for Wilson.[44]

Collaboration had begun in earnest with arrival of the Lunts in London in May 1952. On 6 May Coward read them 'the new bits' he had written: they were 'genuinely entranced' and he 'ticked them off about being tiresome'. At least two of the 'new bits' are represented by three manuscript pages included in the play's business file, which are marked by act, scene and page numbers for insertion in an existing typescript. Both would go some way to redressing the imbalance perceived by Lunt between his character and Hubert. The first is a section in Act Two, Scene Three, in which Axel scorns Hubert's 'high-flown phraseology', insists on 'the language of common sense' and remarks that 'if [he] is unwise enough to indulge in any further equivocation and fiddle-faddle', it will give him 'immense pleasure' to 'knock [him] senseless' (*PP5*, 430/M7, 68). The second enhances Axel's own kind of romantic appeal in the dialogue in Act Two, Scene Two between Axel and Serena, and Axel's rhapsodic account of the brakeman's view of America from the caboose at the rear of a freight train (*PP5*, 459–60/M7, 87–8). Lunt wrote from Paris expressing his satisfaction with the alterations. The 'Come to my country, ma'am' speech might be too long, but he would learn it and, if he wished, Coward could then decide to cut it after hearing it. He also suggested, with the help of a sketch, that Beaton's set for the station buffet might be altered to make credible the 'private' nature of the table where the lovers would sit: with the instinct of a true leading actor, he places the table downstage and centre.[45] Rehearsals went well, and after the 'very exciting' Manchester opening, with a 'lovely audience' and a 'tremendous ovation at the end', Coward was pleased by reactions during the tour.[46] Lunt reported from Liverpool on 1 August that he had revised the opening scene and that Lynne and he had made 'a few little "business" changes' in their first scene together, which he hoped Coward would approve. They had also introduced a new idea for the opening of Act Two, Scene Two that would clarify the lapse of time.[47] In October, during the London run, Lunt reported further adjustments to the first scene, without specifying whether these were in stage business or dialogue.[48]

After its run at the Phoenix, and an additional week at Streatham in South-West London, it was agreed that the New York production should be put off until the autumn of 1954. Perhaps in anticipation of the revival, Wilson had commissioned the copy of the script as 'corrected and brought up to date – June 14 1953' from a New York typing agency. This is likely to represent the play as it stood by the end of the play's first tour and in London, incorporating alterations made with Coward's agreement, with many minor alterations of the kind the Lunts were likely to have made during the run of the play. This is clearly the case with their own roles. A passage in Act Two, Scene Three is representative. Axel and Serena are reflecting on the attempt to make Hubert and Charlotte adopt a relaxed attitude to the journey ahead of them all as they wait for the carriage that is to take them away from the villa. Axel tells Serena that she is a 'truly remarkable woman'. Serena invites Axel to smoke, and the next section of the same scene includes his description of his early career. Serena asks 'You have always worked? All your Life?' He replies:

> Yes ma'am. It has become a habit like smoking; I cannot give it up. My father was an engineer on the early railroads. He drove trains in the dangerous years, through Indian ambushes and storms and blizzards and droughts. We lived in a little village in Illinois which is now a thriving town. I started work when I was thirteen.
>
> PP5, 458/M7, 68

He goes on to tell her that his first job was as a 'news-butcher', selling newspapers and other items on trains, and that he was 'a fairly bright lad', to which Serena replies 'I would never doubt that for an instant, Mr. Diensen'. His next speech begins: 'I worked on freight trains, passenger trains and cattle trains. To me the future always lay at the end of the line. The Iron Horse was my Godhead; as cruel and unpredictable as any of the Gods of Antiquity'. In the typescript (2-2-47), the account of his upbringing is transposed to the beginning of Axel's longer speech. The reflection on tobacco remains – 'Yes, ma'am. It's a habit like smoking. I cannot give it up' – and the transposed lines now form the introduction to his first evocation of the railroad's romantic appeal: 'The Iron Horse was my Godhead; as cruel and unpredictable as any of the Gods of Antiquity.' (2-3-48). The revision gives Lunt a better lead in to his bravura vision of 'the destiny of America', the 'iron hobby-horse' that he apologizes for mounting, but which is clearly a key to Serena's growing admiration for him as a visionary with real practical experience.

Marking the stages of their developing love affair without any expressly amatory scenes is one of Coward's strategies, but, as the Lunts had pointed out, the contrasting romantic rhetoric of Hubert needed to be curtailed to support the effect. The cuts to the play's first scene with which Coward responded to the Lunts' criticisms reduce the delay to their initial appearance on stage. The first moves the dialogue directly from Hubert's insistence 'No regrets. Whatever should happen, no regrets', to Mr. Spevin's approach to the couple's table (*PP5*, 380–3/M7, 8–11). This omits the equivalent of three and a half pages of a love scene between Hubert and Charlotte, including a good deal of exposition describing their relationships. The second cut, amounting to two pages, moves from Hubert's 'To be here with you, alone with you, actually to have the time to squabble. What bliss!' (*PP5*, 388/M5, 16) to a new exchange of ten speeches amounting to 17 lines before picking up with Charlotte's 'It is no laughing matter' and Hubert's reply, 'It is now. All our past sadnesses are laughing matters.' (*PP5*, 390/M5, 18). The changes remove some of Hubert's more would-be romantic flights of fancy, and he is also made less pompous. His explanation to Charlotte of his reason for snubbing Spevin, who seeks his patronage for the Anglican church in Nice, is a case in point. In the published text the speech and her reply are as follows:

> **Hubert** It is a matter of self-preservation. Do you not realize what would happen if he were permitted to achieve his purpose? We should be lost, trapped in a fearful gentility. Besides our secret would be discovered, our romance questioned and discussed and handed round the local tea-tables like petit fours.
>
> **Charlotte** No English churchgoers will call on us, Hubert. Moral attitudes are more potent even than Marquisates. You seem to forget our sinful state.
>
> *PP5*, 386/M5, 14

This is revised to:

> **Hubert** It is a matter of self-preservation. If I had encouraged him our secret would be discovered, our romance questioned and discussed and handed round the local tea-tables like petit fours.
>
> **Charlotte** No English churchgoers will call on us. You seem to forget our sinful state.
>
> 1-1-8

Most of the revisions for both characters are of this order, and Serena's subsequent description of her husband in a speech to Axel as 'a man of charm and wit and sensibility' is cut accordingly. By contrast, very little of substance is removed from the roles of Axel and Serena, while enough is left of Hubert's extravagant language to justify Charlotte's growing impatience with him and to affirm the contrast with Axel.

Coward's diary records the first night in London as a triumph, but the reviews, yet again, praised the actors at the expense of the play.[49] The Lunts were welcomed back after a long absence from the West End, and in many reviews approval for the craft that provided them with a vehicle accompanied more of the continuing narrative of Coward's fall from grace. The headlines of the London dailies on 13 September tell the story: '*Quadrille* is a Rehash of *Private Lives*' (*News Chronicle*); 'The Lunts are back. A Flimsy Play by Noel Coward' (*Daily Telegraph*); 'The Lunts – with Coward trimmings' (*Daily Graphic*). In the *Daily Telegraph* W.A. Darlington described the play as '*Private Lives* with all the modern impudence left out and nothing substituted but Victorian upholstery'. It was a 'simple tale' into which 'Coward [had] introduced no complications, no unexpected twists, in a word, no drama'. In a review headlined 'Coward says it all – twice over', Kenneth Tynan wrote in the *Evening Standard* that this was 'by the author's standards as well as mine, a lame, tame play. You can almost hear, between the lines, the crash of matinée tea cups and the crunch of digestive biscuits'.

On Friday 19 September Coward read the weekly notices. He was especially put out by T.C. Worsley's *New Statesman* review. Among his other strictures – which included the by now familiar complaint about the florid 'period' language – Worsley pointed out that important opportunities for dramatic effect had been missed, so that in the first act Serena's 'abrupt change of front – from standing on her dignity to accepting [Axel's] proposals' was 'absolutely unexplained, although even the faintest hint of a sudden attraction, given us either in the writing or the acting, would have put this right'. The revelation in the second scene of Act Two that, overnight and off-stage, Axel and Serena have prevailed over Hubert and Charlotte, is not dramatized but 'leaks miserably out, almost by mistake'. Ironically, Worsley had identified one of Coward's motives in writing the play, and his observations on the failure to dramatize developments in the characters' relationships identified a problem pertinent to any discussion of Coward's craft.

Anxieties regarding the performance of the roles of Hubert and Charlotte were recalled in May 1954, when the Lunts were requesting alterations for the New York run and returning to the familiar theme of the imbalance between the four principals. On 26 June 1954 Coward wrote from his home in Kent that he had been 'sitting for a week' with 'the original published version and the prompt script with all the cuts' but could find nothing wrong with 'the final version'. He conceded that 'originally the first scene was far too long' and that the cuts were 'a great improvement'. Nevertheless, if they got 'somebody really brilliant' for Hubert some of the cuts might 'conceivably' be restored. In the 'original version' he 'made the technical mistake of making the first scene so long and allowing the character of Hubert to run away with [him], but this [had] been entirely rectified by the cuts already made'. In its final form it seemed to him 'a very charming play indeed' and he could not 'start re-writing it without spoiling its essential structure'. Cutting the first scene entirely 'would leave Mr. Spevin unaccounted for and completely ruin the effect of the last scene'. After further comments on prospective cast for New York, Coward let his frustration appear: 'I know, with complete conviction, that if I started re-writing it and reconstructing and frigging about with it, it would become a shambles and anyway I know that my creative talent won't work unless I really believe in what I'm doing'.[50]

Fontanne's reply reiterated the argument about the first scene, recalling that when he first read the play to them, she and Alfred felt there was a problem with the first scene: it might be that it was too long, and the audience would wonder when they were coming on. This candid but wholly professional appeal to the fact that the audience would be waiting for stars to appear was supported by a more penetrating comment on Hubert and Charlotte: their first scene made it too clear that the affair was going to be a failure, and there had to be a sense that she was madly in love to justify her defying convention. Fontanne also felt that the scene lacked 'atmosphere' Could he do something about that?[51] Coward answered on 10 August that he had thought the first scene was 'crammed full of atmosphere'. He did not believe that Hubert 'is really in love for a moment, or could be. Serena states this herself in the second act. And [with?] his own enjoyment of his own words. He is only in love with himself'. As played by Griffith Jones 'he was a dull, meaningless bore, but if played by an actor with humour and charm he would be neither meaningless, dull, nor a bore'. The play should be given as it was by the time it reached London. Coward had written it for them and it was now theirs to do what they wanted with it, but he would not 'rewrite or alter one more line'. They could 'cut it to bits, play it backwards, engage Shirley Temple to play Octavia'. The message was unequivocal: 'I shall not be pleased but I shan't mind all that much because, unless it is played as I wrote it, I shall never come and see it'.[52]

After this the argument seems to have subsided, although Coward wrote resignedly to Wilson on 13 September that the Lunts, who had been 'dithering, indecisive and irritating to the point of lunacy', would 'get their way in the long run: they always have and they always will'.[53] An example is suggested in a letter from Lunt to Coward on 18 October, reporting that in Boston, on the opening night and since, the audience response had been enthusiastic. He had restored lines that had been cut before the Manchester opening, and had revised the opening of Act Two. Now, as the curtain rose Charlotte was singing some of the Queen of the Night's great aria, so that for the first time there was laughter on Hubert's line 'It isn't that I dislike *The Magic Flute*, Charlotte, it's merely that it goes on for such a long time'.[54] The details of the script's handling by the Lunts amounted to a degree of 'fine tuning' that Coward found irritating, but reflected the care being taken with two actors he loved to articulate the serious, though not solemn, theme of the play. His affection for them was not diminished. In the American and British editions and in *Play Parade*, *Quadrille* is dedicated to them, 'with more than thirty years of love and admiration', and described as having been 'directed by the author with grateful acknowledgement to Miss Fontanne and Mr. Lunt'. Nevertheless, for the text Coward reverted to his earlier version, without the actors' alterations.

Home and Colonial becomes *South Sea Bubble*, 1949–1956

Home and Colonial, 'a comedy in three acts', was first performed as *Island Fling* in 1949 at Westport County Playhouse in Connecticut, where the original title, playing on the name of a British grocery firm, would not have been understood. Revised and retitled as *South Sea Bubble*, it reached London in April 1956. In the archive,

Home and Colonial is represented by an undated typescript prepared by the Rialto Service Bureau, New York, and *South Sea Bubble* by another typescript, also undated.[55] Among other alterations for the London production, Coward removed one character and cut down much of the reactionary and sometimes racist humour, but inevitably this 'comedy in two acts and five scenes' was still an old-fashioned star vehicle designed for the most conservative elements of the West End audience. Given the lapse of years, it was hardly surprising that by 1956 many of the first version's specific political references would no longer be appropriate. These could be altered or removed, but it remained firmly grounded in Coward's amused but deeply felt nostalgia for the colonial past.

The invention of Samolo, documented in detail before he began work on *Pacific 1860*, gave Coward a fully developed background against which to set the comedies of colonial manners in *South Sea Bubble* and – more fully – in the novel *Pomp and Circumstance* (1960). The archive includes a dossier of the historical background, maps, and a vocabulary of the language that even includes a few selected indecencies.[56] (In the course of the late 1940s and the early 1950s, the fictional island and its inhabitants took on more of the characteristics of Jamaica as Coward experienced them). The Samolans have a curiously formal though imprecise grasp of English idioms, are casual and contented rather than efficient, and their attitudes to sex and marriage are not those of the British upper classes. The last of these is very much in their favour. They are also happier, and Coward regards them with a degree of respect not granted by some of the colonialists and their visitors, who have imported the perplexities of their society with which to vex each other. Although it seems unacceptably patronizing (and fundamentally racist) in the cultural climate of the twenty-first century, Coward's treatment of his islanders, reflecting his love for Jamaica and its people, is not merely tolerant and amused but also respectful. They have access to values and beliefs that may count as laxity and superstition, but which their governors cannot comprehend. Arguably, their freedom from prejudice and cant is held in common with the freer spirits of his comedies. Coward's regret for the demise of the Empire – expressed in his fiction as well as here – was qualified by a perception of its inevitability, and a sympathetic appreciation of the differences between Samolan and English ways of life.

They are exploited to comic effect in *Pomp and Circumstance*, but with less of the condescension that lingers in *South Sea Bubble*. The outcome is tragic, though, in the long short story, 'Solali', published in 1965, where the bored and sexually frustrated wife of an 'almost triumphantly dull' planter misunderstands the consequences of what she sees as a casual affair with a Samolan gardener.

In April 1949, when he was 'considering' writing a play for Gertrude Lawrence, a possible plot occurred to him while re-reading Evelyn Waugh's 1930 novel, *Vile Bodies*: 'I constructed it then and there and everything seemed to fall into place. The title is Home and Colonial; theme – Lady 'Sandra' Magnus (Diana-Edwina), Government House, Samolo; scandal with local Bustamente. There is more to it than that, but it's a heaven-sent opportunity to get in a lot of Jamaican stuff'.[57] Little trace of the novel's retrospective satire on the 'Bright Young People' of the 1920s remains in the version revised and produced in London. Lady Diana Cooper had been the inspiration for Julia Stitch in Waugh's novel. Lady Edwina Mountbatten and her husband Lord Louis Mountbatten were old friends, whose style of life had been the inspiration for *Hands Across the Sea* in the second *Tonight at 8.30* programme. The other ingredients of the 'heaven-sent opportunity' included the 'Samolo' background elaborated for *Pacific 1860*. The analogy with Jamaica was transparent: Sir Alexandre Bustamente had been leader of the Jamaica Labour Party, but in 1955, when Coward returned to the play, the JLP had lost the election to the People's National Party, led by Norman Manley.

Home and Colonial, despite the underlying satire directed at the Labour government's support for independence movements in the colonies, had lacked the mild political intrigue that in the revised version turns on the issue of free admission to the island's public conveniences. Without this element, the 'motor' for the action of *Home and Colonial* was simply the freedom from prejudice that in both versions leads the governor's wife to insist on going to a party given by a neighbour who is not altogether respectable. (It is likely to be 'mixed' – that is, with both white and 'coloured' guests.) She allows herself to be driven home by Hali Alani, the 'progressive' son of the conservative grandee Punalo Alani. The crisis is caused by Hali's insistence on bringing her to his 'small shack on the edge of the sea' (*PP6*, 182/M6, 269). After copious draughts of the potent local drink, Kali-Kali, and a frenzied display of drumming on his part, she escapes what is clearly an attempt at seduction by knocking him out with a bottle of the liquor. In the first scene of the final act, after clever prevarication in the face of Chief of Police's report of Hali's injury and the discovery of his car, Sandra admits that she did go to the beach house and 'bash him over the head with a bottle' (*PP6*, 214/M6, 301). This provides a neat 'curtain' for the act's first scene. In the final scene, 'four hours later', the governor is wondering how to deal with the potential scandal. However, the situation is resolved by the arrival of Hali, who has not been seriously hurt. He returns a diamond and sapphire clip that Sandra dropped in the beach house, explaining that after he had driven her back to Government House, he was attacked in his beach house by a thief who stole his car and crashed: this is why the clip was found in his car. The subsequent cover-up and the avoidance of a scandal, effected by the production of a 'suspect' for the assault, demonstrates the usefulness of the casual corruption that operates at a level below (or in spite of) the colonial power. Punalo Alani accepts the situation with good grace, and when a servant announces 'Luncheon is served' he and his son join the company.

After a false start on 7 April, work began in earnest the next day and Coward 'did eleven pages', and by 26 April he had finished the first act, having 'got out of the dilemma' he was in, probably the means by which he would bring Sandra and Hali Alani to the beach house together. On 28 April he finished the 'beach house' scene: 'It's all right I think, and is full of terrifying opportunities for overacting'.[58] On 3 May he 'worked from 7 a.m. onwards and finished the play at five o'clock'. It 'floated' when Lawrence's character was on, but 'the rest [had] been tricky'. His 'only deep fear' was that 'she might overplay it'. It needed 'everything she has got plus taste'.[59] On 4 May, however, Coward received telegrams from both Lawrence and Beaumont to the effect that although they were 'enthusiastic', for tax reasons she could not appear in London until the next April. Her proposal to open the play in America would not be acceptable to Coward, who had written with British audiences in mind. On 24 May she was still prevaricating, and he talked to Margaret Leighton about the possibility of her playing Sandra.[60]

The Lawrence problem seemed to have been resolved by 21 September, when he warned her in a cable that they must start rehearsing in April as agreed as he had committed to 'do [a] picture' (*The Astonished Heart*) in June.⁶¹ Then a letter from her agents in New York, where she was appearing in Rodgers and Hammerstein's *The King and I*, indicated that she was still 'havering', and Coward 'wrote her a letter of extreme firmness, giving her three weeks to make up her mind'.⁶² After re-reading the agents' letter he decided that Lawrence had been 'insolent and idiotic' from the first, and it was 'time she had a sharp lesson'. He would offer the play to Kay Hammond and her husband John Clements.⁶³ These plans fell through in October and in the New Year Wilson reported that Lawrence was 'injured' about the play being offered elsewhere. This cut no ice with Coward. In May the possibility of Vivien Leigh playing Sandra in London was discussed, but Beaumont delivered a bombshell on 27 June: Leigh and Olivier 'violently disliked' the play, which was 'old-fashioned Noël Coward' and would do Beaumont 'great harm'. This was 'a surprising and salutary jolt', and Coward had 'a strange feeling that they [were] right'.⁶⁴

Despite his doubts, he relented in his prohibition of an American production, and in July 1951 it was presented by Wilson at Westport County Playhouse in Connecticut, with Claudette Colbert as Sandra. Wilson cabled that the play was a success and Coward was ready to fly to America to see the production, but Wilson then strenuously dissuaded him from attending the production, occasioning a bitter row between them.⁶⁵ On 30 July, after discussing the matter with Loraine, Coward had decided to take no action, but the next day he cabled the New York producer Max Gordon, asking him to see the production and report on it in confidence. Gordon cabled his verdict on 1 August: 'SAW PLAY OPENING NIGHT REGRET TO ADVISE YOU THAT I CONSIDER IT VERY WEAK AND SHOULD BE ABANDONED AS FAR AS NEW YORK IS CONCERNED. CLAUDETTE GOOD BUT REST OF CAST JUST FAIR'. Coward cabled back that he agreed the play was not ready for Broadway 'BUT WITH RE-WRITING AND "SUITABLE DIRECTION" IT MIGHT LATER ON BE USEFUL FOR ENGLAND'.⁶⁶

Colbert's performance was well-received, but the play's treatment by the critics was lukewarm. The *Stamford Advocate* singled out Edith Meiser as Maud Witterby – a character omitted in the revised version – who had 'three hours of fun being delightfully skeptical about the whole affair', with 'many of the best lines'.⁶⁷ George Freedley, in the *New York Morning Telegraph* paid the play the back-handed compliment of being 'a funnier and better play than *Present Laughter*' and saved most of his applause for Meiser: 'As she languidly pressed her highball against her forehead to indicate the extreme heat and humidity of the South Sea British possessions, you chuckled at the knowingness of the gesture.' (20 August). The *World-Telegraph and Sun* reported 'a wan comedy – synthetic Noël Coward most of the way – an ineffectual mingling of jabs at the Labor Party, flip talk of the traveled British, and a seduction scene straight out of old time melodrama'.[68] Despite this setback, plans for a London production with Lawrence continued, and Coward's affection for her was too strong to be permanently affected by exasperation at her 'havering'. In April 1952, over lunch in New York, Coward advised her to leave *The King and I* and hoped he had convinced her to do a straight play.[69] Lawrence's incurable cancer, the underlying reason for the vocal problems that had been seriously affecting her performances, precipitated her departure from the musical, and she died in hospital on 6 September 1952.

Coward did not return to the script until March 1955, after *Quadrille* had closed on Broadway. He had 'rewritten the whole play except for the hut scene and a few good bits here and there'. It was 'curiously overwritten' and he seemed, 'in later years, to have lost [his] gift for economy'. Nevertheless, by 10 April 1955 he had finished the play, and it now had 'a shape and a plot, which it didn't before'.[70] The work is reflected in a typescript draft incorporating a minimally revised carbon copy of the 'beach house' scene along with newly typed pages of the other acts and a copy of the final scene marked up with revisions that included the excision of dialogue that would now be used in the first-act scene between George and Punalo Alani. At this point, Vivien Leigh entered the picture again, and the process began that would lead to the West End opening a year later.

Coward's most substantial alterations are in the first act. In *Home and Colonial* two visitors arrive to stay at Government House, the Earl of Sharpenhoe ('Boffin') and the Hon. Maud Witterby (Maud). In *South Sea Bubble*, Boffin is an author, John Blair-Kennedy, and Maud is absent: her role in the first version was mainly to assist Boffin in eliciting information about Samolo and providing background on the governor and his wife. It is Maud who has such jokes as the description of the Chinese children on the plane: 'Their general behaviour convinced me that all that well known Oriental imperturbability must be a habit acquired in later life.' (I-1-5). This was retained among the lines given to Boffin in revision. She also prompts a fuller account of Sir George Shotter's origins as a grocer in Huddersfield, his marriage to a Duke's daughter, and identity as an appointee of the post-war Labour government, with references to Herbert Morrison and Ernest Bevin in exchanges that have no equivalent in South Sea Bubble:

> **George** [. . .] How was dear old England when you left?
>
> **Maud** Excessively uncomfortable – thanks to all those incompetent upstarts you support so ardently.

George stands his ground gamely:

> **George** Your class is on the blink Maudie my old cock-robin – you might just as well face it and greet the new world with a smile.
>
> **Maud** God forbid.
>
> 1-1-5–6

The dialogue indicates elsewhere that he has a 'northern accent', and 'my old cock-robin' is one of Coward's sporadic and lame attempts to lend him an appropriate vocabulary. Asked how things are in England by another guest, Maud replies: 'The Socialist Government is doing splendidly – so they tell us. There was a Docker's [*sic*] strike on when we left and a coal strike and a bus strike; the Lyons waitresses threaten to come out next week and there's an agricultural crisis.' (1-1-31). In the second scene of Act One Maud comments that Sandra 'has always been quite unaccountable': 'During the war she struck up the most extraordinary friendships – all that fire-watching you know – it completely bitched her social sense.' (1-2-44). References of this kind placed the action firmly in the immediate post-war years, indicating that Sandra and her friends had been the 'bright young people' of the 1920s: they had to be removed for a production in the mid-1950s, with a star actress born in 1919.

When Sandra appears, it becomes clear that she shares her friends' view of the Labour government as 'a lot of stinkers', and Coward's attempt to depict her relationship with George as one of affectionate raillery is not altogether convincing. None of this would have been topical by 1956, with the Conservatives in power. Still current, however, were ideas about decolonization of the kind voiced by both Sandra and Punalo Alani. In a passage incorporated in *South Sea Bubble*, when George asks Sandra whether or not she wants to help the islanders 'free themselves from the hideous yoke of Imperialist oppression', she retorts that she wants 'no such thing – neither do they'. They are 'perfectly happy as they are'.

> They sing from morning till night – they weave away and make the most divine waste-paper baskets – they never stop boozling [*sic*] and having scads of children who swim before they can walk and have enormous melting eyes like saucers, and whenever they feel a bit peckish and want some delicious fruit and veg: all they have to do is nip it off a tree or snatch it out of the ground.
>
> 1-1-17

This is retained in the *Play Parade* text (*PP6*, 129/*M6*, 127), but with minor alterations. In *Home and Colonial*, the equivalent speech is followed by Maud's comment that miscegenation 'seems to be unavoidable everywhere' and her reminiscence about 'Daphne Pop-Oliver', who before her marriage was Lady Quermerford, 'and had all those dusky languid daughters' (1-1-35).

In *Home and Colonial* the most significant reference to Sandra's membership of a fast 'set before the war' is made by Cuckoo Honey, the wife of the Colonial Secretary and a 'mixture of Bangalore and Earl's Court' (*PP6*, 124–5/*M6*, 212). She tells Christopher, the governor's aide-de-camp, that 'her name was always in the papers'.

> They used to have treasure-hunts and climb up fire-escapes and take negroes into Claridges. Lady Alexandra was one of the ringleaders. H. E. [i.e., George, now His Excellency] once made a slashing speech about them – that was before he met her, of course, when he was in the Office of Works – 'Bright Young things' he called them – ironically you know.
>
> 1-1-23

Cuckoo's gossip includes an explanation of the arrival of Boffin and Maud together as a couple – it has already been alluded to with reference to their possibly taking a house together. They are having an affair, and 'It all started at the beginning of the war when he was still Lord Saddle and got into that trouble with the Trouncer girls.' (1-1-23). In *South Sea Bubble* Coward developed Sandra's background along more 'respectable' lines. From her schooldays at Roedean she has acquired the knack of capping conversations with quotations along with their authors' birth- and death-dates, and can sing the school song – 'It's very rousing.' (*PP6*, 194/*M6*, 281). She is endowed with something of the gift for flippant repartee that Lawrence and Coward had shared in *Private Lives*:

Sandra   Do you always drive as fast as that?

Hali   Only when I am gay and happy.

Sandra   I must try to think of something to depress you on the way back.

PP6, 183/*M6*, 270

There is even a reference to Coward's earlier mode of subverted country-house comedy, *Hay Fever*, in Sandra's apology for her husband's 'barbarous idea of having communal breakfast [. . . .] He saw a country-house comedy once in which everyone was frightfully witty all through the last act and kept on helping themselves to kedgeree'. She goes to the side table, lifts up the cover on a dish and exclaims 'My God, there really is kedgeree.' (*PP6*, 201/*M6*, 288).

In both versions, Cuckoo represents the worst aspects of the 'colonial' mentality: 'I was brought up in India, you see, and I expect a sense of the importance of British prestige is more or less ingrained in me.' (*PP6*, 163/*M6*, 251). A notable alteration concerns Boffin, in *Home and Colonial* a colourless and flippant aristocrat who, together with Maud, represents the 'Bright Young People' past of Sandra. (Maud mentions that he had been 'an ace pilot in the war' [1-1-24].) In *South Sea Bubble* he is a successful writer, who has come 'to collect data and make notes for a satirical novel about British Colonial Administration' (*PP6*, 123/*M6*, 211), a project strikingly similar to Coward's long-standing plans for the novel published in 1960 as *Pomp and Circumstance*. Like the novelist Mortimer Quinn in *Point Valaine* (1934), the new Boffin resembles the detached observer of human nature who is Maugham's avatar as narrator of many of his stories. (*Point Valaine* had been dedicated 'affectionately' to the older playwright.) Cuckoo Honey, tactless on all topics, makes the 'dreadful confession' to him that she has read all his books but 'didn't care for them'.

> **Cuckoo** Of course, I know they're frightfully clever and all that, but you must admit they don't 'contribute' very much, do they?
>
> **Boffin** They contribute a hell of a lot to me.
>
> **Cuckoo** I wasn't speaking commercially.
>
> **Boffin** I was.
>
> **Cuckoo** With the world in its present state there are so many really important things to write about.
>
> **Boffin** Name three.
>
> *PP6*, 159–60/*M6*, 247–8

She comes off badly in a similar conversation with Christopher, the governor's aide-de-camp, in Act One, Scene Two, when she is expressing her anxiety about Sandra's holding 'too many mixed parties' with white and 'coloured' guests (*PP6*, 146/*M6*, 232). Sandra has been asked by her husband to 'charm Hali' and get him on side in political matters, and at the end of the evening's dinner she takes him into the garden for this purpose. Afterwards, she dances with him. It is Cuckoo's indignation on seeing this that prompts Sandra's decision to go off with Hali to the party that ends with her visit to his beach house. In the exchange with Boffin, though, Cuckoo's function is principally to allow Coward to respond to critics who reproached him with a lack of engagement with 'serious' issues. Boffin specializes in the kind of quick-witted response associated with Coward's own performances, but some of his lines are off-handedly racist. Told soon after he arrives that the Samolans are 'a sweet people, in many ways', with 'a lot of charm, but [. . .] a bit backward politically', Boffin responds with 'Like the Irish' (*PP6*, 118/*M6*, 206). In the final scene when Hali, returning the clip to Sandra, remarks that 'It is most dismal to lose something of sentimental value', Boffin adds 'Yes. Like India' (*PP6*, 228/*M6*, 314).

Even though attitudes as thoughtless as Cuckoo's are contested within the play, her casual racism remains unpleasant, and the issue of class is bound up with it. There is a sense that ignorance and lack of tact are her most reprehensible traits, rather than the assumption that the 'natives' are for the most part inferior to the colonialists. The trivial dispute at the centre of the intrigue regarding public conveniences represents a wider issue, concerning the alleged benefits of class distinction. Punalo Alani points out that if the lower classes are given easy access to the toilets, not only will this be repugnant to wealthier islanders but the fixtures and fittings will soon be stolen: 'Have you envisaged, from the point of view of hygiene alone, the state of the water closets after a week's gratis promiscuous occupation?' (*PP6*, 138/M6, 124). George's support for this measure will only strengthen the Samolan Socialist Nationals, 'who wish to emancipate us from the cosy Imperialism that has gently guided us for so long'.

> [T]o endure, unprotected, the fearful discomforts of democracy, which are so racking Western civilization. Believe me, we are too young yet for such brave experiments. Too young and gay and irresponsible to be able to do without our old Nanny.
>
> *PP6*, 140/M6, 228

He even 'thanks God' that Samolo 'is not yet a Welfare State, and it is still permissible to speak freely without fear of reprisals', a somewhat extreme version of Coward's own chafing, in private and public, at the changes brought about in post-war Britain (*PP6*, 136/M6, 224).

On 7 September 1955 Leigh wrote from Stratford-upon-Avon, where she was playing Lavinia opposite Olivier's Titus in Peter Brook's production of *Titus Andronicus*, to tell Coward how enthusiastic she was about his 'wonderful new play'.[71] Despite his misgivings about her state of mind, he told Beaumont to go ahead.[72] The limitations attached to his non-resident tax status prevented him from attending rehearsals in London. He had written to Loraine in September, referring to a 'really enthusiastic letter' from Leigh, and hoping that (as she had suggested) Peter Brook would direct the play. However, Brook was not available and the experienced dancer, actor and director William Chappell was appointed. On 24 December Coward had expressed his misgivings in a letter to Loraine: 'I do not think Billy Chappel [*sic*] is the ideal director of *South Sea Bubble* on account of his view of high society being confined to the area between Charing Cross and Dean Street'.[73] The pre-London tour began. A report from Leigh on 11 April 1956 from the Central Hotel, Glasgow included troubling information: she had been delayed in writing by being depressed about her performance, and (she cheerfully informed him) Olivier had been coming up every weekend to give the company the benefit of his advice and criticism.[74] (This was news that was not likely to please Coward.) The London opening took place at the Lyric Theatre on 25 April.

Although the satire is no longer directed at the current government, Sir George is still a Labour appointee, and there is criticism of the Welfare State and reactionary humour at the expense of the aspirations of remaining colonies. As regards construction, until the beach-house scene the stage is dominated by more-or-less witty dialogue and exposition. In the final act the resolution of the situation through Hali Alani's chivalrous intervention seems perfunctory to a degree that some of the critics found puzzling. *The Times* summarized the faults of 'a minor but not unpleasing Coward, striking out at the outset in several quite promising directions and getting in the end nowhere in particular but entertaining as it meanders along with talk well filled out with amusing extravagances'. A 'stronger solution' to the embarrassment of the final scene might have been found by having Sandra blame her husband or Cuckoo for her admitted indiscretion, rather than 'simple recourse to native chivalry'. The playwright seemed to be 'on the verge of political comedy' in the confrontation of the idealistic governor and 'the dusky Etonian with his intellectual grasp of realities', but he 'turn[ed] away with a slight shudder from the prospect'. As for 'the brittle thinness of the first act' it was indicated by the whole company playing at 'a speed which shorthand experts are ready to estimate at a steady 250 words per minute, a speed the like of which has surely never been known before on a West End stage'.[75]

The weekly notices further confirmed Coward's usual expectations. Harold Hobson in the *Sunday Times* found it 'typical of Mr. Coward's provocativeness that he should make the political issue depend on the question of public conveniences'. In *Cavalcade* he had been 'imbued with a sense of the glories of British imperialism', but here he had 'made the loss of India the subject a joke that is only a little wry'. In an interesting glance at reactions to the play, he suggested that 'the heroine of *Cavalcade* would have been as shocked by Lady Alexandra Shotter's behaviour as were some of Wednesday night's audience'.[76] Coward reflected on the likelihood that the production was 'a lash-up', with 'fussy, insecure direction' and 'inadequate comedy acting'.[77] Nevertheless, Leigh's presence seemed to guarantee a good run at the Lyric. As for Olivier, Beaumont visited Coward in Paris in May and told him about 'all the trials and tribulations of "S.S.B." and how Larry interfered and wanted to cut this and that etc. Oh dear'. This made him glad that he had not been there to be involved.[78]

In July there was an unwelcome surprise in the form of a 'long and affectionate letter' from Leigh explaining the 'tender secret' that she was leaving the production to have a baby. Olivier had intended to come over to Paris to tell him, but commitments in London prevented it. Their doctor had told them that she should leave the play on 1 August.[79] Coward 'rose above' his anger, and sent his congratulations.[80] Leigh left the cast on Friday 11 August, and after a farewell party, drove home to Notley Abbey, the Oliviers' country home. She had a miscarriage on the Sunday. Coward was by now particularly incensed by the way they had jeopardized a production that 'if only they had had the sense to see it, was a life-saver for Vivien'.[81] Elizabeth Sellars took over from Leigh and *South Sea Bubble* ended its West End run after 276 performances. Comparison with the London figures for *Relative Values* in 1951 (477) and *Quadrille* in 1952 (329) suggests that Coward's chagrin was justified, as a run ending at Christmas would have brought the number of performances up to at least a respectable 400. Nevertheless, Coward's deep-seated affection for Leigh survived this setback, and he remained a loyal and supportive friend through the rest of her increasingly unhappy life.

The New York production did not materialize. In a letter to Loraine, Coward had described plans he was already making for an opening in October, but by 16 September these had been abandoned for want of an appropriate substitute for Leigh.[82] He still had faith in the play, but was happy not to pursue the plan for Broadway: 'It is a wonderful play and it won't date me, [but] having seen the red lights flickering incessantly in the writing on the wall, I suddenly decided to get out under the wire and if that isn't a nice little nest of mixed metaphors I don't know what is'.[83]

Volcano: Passion and betrayal on an island

Despite his disappointment at the notices for *Nude with Violin* in New York, in the early New Year, 1958 Coward took the play to San Francisco and Hollywood, playing alternately with a revival of *Present Laughter*, using the same set but with some modifications.[84] By 13 April he was back in Jamaica at Blue Harbour and ideas for plays were beginning to suggest themselves.[85] One of these was *Waiting in the Wings*. The other, not referred to in the published *Diaries*, was *Volcano*, a 'serious play' about passion that, like the ill-starred *Point Valaine*, featured the forces of nature as a catalyst for human passion.

On 10 March 1957 Coward had been 'half way, or nearly half way through a new play'. The idea had been 'prompted vaguely' by the 'goings on' of his neighbour Ian Fleming and his friends, and 'came to [him] quite suddenly'. (Fleming's wife Ann had come to Jamaica, as usual travelling separately from him, and was incensed at his growing intimacy with another woman, Blanche Blackwell.)[86] He discussed it with Loraine, who 'thought it very good indeed' and 'in about twenty minutes the whole story had set itself into three acts and six scenes without any conscious effort'. The title, *Volcano*, 'obligingly dropped into [his] mind', and he 'started right away and wrote the first scene, then a day or two later, half of the second scene'. He thought it 'a serious play', that so far was 'very well written'. He was gratified by the thought that his recent 'concentration on verse' had 'enriched' his vocabulary and 'improved' his style: 'I know that my psychology is sound and, for the first time for a long while, I am conscious of the real magic of my gift. [. . .] I am sure, by the way this is absorbing my mind and by the pleasure it is giving me to write it, that it is intrinsically right, all of which, not unnaturally, makes me very happy'. Cole Lesley sent a copy of script to Loraine on 29 March.[87]

The archive's 'second' draft of *Volcano* opens with an early morning scene in which Adela, a widow in her early forties, in whose house the action takes place, explains to Guy 'Guido' Littleton (age 38) – the Fleming character and a notorious philanderer – why she has not been prepared to 'give herself completely' to him despite his ardent pursuit of her. They must remain no more than friends. Moreover, Guy's wife Melissa is expected to arrive from London. In the second version, as reproduced in the Methuen edition, this scene is omitted, and the implication throughout is that they have been lovers in the fullest sense. In the second act, members of the house party (not including the newly-arrived Melissa) have flown to a neighbouring island to view the dawn from the slopes of the volcano Fumfumbalo. It erupts, and they are lucky to escape with their lives, but during the emergency Guy and Ellen, a married woman whose husband is away on business in Honolulu, take shelter and spend the night together before making their way down to the airstrip. In the final act, back at her house, Ellen confesses to Adela, who tells her she has three alternatives: she can continue an affair with Guy; move into a hotel, confirming the rumours a local newspaperman has already picked up; or 'stay here, be quiet, and behave outwardly as though nothing had happened' (M9, 252). Matters are further complicated by the arrival of Ellen's husband. After Guy's wife Melissa has decided that she will go back to England to think about a divorce, the play ends with a scene in which Guy and Adela seem to have reached a common understanding. But just before the curtain falls, she picks up the shells he has brought as a peace offering 'and, taking them out of the basket one by one [. . .] smashes them violently on the ground' (M9, 271).

The completed draft was sent to Loraine, now in London, who responded on 18 April that she was 'really thrilled' that it was 'so frightfully good'. She admired 'the taut economical writing, and the wonderful atmosphere and tension of the scenes on the mountain, the sharp clarity and truth of the characters'. Moreover 'the play and the people in it' had 'certainly worked themselves out a treat' and she 'couldn't be more delighted'. However, by 30 April she had heard from Beaumont, and was 'extremely disappointed' that 'while being impressed by a lot of it', he did not 'care for it a hundred per cent and [had] a good deal of criticism to make'. The most important was his feeling that 'Adela's continued friendship with Guido plus her continued refusal to let him be her lover makes her an unsympathetic character'. Beaumont seems also to have expressed reservations about potential critical response to the social milieu, and Loraine bridled at 'this prevailing idea that the only people worth considering in serious plays are those who either live in squalor or, at the highest, do their own housework and take the washing to the launderette'. The 'slightly more leisured classes' were 'presumed to be acceptable to an audience when in farce or light comedy but not when their deeper emotions are involved'.[88] By 5 May Coward had received a letter from Beaumont, '*not* liking "Volcano" and saying that I should have written it as a comedy and that such people (i.e., cultured and articulate I presume) no longer exist and if they do are apparently not acceptable as serious characters'. He knew Beaumont was 'possibly right' but he had 'no faith in the trend of squalor and dreariness lasting much longer'. There were still 'many million middle-aged middle class English people who would [. . .] appreciate the values of "Volcano."' He admitted that perhaps he was 'more old-fashioned' than he realized.[89] It seems likely that, as the potential producer, Beaumont may have felt not only that *Volcano* was unsatisfactory in itself, but that this was not the time for yet another play, even a 'serious' one, about the intrigues of English expatriates in a thinly-disguised Jamaica.

In September, when Coward was preparing for the New York run of *Nude with Violin* and writing the additional scene for himself and Clinton Preminger, he was engaged in the 'far more gruelling' task of revising *Volcano*. Adela was now 'much more sympathetic and no longer a self-righteous, boring prig'. Among the early manuscript drafts for the first scene is a version that begins with Adela physically as well as verbally fending off Guy's attentions: 'When the curtain rises Adela is in Guy's arms. She is struggling and beating his chest with her hands. Finally she breaks free'. Another draft has the couple sharing a 'night-cap, or rather a morning-cap' after their night of unconsummated passion, and wistfully quoting the lovers' awakening scene from *Romeo and Juliet* to each other. Neither of these openings made it into the subsequent typescript, which avoids both violence and lyricism. In the first, when Adela sends Guy home she has a speech that is probably representative of the 'thousands of adroit carefully phrased metaphors and similes' Coward 'ruthlessly' discarded as he reworked the play:

> At the risk of you accusing me of being 'superior' again, I must explain that the secret of our mutual attraction is that we do not speak each other's language. We are like people sitting in a foreign theatre watching a foreign play. Once in a while we are assailed by a familiar phrase, a slight indication of the plot and

for a moment we are deluded into the belief that we know what's going on, but we don't, the moment of near understanding is whisked away, and we are content to let it go and allow ourselves to be beguiled by differences and strangeness and the charm of alien sounds.[90]

He reflected ruefully that '[t]hree quarters of the play was pompous and so "beautifully" written that it had no reality'. This was '[n]othing but literary smugness' and he must 'never again write careful polished dialogue with poetic and literary overtones'. If his characters did not 'talk realistically and naturally' they would 'cease to be characters and become over-articulate puppets' After this 'salutary lesson', in future he would 'keep [his] beautiful thoughts for [his] verse or, perhaps, [his] prose'. He reiterated his credo: 'I believe in the Theatre being primarily a place of entertainment and I believe in trying to create characters swiftly and surely in the two hours and a half that the formula allows me'.[91]

5

The 1960s: A 'rendezvous with the past' and new directions

Cora Deirdre can make even a game of draughts sound like a Lyceum melodrama.

Deirdre And what's wrong with that I should like to know. The Lyceum melodrama at least gave you your money's worth. An honest bit of blood and thunder's a lot more healthy and entertaining than all this modern creeping about in the pitch dark and complaining.

May For once I am in complete agreement with Deirdre.

Waiting in the Wings, Act Two, Scene Three:
PP6, 498/M5, 312

The 1950s had ended inauspiciously for Coward with *Look After Lulu*, the collision between his comic dramaturgy, and farce as practised by Georges Feydeau. In his next stage comedy to be performed, *Waiting in the Wings*, begun in 1958, Coward paid tribute to the theatre of the past, shaping his dramatic action according to its methods while recognizing them as well-honed and perhaps hackneyed techniques for eliciting humour and pathos. As the exchange between Deirdre, Cora and May suggests, even the Lyceum melodramas popular from 1909 to the 1930s, under the management of Frank and Walter Melville, had a vitality and entertainment value of the kind Coward found lacking in contemporary theatre.[1] Although he continued to be at odds with much of the work of emerging playwrights – the 1960s brought a 'second wave' of the kind of innovation he found distasteful – he turned in his final plays, the trilogy *Suite in Three Keys* (1966) and the uncompleted *Age Cannot Wither*, to a theme that had concerned him since the 1920s. In his 'Preface' to the unpublished *Semi-Monde* he had inveighed against the hypocrisy that denied the theatre the opportunity to depict 'types and characters which, although constituting a comparatively small section of civilized society', were 'nevertheless just as valuable as factors in human drama as Gentleman Burglars, Lancashire Homicides and Elizabethan Harlots'.[2] Now a relaxation of the censorship's prohibition of direct references to homosexuality opened the way to a franker treatment of the victims of institutionalized prejudice. In their formal qualities the three plays continued to be conventional: John Russell Taylor describes *A Song at Twilight* as 'a straightforward well-made play such as Pinero would have thoroughly approved, but with a mid-century twist' in the revelation that the leading character had 'a homosexual past'.[3] In two of the *Suite* plays the professional lives of the protagonists, a novelist and a publisher, both played by Coward himself, permitted the characters to appreciate the values in fiction and life of comedy and pathos, if not quite of tragedy.

Waiting in the Wings, 1958–1961: Theatre in 'the old days'

On 13 May, when he was sufficiently recovered from his journey from New York to Jamaica to contemplate writing, among Coward's ideas was 'a play called "The Wings"' about a home for retired actresses'. By 1 May, 'suddenly, in a wild resurgence of energy', he had 'rushed at' the play, now with its eventual title, *Waiting in the Wings*, but he had 'started too soon and too quickly, without taking enough care to construct properly'. After talking it over with Cole Lesley he knew he had made the right decision. He was 'no longer twenty-eight but fifty-eight', his 'processes' were 'inevitably a little slower'. He set the play aside, but 'ideas about how it should be done' were 'beginning to flow into [his] mind'.[4] On 21 May, on his way by sea from New York to Bermuda, he wrote to Lorn Loraine that he couldn't wait 'to get into his cosy little cabin' to work on the play, but on 1 June he admitted to his diary that he 'intended to write during the voyage' but 'was too tempted' by the books he had brought with him, including *Pride and Prejudice* ('more entrancing than ever'): 'I have thought about "Waiting in the Wings" and I hope I shall feel like attacking it when I get settled'.[5]

'During this period', Graham Payn recalled, 'projects were forever stopping and starting'.[6] Coward's attention turned to three in particular: the New York and London productions of *Look After Lulu*; *London Morning*, the ballet for London Festival Ballet; and a musical, *Later Than Spring*, which in due course became *Sail Away*. *Waiting in the Wings* was not 'revisited' until early April the following year, when he 'found it much better than [he] thought it was' and 'set to work and finished it'.[7]

As he prepared to leave for Cuba for location shooting on Carol Reed's film of *Our Man in Havana*, he wrote to tell Loraine that *Waiting in the Wings* had been completed.[8] In London he read the play to Beaumont, whose initial response was that he 'loved it', but at their next meeting he 'was a little too full of suggested alterations'. The discussion went sour', and after Beaumont finally said that he would not produce the play, Coward 'took this angrily at face value and flounced out with [his] lovelocks flowing'. An 'anguished telegram' arrived the next morning and 'everyone forgave everyone'. The choice of directors was discussed, and it was agreed that the play would be sent to Frith Banbury, whom Coward 'consider[ed] the most appropriate director'.[9] In the event it was Margaret ('Peggy') Webster who agreed to direct.[10] She wrote enthusiastically to the co-producer Fred Sardoff on 7 February: 'Noel's play is for me – as it must be for Michael – full of ghosts!'[11] The play would be produced by the 'newly-formed partnership' of Sardoff and Michael Redgrave, as Barry Day notes, a 'less than ideal combination' with Sardoff 'inclined to be doctrinaire and Redgrave, indecisive'.[12] Coward had told his long-standing friend Edna Ferber, to whom he had sent a copy of the script in August 1959, that he had 'wanted to set down this play as Chekhov did his plays – without tricks and without the observance of trite usage'. Nevertheless, the play as it emerged after his revisions in the light of the consultation with Webster and her partner the novelist Pamela Frankau was as artful as any of his other works in its theatrical self-consciousness.[13]

By 15 April Sybil Thorndike and her husband Lewis Casson had signed up to play Lotta and Osgood. Meanwhile Webster had 'given

[him] some really constructive criticism of the play' which he would follow: 'It means a little rewriting and transposing and one short extra scene, but I know it will improve the play enormously'.[14] By 22 April he had 'reconstructed' the play 'really satisfactorily'.[15] At the end of April he was in London, where he and Webster 'discussed the play and casting ad nauseam'. Rehearsals were to begin on 11 July, to open in Dublin on 8 August for two weeks. On 30 June 1960 he had finished the music and lyrics of the play's songs, and by 21 July it had been confirmed that in London it would go into the Duke of York's Theatre.[16]

A letter from Webster on 25 July described some of the problems presented by the more forgetful members of the cast, in particular Mary Clare (as Almina Clare), who was 'a serious worry – and I think also a serious tragedy – like one of those pieces of dead coal that you find in the grate the next morning'. But she was 'also, sometimes, quite pixie', and given to suddenly coming up 'from left field in a firm, bright, voice' with one of someone else's lines, 'leaving the real speaker stupefied'. It was decided that in each of her scenes she would carry 'a brightly coloured paper-back thriller, inside which is – guess what!' (Production photographs show her holding a science-fiction magazine). Webster observed that the 'minor troubles' caused by confusion on the part of the cast were a consequence of the play, which was itself 'very confusing [. . .] with so many scenes following a pattern that is the same-only-different, and further befogged by having been changed around after the first time it was set'. The result was 'some rather unequal cookery', with 'the duologue scenes . . . a bit over-cooked', and 'general scenes' not having 'begun to brown'. It would, she hoped, 'come with security'.[17] In Dublin the play was indeed a success. Coward wrote that he and Webster had done 'a little snipping and tightening here and there', and the individual performances were strong. With one exception the reviews had been favourable, and although he was as ever pessimistic about the London reviews, after seeing how it was received by an audience, he was confident.[18]

'The Wings' is 'a small charity home in the Thames Valley, not far from Bourne End' – as Coward specifies with his habitual precision – and is administered by a superintendent, Sylvia Archibald ('Miss Archie'), with a secretary, Perry Lascoe, acting as a channel of communication with the board of trustees. Coward specifies that the charity, founded in 1925 by the actor-manager Sir Hilary Brooks, 'only provides from public funds for those who have been stars or leading ladies and who, through age, lack of providence, misfortune, etc., have been reduced to poverty' (*PP6*, 425/M5, 239). By the terms of the trust, all residents must be over sixty years old. Funding for the home is supported by an annual 'midnight matinée' at which present-day stars give their services for free. In the course of the play, most of the residents go to London to see the dress rehearsal of this event. A regular visitor to the home is Osgood Meeker, a veteran playgoer who comes every week to see a bed-ridden resident, Martha, who never appears on stage. Played by Lewis Casson (born in 1875), Osgood is said by Perry to be 'just a kiddie of seventy', twenty-five years younger than the object of his faithful attentions. Two issues provide the overall arc for the play: securing the trustees' agreement to spend a recent legacy on a 'solarium' (or sun-lounge); and the resolution of the long-standing enmity between one of the established residents, May Davenport (Marie Löhr), and a new arrival, Lotta Bainbridge (Sybil Thorndike). The solarium issue gives rise to a subsidiary plot development: in an attempt to secure publicity that will force the trustees' hand, Perry brings a notoriously intrusive newspaper columnist, Zelda Fenwick, to the home. This unauthorized action puts him in danger of losing his job, as the house rules forbid interviews with the residents.

In addition to the play itself, the manuscript material includes detailed summaries of each act and scene, biographical information on some of the characters, a draft of the opening stage direction, and a cast list.[19] Among the script pages are several in which characters provide biographical vignettes not used in the final script, and the original version of the final act, with the division into two scenes discussed below. As usual, in the scripts and the published play Coward took pains to identify characters with detailed stage directions on their first appearance. The relative ages and status of the residents are specified, with some indication of their personalities. Two actresses have a higher professional status. May Davenport was 'an authentic star in her day and specialized in Shakespeare and the more ponderous Restoration comedies'. Her 'movements are immensely dignified and she wears a black velvet dress which in earlier years might have been described as a tea-gown' (*PP6*, 428/M5, 242). Lotta Bainbridge is 'a well-preserved woman in her early seventies [. . .] well made-up and calmly cheerful' (*PP6*, 443/M5 257). Perry Lascoe, a former juvenile lead who gave up the stage when he realized he was not going achieve stardom, was played by

Graham Payn, bravely taking on a role that had parallels with his own career. The superintendent of the home, 'Miss Archie' is described as having 'a gruff and rather masculine manner [that] conceals a vulnerable heart and amiable disposition'. She favours 'corduroy trousers and rather tight woollen sweaters' and tends to revert to the language and demeanour of her rank as colonel during wartime service in ENSA (*PP6*, 430/*M5*, 250). She strikes up a degree of rapport with the journalist, Zelda Fenwick, who arrives wearing slacks and shares her lively interest in sports cars with Miss Archie. There is a strong implication (in the code of the time) that they are both lesbians.

The play's crises and opportunities are managed adroitly, although important adjustments were made after the first full draft, referred to here as the 'first version'. In the first scene the arrival of Lotta is anticipated, the enmity between her and May is accounted for, and she arrives after the delay appropriate before a star's entrance. The scene ends with her tearful parting from Dora, her faithful dresser and companion of many years, and as the curtain falls, she slowly mounts the stairs to her room. Act One, Scene Two ends with a confrontation between Lotta and May, with May 'making an exit' up the stairs to her room as Lotta stoically 'bites her lip and forces a smile'. The self-conscious theatricality is underlined when Bonita, one of the other residents, comments 'Once a ham always a ham' (*PP6*, 464/*M5*, 278). The second act begins in 'the following September', and Perry introduces the first outsider, Zelda, presenting her as a friend, 'Miss Starkey', a reference to the character in Barrie's *Peter Pan*, in which, like Coward, Perry once appeared. Confronted by the dignified reproaches of Lotta and the more vehement denunciation delivered by Deirdre, who 'rises dramatically' to do so, Zelda leaves. At the end of the scene Sarita, lively but barely in her right mind, and living in the past to a greater extent than the others, sneaks downstairs to fetch a box of matches. Scene Two begins 'several hours later' with the discovery that she has set fire to her room. With appropriate alarums and excursions the blaze is contained, and in the aftermath, sharing the whisky that 'Miss Archie' has provided, Lotta and May have their scene of reconciliation. They toast one another – 'Happy days!' – and then '*stand quite still for a moment looking at each other. In their eyes there is a glint of tears as* – *the* **Curtain** *falls*' (*PP6*, 496/*M5*, 310). At the end of the third scene Sarita is taken away to a nursing home, still in her world of memory and saying goodbye to the others as though they were a company parting the end of a theatrical engagement. In the manuscript (p.31) May and Lotta discuss her career:

> **Lotta** You knew her in the old days, didn't you May?
>
> **May** Yes. We were in a play together at the Garrick just before the first war – I forget the name of it – she made quite a success in it.
>
> **Lotta** Was she good?
>
> **May** Great heavens no. But It was a good part.
>
> **Deirdre** I can remember her, pretty as a picture she was, but too chocolate boxy for my taste.
>
> **May** No sense of timing whatever No better ear poor thing – she stamped on laughs when they came and waited for them when they didn't. She used to drive poor old George mad, he had a long scene with her in the last act. He used to come off the stage every night swearing like a trooper Navvy.

This is typical of a number of biographical details subsequently removed from the script.

The first of the final act's two scenes takes place at the Christmas party. Zelda, now repentant about the report she wrote for the 'Clarion' and chastened by a rebuke from her boss, who vetoed a threatened television programme, brings a case of champagne and leaves an envelope containing his cheque for £2,000, enough to pay for the solarium. The scene develops into an impromptu concert party, with the ladies joining in songs from an old musical comedy, 'Miss Mouse' and 'Over the Hill'. Perry is persuaded to sing a number from his days as a juvenile, 'The Wild, Wild Weather'. Deirdre obliges with an Irish jig, but this brings on a fatal heart attack. She is lifted onto the sofa. As *'everyone stands in silence'* May *'takes Deirdre's hands and folds them on her breast, then straightens herself'*, delivering the curtain line: 'The luck of the Irish'. In the play's final scene, Lotta receives a visit from the estranged son she has not seen for thirty-three years, who urges her to come back to Canada with him to live with his wife and family.

This old-fashioned melodramatic situation is resolved by her dignified refusal, but in the final moments of the play the tone shifts as a new resident, Topsy Baskerville, is welcomed to 'The Wings' with a rendition of her famous number 'Oh Mr. Kaiser'. The play's celebration of the theatre of the early 1900s is thus complemented by the kind of emotional situations, set-piece entrances and exits, and 'strong curtains' familiar from the theatre of the past. Musical comedy is evoked in numbers in the pastiche mode Coward had shown in the musical-comedies-within-plays of *Cavalcade*, *Bitter-Sweet* and *Operette*. Although Marie Löhr and Sybil Thorndike were unquestionably the play's 'leading ladies', this is an ensemble piece, one that would tax Webster's skill in rehearsing the veterans, not all of them as quick of study or certain of moves as they had been.

In a passage omitted from the published diary, Coward specified the changes referred to in the entry for 22 April:

> I have transposed the Lotta-May reconciliation from the end of the first act to the end of the second scene of the second act. There is a new scene [Act Two, Scene Two] about the fire and I think it has come out well. I have also telescoped the two last scenes of the play into one and this is also a vast improvement.[20]

The 'snipping and cutting' included the removal of Ted, the home's 'house boy'. (The term has an oddly colonial ring.) The alleged unreliability of Deirdre, the persistently mournful Irish actress ('She's never played a scene the same way twice') is ascribed in the typescript to drink (1-1-6). Estelle's reminiscence that she was 'an ingénue for years' (*PP6*, 454/*M5*, 248) is elaborated: 'I was an ingénue for years and played all those dull love scenes with young men in white flannels. I always made my first entrance with a croquet mallet and, later on, with a tennis racquet.' (1-1-10). The description of the maid Doreen's predecessor, Gladys – 'she was like a bad character performance in Act Three' (*PP6*, 438/*M5*, 252) – replaces 'she was sort of Hogarthian' which had been followed by a mild double-entendre from Cora and Bonita's reply: 'We were always finding her fumbling in our drawers' – 'You put things so delicately dear'. (1-1-14–15) A more significant alteration is the deletion from the opening of the second scene of a conversation between Ted and the maid Doreen, as they prepare at three in the morning for the return of the party from their 'annual treat' at the rehearsal for the 'midnight matinee':

> **Ted** You'd think the old geysers would be beyond wanting treats wouldn't you? Let alone stopping up all night.
>
> **Doreen** They're used to that I expect.
>
> **Ted** I bet some of them was hot stuff in their time, champagne suppers and patty de foir grar and carrying on stinking. This cocoa and sandwiches lark must be a bit of a come down. [...] Do you think they like it here? Living in a sort of workhouse?
>
> **Doreen** It wouldn't do much good if they didn't like it would it? They haven't got anywhere else to go, poor old things.
>
> 1-2-35–6

The crudely patronizing view of the home is out of keeping with the play's tone, and Coward wisely reserved the expression of an outsider's attitude for the journalist Zelda Fenwick, whose readiness to depict the actresses as victims is a potential threat. He may also have realized that the device of having servants provide this kind of exposition was too shop-worn.

In the typescript, the second scene of the act ends with a protracted argument between Lotta and May, in which the physical struggle between them is stronger than in the completed play: as well as 'grabbing her by the shoulders' Lotta even gives May 'a slight slap on the face' as she restrains her from going to summon Miss Archie. Her plea for the resolution of their feud – 'Let's for God's sake forget the past and welcome our limited future with as much grace as possible'. (1-2-52) – corresponds in all but a few details to the equivalent in the final version, and is followed by the 'reconciliation scene' (four typescript pages) later moved to the end of Act Two, Scene Two, in the aftermath of the fire emergency. The structural advantage of postponing this resolution is clear, but Coward also seems to have wished to modify the physical interaction between the two women. The alteration gives more point to the episode of the fire, as it now prepares for a change of tempo leading into the change of attitude on May's part. She has also been given fictional time for this to develop, more than a month out of the time-scheme's twelve.

To accommodate the postponement of the reconciliation, in revising the first scene of Act Two Coward removed Lotta from the group to whom Perry introduces Zelda on her arrival, and cut a line in which Miss Archie assured her that although Lotta and May 'didn't speak for years. [. . .] It was a bit tricky when Lotta came at first but it's been all right lately.' (2-1-6). The typescript's Act Two, Scene Two, (subsequently adapted to become the first scene of Act Three) takes place a week after the day of Zelda's visit. Perry describes his treatment at the hands of the committee, the threat of dismissal for breaking the terms of his contract, and his eventual reprieve. The fire started by Sarita has already taken place. Perry has 'just been having a look at Miss Archie's official report', and the details are supplied by Lotta and Bonita, with gloomy interjections from Deirdre. (2-2-34–5) The scene ends with Sarita being escorted from the home by the kindly Dr. Jevons. In the added scene – the new Act two, Scene Two – Coward dramatizes the (offstage) accident and its aftermath and, as noted above, ends it with the May/Lotta reconciliation. In Act Three, Scene One, the few revisions included the omission of an exchange following Cora's recommendation that Deirdre 'stop overacting' (*PP6*, 517/ M5, 331):

Deirdre So I'm overacting now am I?

May (*majestically*) Yes Deirdre you are, and you always did.

Deirdre (*with spirit*) And what about you I should like to know? I've heard you ranting an roaring until my ears crackled – perhaps you've forgotten what they said about your Lady Macbeth at Stratford?

3-1-10

As he noted in his diary, Coward combined the two final scenes of the manuscript and typescript: the first consisted of Alan's visit with his mother's refusal to go to Canada and ended with their parting. In the second scene, the episode had been discussed by the other residents, providing an opportunity for them to reflect on their own respective situations. When Lotta entered they expressed their pleasure at her decision. This was followed by the arrival of Topsy Baskerville. In the process of making these scenes continuous Coward removed a series of exchanges that would merely have revisited topics previously aired when the play needed to move swiftly to its conclusion. In the first version, when Lotta enters and asks 'What's the argument about?' Maudie blurts out that the discussion has been about her, 'and then it got sort of general'.

Cora (*irritably*)   How can you be so tactless Maudie.

Lotta   About me? What a waste of time.

Bonita   What it boils down to is that we're all delighted that you decided not to go away and leave us.

Lotta (*after a slight pause*)   Thank you Bonita. Has anybody seen my work-bag? I left it on the piano.

Maudie (*producing it from the sofa*)   Here it is.

3-3-39

As revised, this becomes a moment of tactful kindness on May's part and stoicism on Lotta's. After Alan's departure she 'sinks on the sofa buries her face in her hands and bursts into tears'. May comes in from the television room and comforts her. Lotta tells her about the offer and her refusal:

May   And you said no?

Lotta (*sitting up and speaking without emotion*) Yes, I said no.

May   I see. (*A slight pause, she puts her hand on* **Lotta's** *shoulder.*) Is there anything I can do to help?

Lotta (*resting her hand for a moment on* **May's** *hand*)   Yes, dear May. You might pass me my knitting, it's on the piano.

There is the noise of a motor-bicycle outside.

PP6, 534/M5, 348

The first version also includes a sequence in which Lotta is disturbed by the prospect of welcoming a new resident. Told that Topsy is arriving she '*bites her lip and looks suddenly unhappy*'. Perry reassures her with 'She's a sweet old girl – you'll love her', and she replies 'I'm sure I shall Perry dear'. May senses Lotta's unhappiness and, '*firmly putting down her embroidery frame*', gets up and suggests they go out for a stroll in the garden:

Lotta Yes May – that would be very nice.

May (*briskly*) I always dislike seeing people arriving here for the first time, it depresses me. We can walk as far as the lower fence, Miss Archie says that they've mended it at last.

Lotta (*with a strained smile*) Guard my knitting with your life Maudie.

Maudie All right.

May We'll be back in time for tea.

(**Lotta** *and* **May** *go out through the garden arm in arm.*)

3-3-40

The final version adds Maudie's rendition of Topsy's old song, and '*with a wry smile*' Lotta agrees with Perry that she is sure they will 'love' the 'sweet old girl':

Lotta [. . .] I expect that's what you said a year ago when I arrived.

Bonita Yes, I expect we did. A whole year ago! It doesn't seem possible, does it?

Lotta I was in deep despair, lonely and hopeless and feeling as though I were going to prison, and now, after a year of prison, I feel suddenly free. Isn't that curious? (*She returns to her knitting.*)

PP6, 537/M5, 531

In French's edition the feeling of the 'moment' between the two is further underlined by action: Lotta crosses to May before 'I remember I was in deep despair', at which May holds her hand. Lotta does not 'return to her knitting' (Fr, 83). As revised, the play's conclusion is simplified, with Bonita coming forward to greet Topsy, who exclaims, '*in a tremulous voice*', 'My song!' as everybody runs forward to greet her as the curtain falls. This is less sentimental than the scene in the typescript, in which Maudie, Estelle, Cora and Almina approach her and Topsy, distraught, bursts into tears. As she is being helped upstairs by Perry and Miss Archie, Maudie goes to the piano and begins to play 'Oh Mr. Kaiser'.

Topsy *stops at the top of the stairs and turns. She steps forward and sings, in a quavering voice, the last couplet of the song with* **Maudie** *and* **Bonita** *and then, with a gallant effort, she gives a saucy little back kick and disappears with* **Miss Archie** *and* **Perry**. *Everyone applauds.*

Curtain

3-3-42

The simpler stage directions in *Play Parade* and the earlier Heinemann edition – which correspond with minor differences to those in French's edition – suggest that it was decided to avoid a potential 'laugh' moment that might have detracted from the effect of the exchange between Lotta and May. In her letter of 25 July, Webster told Coward that the new ending 'work[ed] miracles': 'You were a wonder-boy to do it so quickly and so beautifully. It's very good for both Sybil and Marie and also for Topsy herself'.[21]

It was inevitable that Coward's forty-second play, produced on the London stage in his sixtieth year with a principal cast of elderly actresses playing ageing stars in a theatrical retirement home, should evince reflections from the largely hostile press on Coward's own 'twilight years', and on the distance between his work and that of the new generation. When he emerged from the theatre after the opening night's performance 'there were cheering crowds on either side of St. Martin's Lane', but he was, as ever, right to be pessimistic about the reviews, some of which reflected his own misgivings. Under the headline 'A Play About Nothing at All', Bernard Levin in the *Daily Express* complained that the play was 'an exercise in grisly nostalgia so awful as to defy analysis, a defiance reinforced by the fact that in it Mr. Coward has achieved what I would have said was the impossible, and written a play that is about nothing'.[22] As if this were not wounding enough, Levin attacked the craftsmanship on which Coward prided himself: *Waiting in the Wings* 'appears to have been constructed on the do-it-yourself principle out of fully interchangeable pieces'. Levin objected that 'almost any line – indeed any scene – could be taken out and replaced anywhere else in the play, and much the same is true of the characters'. The *Daily Mail*'s Robert Muller complained that the action 'meander[ed] along placidly', with 'long arid patches in which the old actresses are bitchy to each other or remember the old songs they sang'.

Coward had been 'content to carpenter diligently', but did not 'give of himself', and all that was conveyed was 'prattle, prattle, prattle. And timeless, rootless prattle at that'. Several of the other reviews were remarkably abusive.[23]

Among the more sympathetic critics, Philip Hope-Wallace in the *Guardian* struck a rueful note – 'The play may seem a waste of talent but it is likely to please those who are drawn to go to see it' – while at the same time pointing to dramaturgical failings: 'The sudden death of one of the inmates quite fails to make a curtain: and not even Dame Sybil Thorndike can salvage a fatally tardy mother-and-lost-son scene'.[24] In the *News Chronicle*, Alan Dent noted that 'Every now and then the Master runs out of plot. But his recoveries are in his best and most alert style'.[25] The most detailed commentary on the play, situating it in the context of Coward's career and – most importantly – his craftsmanship, was R.B. Marriott's in the *Stage and Television Today*. Acknowledging that Coward 'still continues to try his best, and does care about his craft', Marriott suggested that the theme 'could, of course, have been treated in the style of Osborne or Wesker, or there could have been a Chekhovian approach'. But the play had 'magic: the essential quality', despite 'many poor lines, characterization that goes only skin deep, craftsmanship which, although expert in its way, could be called dated, and complete remoteness from the atomic world of today'. Marriott praised the 'workmanlike direction [that] fits the design of the play, like the décor by Motley', but it was the performances that 'lift[ed] it to a higher level'. Thorndike's Lotta was 'a finely sensitive characterization, delightful in its quiet humour and moving in depth of understanding', and Löhr was 'most effective when obliquely revealing that behind the woman's ferocity lie fear and mortification'. He was not the only reviewer to single out the 'still, radiant performance' of Mary Clare, which justified the casting of an actress who had been so uncertain in rehearsals, and most of whose lines had in fact been cut. (They would be reinstated in the published texts): 'Her loose white hair, her ashen face, lovely and with a faint shadow in its serenity, her slow but graceful movement, all express thoughts and feelings which require no words'.[26]

On 22 September the *Stage and Television Today* reported that, before leaving for Switzerland after the first night, Coward had predicted that his play would 'capture the imagination of the public and run for two years'. This was not unreasonable, given the popular success of *Nude with Violin* and (before Leigh's premature departure from the cast) *South Sea Bubble*. Nevertheless, reviewers who suggested that *Waiting in the Wings* would find its most appreciative audience among the 'over-60s' were not wide of the mark. On 6 October Lorn Loraine wrote to Coward that 'Apparently every elderly and middle aged lady in the United Kingdom is determined to go to a matinée of *Waiting in the Wings*'.[27] Nevertheless, the customary 'pre-Christmas slump' in theatre attendances took its toll, and Loraine reported on 31 January that the audiences had just 'dwindled': 'The box office think this is due, to a certain extent, to the effect of winter weather because there is no doubt that a high percentage of our audiences have been oldish people – the good matinees prove that – and they don't go out much in the winter'. Because a month's rent-free use of the theatre had been negotiated to take them up to 18 February, they had reached a six-months run of 188 performances, and 'there would be 'a small profit'. Auditions were in hand for a post-London tour.[28] Coward's 'Consider the Public' articles, attacking aspects of the contemporary theatre, had appeared in the *Sunday Times* on 15, 22 and 29 January, and he reflected that in the resulting 'uproar' it was unfortunate that the closure of *Waiting in the Wings* had given 'some of the enraged correspondents a handle'.[29] In her letter of 31 January Loraine had assured him that the articles had been 'a great success' and that everyone she knew of had been 'greatly impressed and in complete agreement'.

Suite in Three Keys, 1965–1966: 'Coward Triumphant as of Old'?

After *Waiting in the Wings*, Coward's attention turned, as usual to a variety of projects, including the publication in 1960 of his 'Samolan' novel, *Pomp and Circumstance*. Early in the year he had been contemplating a play that would deal directly with homosexuality. The Lord Chamberlain had let it be known that the 'supposedly blanket ban' on 'explicit references to homosexuality' was to be removed, and plays submitted would be 'considered individually on their merits, rather than on principle'.[30] On 10

February Loraine wrote a letter, hitherto unpublished, to 'Darling Master':

> I have thought a lot about this play outline and I feel strongly that is [*sic*] must be treated entirely psychologically and with restraint and no sign of melodrama such as the Admiral threatening to shoot Trevor. I feel that it is part of a different play about quite other people. I think all your characters are too intelligent and civilized to imagine violence would help. I have been wondering whether it would be a good idea for Trevor to have had an affair with Owen Fletcher but to be *really*, all the time, deeply and jealously in love with John – a love which John has never returned and which has therefore turned sour. I think that would possibly be a stronger motive for his behaviour than Owen's death alone and might also give us a convincing end – that when it came to the final point he could not bring himself to smash John's life. I don't know what actual end there could be – possibly a telegram to Judith – I am not sure and of course you may not agree with any of this.[31]

This suggests that Judith would have been Owen's wife and possibly the daughter of the Admiral, and that Coward seems to have envisaged a return to the 'well-made' formula. He may have been further discouraged by the reception of Joan Henry's *Look on Tempests*, reviewed in the *Stage* with the headline 'First Homosexual Play Presented in Public'. The story of a wife's support of a husband who has been accused under the legislation against homosexual acts (not repealed until 1967) was in Coward's opinion 'an excellent play impeccably acted', by Gladys Cooper as the man's mother and Vanessa Redgrave as his wife. In the *Stage* it was described as 'a dullish conventional drawing-room drama with bloodless people, plus an unusual theme'. Coward found the notices 'idiotic, principally, I suppose, because the ambience was educated middle class, and not forbiddingly squalid'.[32]

One of his own least promising – and resolutely heterosexual – projects, first mentioned in his diary in 1962, was a new three-act comedy, provisionally called *Three for the Money*. He would play 'a ramshackle Irish lord', burdened with 'a ramshackle castle' and three 'beautiful but undisciplined daughters, upon whose charms he relies to save the family fortunes', and whom his ex-mistress would take to France in search of rich husbands.[33] Cole Lesley reported to Loraine that the idea was originally for a film script, and a synopsis had been written, but that Coward would not act in it himself.[34] In the event, over the subsequent three years his theatre work was dominated by *Sail Away*, the score for the musical *The Girl who Came to Supper* (from Terence Rattigan's play *A Sleeping Prince*), and overseeing *High Spirits*, Hugh Martin and Timothy Gray's musical based on *Blithe Spirit*. In 1964 he published a collection of short stories, *Pretty Polly Barlow*, and directed *Hay Fever* for the National Theatre at the Old Vic, in a production that contributed considerably to what he and his professional family liked to call 'Dad's Renaissance'.

Between March and October 1965, Coward wrote the three plays, each with three characters, that make up *Suite in Three Keys*, first performed in April 1966 with Coward himself in all three leading male roles. (In August 1962 he had conceived the idea of a group of plays, two to be performed each evening, under the collective title *Neutral Territory*.)[35] Each play is set in the same suite of a luxury hotel in Lausanne, where the guests are served by the same floor waiter, Felix. Although there are passages of wit in all three, two are predominantly dark in tone, and the alterations made during their composition reflect Coward's continuing desire to find his own way of engaging with serious themes. Each play features a version of the 'lovers' triangle' that had recurred, often with radical variations in some of his earlier plays, including the creation of a four- rather than three-sided configuration in *Private Lives*, *Design for Living* and *Quadrille*. In two of the *Suite in Three Keys* plays there is an added clarity and frankness in treating the issues of emotional loyalty and betrayal and, in one instance, the consequences of concealing one's true sexuality.

A number of Coward's published and performed plays had included identifiably (if not explicitly) gay or lesbian characters, as well as the more or less implicit relationship between Otto and Leo (and conceivably Ernest) in *Design for Living*. The narrator of the short story 'Me and the Girls', published in 1964, is a gay variety performer, dying in a Swiss hospital, whose reminiscences make frank reference to his various affairs. But the emphasis in *A Song at Twilight* would not be on the central character's homosexuality in itself, but the subterfuges by which he had managed to pass as heterosexual, the consequences for the women in his life, and the cruelty with which he had treated a former lover. In this 'comedy in two acts' – a somewhat ironic indication of genre – the elderly author Sir Hugo Latymer, who has kept up the pretence of being exclusively heterosexual, is confronted by an ex-wife, the actress Carlotta Gray, with evidence of his cruelty to a discarded male lover. This is the 'rendezvous with the past' (M5, 363) for which he is preparing when the play opens. Her motive in wishing the incriminating letters to be available to a biographer is not blackmail but a desire to see justice done, and he is protected by Hilde, his German second wife. In *Shadows of the Evening* ('a play in two scenes') Anne Hilgay, the estranged wife of a publisher diagnosed with terminal cancer, has been summoned to the hotel by his long-established mistress, Linda Savignac. Coward reflected that this was 'a sad theme but not entirely a sad play'.[36] (It is the only one of the three identified as a 'play' rather than a 'comedy'.) In *Come into the Garden Maud*, a 'light comedy in two scenes', a romantic involvement with Maud Caragnani, a sophisticated cosmopolitan Englishwoman who is an Italian princess by marriage, rescues the rich American businessman Verner Conklin from his loveless marriage to Anna-Mary, his vulgar, snobbish, insular and selfish wife. In their respective concluding moments, the characters of all the plays achieve some kind of resolution, with Hugo Latymer 'deeply moved' as he reads the letters Carlotta has surrendered to him and George Hilgay leading his wife and mistress off to an evening at the Casino to spend some of the precious time remaining to him in a little gambling. Verner is allowed to make his escape from Anna-Mary in a moment of satisfying and long-overdue confrontation:

> **Anna-Mary** (*furiously*)   Go away, Verner. Go away and leave me alone.
>
> **Verner**   Okay...Okay...That's just exactly what I'm going to do. Good night, sweetheart.
>
> **Verner** *picks up his tie and shoes, flings his coat over his arm, looks at her quizzically for a split second, and goes swiftly out of the room.* **Anna-Mary** *sits glaring at him balefully as the* **Curtain Falls.**
>
> M5, 539

She thinks he is simply going to his own room, but the audience knows he is going to join Maud in her drive to Rome.

In each play the young Swiss-Italian waiter Felix appears: their treatment of him is a touchstone to the social attitudes and sophistication (or lack of it) of the main characters. Hugo treats him with a mixture of arrogance and surreptitious fascination that hints at his concealed sexual preferences: told that Felix has a friend who is a champion swimmer he remarks 'You look as though you should be a good swimmer yourself, with those shoulders' (M5, 371); Carlotta's easy confidence with Felix draws a rebuke from Hugo – 'I hate familiarity with servants' (M5, 398). Linda, in *Shadows of the Evening*, clearly knows how to speak to a servant, and takes a polite interest in the plight of Felix's friend, who has been involved in a crash on his motor-scooter. Anna-Mary's brash ignorance – 'Neither Mr. Conklin nor I speak Italian and the sooner the staff of this hotel realises it, the better it will be for everybody concerned' (M5, 495) – contrasts with the more sympathetic and engaged manner of her husband in his conversation with the waiter.

Coward chose his titles from Victorian parlour songs for *Come into the Garden Maud* and *A Song at Twilight*, and a hymn for *Shadows of the Evening*. The lyrics were current in his youth and still familiar in the 1960s, and the implicit allusions to the plays' themes would be intelligible to many in the original audience. In the song from Tennyson's long poem *Maud* the lover is 'here at the gate alone' and 'the planet of Love is on high'. 'Just a song at twilight' is the first line of the refrain of 'Love's Old Sweet Song', in which the subsequent reference to 'the dear dead days beyond recall' would amount to an ironic comment on the play's action. Given that the dying publisher in *Shadows of the Evening* has no faith in the afterlife promised by religion, he would be unlikely to have found any comfort in the words of Sabine Baring-Gold's hymn, 'Now the day is over' in which Christ is entreated to 'give the weary / Calm and sweet repose' now that 'night is drawing nigh' and 'Shadows of the evening / Steal across the sky'.

The first act of *A Song at Twilight* had been completed by 1 March 1965, and on 21 March Coward noted that the play was 'nearly finished', but he felt that further work was now necessary. By 14 June he had finished the first act, and by 23 July the revision was complete.[37] Nevertheless, work on the script continued through the first two weeks of July.[38] On 17 July he wrote that he had read it to Robin Maugham, Somerset Maugham's nephew, who was 'deeply impressed', but concerned because it might seem to be based on his uncle.[39] In his 'Foreword' to Garson Kanin's *Remembering Mr. Maugham* (1966) Coward wrote that Maugham was 'a complex man and his view of his fellow creatures was jaundiced to say the least', and that despite this he was 'a man of almost painful sensitivity and was a great deal more shy and vulnerable than he would have us believe'.[40] In her biography of Maugham, Selina Hastings suggests that a letter he sent Coward after the death of his lover Gerald Saxton may have suggested Latymer's response to the letters returned to him at the end of the play.[41] Although Maugham's increasingly cantankerous behaviour and his concealment of important aspects of his private life informed the character of Hugo, the principal inspiration for the play's situation was the account in Lord David Cecil's biography of Max Beerbohm of the reappearance at his home in Rapallo, 'after years of non-contact', of the actress Constance Collier.[42]

Meanwhile, on 4 April he reported that he had 'been racking [his] brains to think of two other long-short plays to go with "A Song at Twilight," but so far to no avail', and had started work instead on *Past Conditional*, the third volume of his autobiography.[43] Within the next few days, *Past Conditional* was set aside, and on 19 April *Come into the Garden Maud*, the shortest of the three, was completed.[44] On 14 June he was busy rewriting *A Song at Twilight*, and reported an idea for the third play of the series, although he had not yet begun to 'construct' it. It would be about 'a celebrated actor and entourage who settles [sic] in Switzerland to avoid the English tax situation'. It would be based on his own experiences and he could not see that he could 'fail to make it fairly funny', and once he had worked out the 'shape' the dialogue would take care of itself.[45] He may have lost confidence in what might seem a potentially hazardous revisiting of the topic that had caused so much unwanted and unfair publicity when he acquired non-resident tax status, or maybe he felt that another version of the actor and his 'entourage' would be overly reminiscent of Gary Essendine's situation in *Present Laughter*. In any case, this line was not pursued.

The two scenes of *Shadows of the Evening*, which would play on the same bill as *Come into the Garden Maud*, were written by 20 August.[46] Nevertheless, in September he revised the play again in the light of comments by Lilli Palmer – who was to eventually to share the women's roles with Irene Worth – the playwright and anthropologist Robert Ardrey, and the newly appointed director Vivian Matalon. Ardrey had echoed Palmer's objection that 'there was not enough conflict between the two women and that the whole thing was too fucking noble'. By 3 October Coward had rewritten it and 'kept all the good bits but ruthlessly cut out all pretension and nobility'.[47]

Margaret Leighton had prevaricated over accepting the offer to appear in the plays, making 'silly telephone calls' and trying to have Michael Wilding, her third husband, brought to London as part of the contract. Coward had lost patience with her. By 7 September, Palmer and Worth had been confirmed for the female roles. At his request on 8 October Loraine had sent the Lunts copies of all three scripts, now in the Alfred Lunt and Lynn Fontanne Collection at the Wisconsin Historical Society. These represent the state of the plays before they went into production. Variants in the earlier drafts are from copies of the 'first version' of each play in the Birmingham archive, marked up with corrections carried over into the script sent to the Lunts.[48]

Almost all the changes made in *A Song at Twilight* between October 1965 and April 1966 were cuts, amounting to the equivalent of 6 out of 67 pages of typescript in the first act and 2 out of 44 in the second: a total of some 7 per cent across both scenes. Apart from one passage of dialogue between Hugo and Hilde – 'Hildi' in the early drafts – the cuts to the first act are in the long dinner scene between Hugo and Carlotta. Most of the omitted lines, including those from an exchange between Hugo and Hilde, deal with circumstantial details of the respective pasts, including the equivalent of two typescript pages, referring to their difference in ages and the length of time since their last meeting. The most important alteration in Act One comes immediately before the end of the act, when Carlotta describes her relationship with Perry Sheldon, Hugo's discarded lover. Hugo asks what she knows about him, and in the October draft her answer is as follows:

> A great deal. I have known him on and off for many years. He had a little one-room apartment in Hollywood you know. We used sometimes to go to the movies together. On several occasions I took him to the Hollywood Bowl. You remember he adored music. He could be gay and charming company but I know how

haunted he was by his inner consciousness of failure, and how tired and sad and lonely he was, particularly towards the end when he was ill and penniless and had no one to turn to. I also know that he happened to be the only true love of your life. Good night, Hugo, sleep well.

After this 'CARLOTTA *goes out, closing the doors behind her*'. Before the curtain falls 'HUGO *stands transfixed for a moment staring after her. He makes a movement to follow her and then sinks slowly into his arm-chair.*' (I-67). In the published play this becomes: 'Among other things that he was the only true love of your life. Good night, Hugo, sleep well'. The curtain falls as she '*turns upstage, exiting through the door*'. (M5, 402) Whereas the other long cuts seem designed to remove extraneous information and improve the pace, the shorter version of this speech leaves the question of Perry Sheldon's personality and career hanging in suspense until after the interval: Coward is marshalling the play's revelations more carefully. In Act Two little is said about Sheldon, though Carlotta discloses that he died from leukaemia, exacerbated by drink. The emphasis shifts to Hugo's treatment of him and, more particularly, the manner in which he has excised their relationship from his autobiography and all statements about his past, in order to present himself as exclusively heterosexual.

Between October 1965 and the first London rehearsals in early March Coward had been on one of his habitual wanderings to remote parts of the Globe and had become seriously ill, and plans to open in Dublin before the London premiere had been abandoned. Nevertheless, the play had been tightened and made more effective in the disclosure of information, making possible a better springboard for the reversal in Act Two, by which, as a result of Hilde's revelation that she has always known about Sheldon, Carlotta relents and Hugo is left with the incriminating letters. Coward seems to have been wary of any hint that the situation was evocative of melodrama, or the language inappropriately elevated – even when expressed humorously. This applied particularly to Hugo, whose habitual sarcasm and pomposity needed to be carefully adjusted. One example in the first version occurs in the exchange between Hugo and Carlotta that reappeared in a modified form in revisions to the October script but was excised altogether in the published text. Carlotta, asked what she wants from him, replies

'Oh I don't know. A moment of truth perhaps. A sudden dazzling flash of self-revelation. Even an act of contrition' (M5, 419, which adds 'Even . . . contrition'). Before Hugo's reply, 'That, if I may say so, is pretentious twaddle', the October script has the following:

Hugo   You talk like a sententious Victorian novelist.

Carlotta   I feel that many of the major Victorian novelists would have a shrewder idea of what I am driving at than you.

Hugo (*sarcastically*)   I have little doubt that Ouida, Marie Corelli and Hall Caine might have saluted your high-minded moral crusade, but I suspect that their more realistic contemporaries would have dismissed it with the contempt it deserves.

Carlotta   I was right. The stronghold of your complacency is still impregnable. My small slings and arrows have barely dented the outer walls.

II-20

(In the first version Hugo refers to the 'high-minded moral crusade' as 'this gratuitous moral crusade upon which [she has] embarked with such high-minded enthusiasm'.) Another self-conscious reference to literary and theatrical genre was removed from the opening of the second scene. Carlotta has ordered another bottle of champagne, and Hugo comments that she has 'decided to set the mood in a light vein' – in the first version the phrase was 'vein of light comedy'. This minor emendation leaves the reference to dramatic genre for Carlotta's insistence that the situation is not tragic: 'All the tragedy was drained out of it when Perry died. There's only comedy left now. Rather bitter comedy, I must admit, but not entirely unenjoyable'. Her response to the accusation that she is blackmailing him continues the theme of dramatic genre: 'Blackmail! Really, Hugo! I had no idea you had such a highly developed sense of melodrama.' (M5, 405; 406).

After the revelation that Carlotta has Hugo's letters to Sheldon, the point of suspense on which the first scene ends, the play's subsequent reversals and revelations are carefully plotted. All devolve from Hilde, who has been offstage during the central scenes between Hugo and Carlotta. She tells them she has been in communication with Chandler, the American would-be biographer. She has known about the letters all along, having found Sheldon's replies. She has put these in a safe deposit box in a bank. Her motivation in this was her conviction that Hugo is 'a great writer and a famous man' and 'nothing that concerns [him] should be destroyed' (M5, 435). Hilde describes Sheldon in terms more ruthless than any used by her husband: 'He was a creature of little merit; foolish, conceited, dishonest and self-indulgent', his only claim to attention being 'his early relationship with Hugo' (M5, 440). By discounting any image of Sheldon as a romantic victim, Hilde also discounts the threat from the letters. In the course of the play Carlotta has moved from what seems like blackmail to a moral crusade and then to acceptance of the strength of Hilde's bond with Hugo, despite his often cruel and dictatorial treatment of her. Her account of her past (M5, 438–9) is also reserved for the closing section of the play. After she has snubbed Carlotta by insisting on addressing her formally, the surrender of the letters prompts her to respond at the end to the latter's 'Good night, Lady Latymer' with 'Good night, Carlotta'. This is the kind of social nuance that Maugham excelled in. Here, it reinforces the sense of *A Song at Twilight* as a well-made play.

Another satisfyingly 'well-made' element is the manner in which the final moments before the fall of the curtain add to the sense of Hugo's lifelong suppression of feelings and Hilde's compassionate understanding. After the women have left, with Hilde taking Carlotta by the arm and insisting that she would like to accompany her to her hotel room, Hugo is left alone:

> **Hugo** *stands looking after them for a moment, then he glances at the bundle of letters in his hand and sits down in his armchair. He puts on his glasses, selects a letter at random from the package and begins to read it. Having read it, he takes another. As he begins to read this second one, he frowns slightly and looks up. It is apparent from his expression that he is deeply moved. He starts to read the letter again and then, with a sigh, covers his eyes with his hand.* **Hilde** *comes quietly back into the room. She stands looking at him for a moment and then sits down silently on the edge of the sofa.*
>
> **Hugo** (*after a long pause*)   I heard you come in.

Hilde (*almost in a whisper*)   Yes, I thought you did.

Hugo *continues reading the letter as*

The **Curtain** *slowly falls*[49]

M5, 441

French's acting edition (1966) indicates that Hugo '*wipes away a tear*' after taking off his glasses (Fr, 55).

This final tableau qualifies some of the more glaringly negative aspects of Hugo's character and confirms a degree of compassion underlying Hilde's relationship with him. Of the plays' three male leads, he is the most complex. His offhanded cruelty to Hilde includes such insulting references to her being German as 'Turn round Hilde. I don't like talking to your back. It's such a Teutonic, uncompromising back.' (M5, 365). When he rebukes her for 'looking hurt' because it 'infuriates' him, she replies, 'If you do not wish me to look hurt you should not try so hard to hurt me.' (M5, 269). Carlotta's analysis of his temperament is clear-eyed:

> I don't remember him being overstrung exactly. On the contrary, his studied calmness used occasionally to irritate me. It was as though he had made a private vow to remain Captain of his Soul no matter what emotional hurricanes he might encounter. [. . .] The continual demands made upon his time, the constant strain of having to live up to the self-created image he has implanted in the public mind.
>
> M5, 374

She sees this as directly related to his approach to fiction:

Carlotta   [. . .] You take a fairly jaundiced view of your fellow creatures don't you, on the whole?

Hugo   Perhaps. I prefer to see people as they are rather than as more sentimental minds would wish them to be. However, I am a commentator, not a moralist. I state no preferences.

M5, 379

The reference to Maugham is even clearer in her recollection of his being 'away in the Far East' on one of his 'excavating expeditions

[...] digging for treasure trove in the minds of the innocent' (M5, 390). (The real-life origin of such stories as 'Rain' had been made public by Maugham in *A Writer's Notebook*, published in 1949.)

Hugo's exaggeration of his infirmity, which Hilde firmly contradicts in their first scene together, and the 'indestructible elegance' of his speech, which Carlotta says is 'flustering' her and making her talk too much, are elements of a carefully assumed persona. His disdain for 'the young of today' is part of this, and he claims he is 'too old to make allowances'. Carlotta will not let this pass: 'Oh Hugo! You're positively stampeding towards the quiet grave, aren't you?' (M5, 385). Deflating his claims to the privileges of seniority – he is no more than five years older – is part of the campaign to unmask his more serious pretences, which have included using their marriage to camouflage his sexual identity and the celebration of heterosexual passion in his writings. Carlotta points out that the letters were written 'in [his] earlier years [...] before [his] mind had become corrupted by fame and [his] heart by caution' (M5, 406). The closing moments suggest a change in Hugo, in a private surrender of his mask of ironic and acidulous detachment as well as confrontation with his emotional past.

Shadows of the Evening presented different challenges: the anxiety regarding 'nobility' and the need to sharpen the initial conflict between the two women. The annotated script identified as the 'first version' in the Birmingham archive shows alterations to tone down the 'nobility' by removing lines or complete speeches in which characters express emotion in a register that sounds dangerously similar to the voice of Laura in the film *Brief Encounter*. Thus, after George's account of his reaction to news of his diagnosis, ending 'But I think I'm alright now', Linda 'brokenly' exclaimed 'Oh my dear darling'. To Anne's explanation for not having divorced George, 'I didn't want to get rid of you once and for all' (M5, 466), the first version adds 'I wanted to hang onto every little bit of you I could'. The reduction in 'nobility' has the effect of foregrounding the uneasy nature of the women's situation as they cope with their respective feelings towards him while at the same time negotiating their mutual resentment. It is this, rather than the addition of only a few especially sharp exchanges, that increases the tension between them in the play's opening movement.

As well as making changes that modified the women's emotional language, Coward deleted passages of self-conscious stoicism in

George's account of his response to the doctor's admission that his cancer was unavoidably terminal. In the final version, his immediate reaction is described simply: 'After he'd gone I had a glass of water and smoked a cigarette and lay there staring at the white ceiling, and thought harder than I'd ever thought before' (M5, 465). This appears as follows in the October script:

> I lay there after he'd gone, staring at the white ceiling and waiting for self-pity to engulf me. I even managed to cry a little, but my tears were only a token gesture. I found I couldn't weep with any conviction because I was too preoccupied with the challenge I had been forced to accept. Then I had a glass of water and smoked a cigarette and waited for the fear to come, for the goblins to get me. They came all right, but they were surprisingly courteous and almost apologetic, they seemed more embarrassed by me than I was by them. I informed them, with some asperity, that I had a great deal to think about and had no time for them at the moment, whereupon they bowed, a trifle cynically, I thought, and scuttled away.
>
> I-24

Coward seems to have been anxious not to lend his character a degree of fanciful imagination that might vitiate the effect of the genuine eloquence he achieves in other speeches. (It also resembles the kind of 'poetic' metaphor removed in the revisions to *Volcano*.) This results in a leaner, more direct mode of address that suits the impatience George expresses elsewhere with the emotional self-indulgence he refers to in the 'bloody performance' of 'ghastly politeness' on the part of Anne and Linda. (M5, 480–1). How to talk about their situation and his condition is the play's dominant topic, and Coward successfully allows himself a simpler metaphor in the play's concluding speech, as the three characters prepare to leave for their evening at the Casino across the lake in France: 'Come my dear ones, you have your passports. I have mine. It is still valid for quite a while.' (M5, 489).

Most of the differences between the October script of *Come into the Garden Maud* and the published version are minor adjustments of the usual kind: inserted or transposed lines reflecting the experience of rehearsal and performance. One substantial change is the deletion of elements of Maud's account of her experiences in the

Second World War. In the published text she tells Verner that her Italian husband was killed in a car crash in 1940, moving immediately to 'I managed to get myself onto a ship going to Lisbon, and from there back to England.' (M5, 524). The typescript adds details:

> We were living in a dilapidated old Palazzo just outside Palermo. In addition to his mother there were two dotty spinster aunts. It wasn't very comfortable because by then Italy had come into the war against the Allies and so I became an enemy Alien. Finally. I managed to get myself onto a ship. . .
>
> I-2-27

In itself the information does not lead anywhere, and it is reasonable to suppose that the omission was simply a matter of pace and giving the audience only what it needs to know.

Although it is by far the 'lightest' of the plays, these alterations in the account of Maud's life are symptomatic of Coward's careful management of the past of his characters in all three: with the exception of the banal experiences of Verner and Anna-Mary, who is naively anxious to achieve social status through her trip to Europe, none of them has led a life that can be described as conventional, and the marriages of Carlotta and Hilde to Hugo have been subterfuges to hide his homosexuality from the public. In *A Song at Twilight*, Coward handles Hilde's experiences in Nazi Germany and her marriage of convenience to Hugo with careful revision in successive drafts. At the same time, these characters, men and women each 'with a past', lack the freewheeling independence of spirit with which the world is challenged by Elyot and Amanda in *Private Lives* or Otto, Gilda and Leo in *Design for Living*. In *Suite for Three Keys* the imperatives of getting and spending, and of maintaining stable relationships and (in Hugo Latymer's case) a posthumous reputation, are unavoidably present.

On 10 April Coward wrote in his weekly journal that the press notices of *A Song at Twilight* had, 'on the whole, been extremely good'.[50] 'On the whole' seems appropriate: his acting was praised, and Irene Worth was singled out with superlatives by many reviewers, but judgements on the plays read like a representative selection from the press's reception over the preceding two decades. Herbert Kretzmer in the *Daily Express* ('Brilliant Noel Coward at his Zenith') wrote that each of the plays 'glistens with wit, perception and compassion'. W.A. Darlington in the *Daily Telegraph* celebrated Coward's achievement as author and actor under the headline 'Coward Triumphant as of Old'.[51] Harold Hobson claimed in the *Sunday Times* that *Shadows of the Evening* 'penetrates as deeply into personal problems and emotions as anything now to be seen in London, or that we may expect to see for some time'.[52] In *The Times* 'Our Drama Critic' (still traditionally anonymous) observed that 'for all their determined glitter' and 'the author's disclaimers of any purpose', his plays were 'among the most earnestly moral works to be found anywhere in modern drama'.[53] On the debit side, Hilary Spurling in the *Spectator* found the structure of the plays in the second bill 'tenuous to vanishing point', and the dialogue 'a mishmash of cliché, stilted purple passages and sharp descents into bathos'.[54] In the *Guardian*, Philip Hope-Wallace grudgingly admitted that *Shadows of the Evening* 'kept going perfectly decently' in a 'brittle, outdated way'[55] In the *Stage and Television Today* R.B. Marriott, after commenting that *A Song at Twilight*, despite 'taking a little too long to accomplish its first unfolding' and having 'tedious passages elsewhere', admitted that it was 'nevertheless the work of a master playwright'. For this reason, 'the *longeurs* and a rather old-fashioned air [did] not matter'. He noted, though, that there was 'an odd sidelight' in Coward's 'speaking on a controversial subject' after 'condemning the writers who in the past few years [had] made such a subject possible in our theatre', and that 'not long ago' Osborne's *A Patriot for Me*, which had opened as a 'club' performance at the Royal Court in July, had 'put the case more forcefully', with 'a striking depth of emotion and dramatic intensity'.[56]

Age Cannot Wither, 1967: Sex and good sense

On 10 January 1967 Coward had started the second act of an adaptation of 'Star Quality', his story of a playwright's ordeal at the hands of a sublimely egotistical and capricious leading actress. A complete second act was ready by 22 January and he was satisfied with the dialogue, but it would need some revision.[57] When he returned from New York in early March, he dined with Beaumont, who was 'not enthusiastic'. Although 'highly amused by it personally', he 'thought it too esoteric for the great public'. He was 'rather flummoxed' when, over dinner in the first week of March, Coward 'entirely agreed with him'. It had not been 'a waste of time' because he had enjoyed writing it.[58] On 20 April 1967, Coward had written the first scene of 'a new comedy', *Age Cannot Wither*: 'So far it is good and funny, but whether I can keep it up or not remains to be seen. Gone are the days when I could cheerfully polish off a complete play in a day. Perhaps my standards are higher. At any rate, my impetus has lessened'. Work progressed through May and early June, but by 22 June he still had not begun the second act: 'I've been too agitated by everything. I shall get after it when I'm good and ready'.[59] At this point, the play seems to have stalled.

In the first scene, three ladies, school friends some fifty years ago, are meeting for their annual lunch, to gossip and reminisce. The hostess of what her husband calls 'this gruesome party' is Naomi Kemble, and Stella and Judy share her enjoyment of stories and badinage of a kind that would have seemed too risqué to the inhabitants of 'The Wings'. Much of the talk turns on sexual adventures in the past, with an amused tolerance of homosexual and lesbian relationships. The scene ends with them deciding for 'another teeny little drink' before their delayed lunch. This is the point at which Barry Day's edition in Volume Nine of the Methuen *Collected Works* ends, making it an actable though tantalizing entertainment, and there is no indication of how the play would have developed. But the Birmingham archive's 37-page script includes the second scene, with the suggestion of at least one likely plot line.[60] After lunch, the ladies have moved on to other topics, including opera:

Judy You don't exactly have to be *warned* about 'Norma', it's fairly jolly compared to some of the other operas.

Stella Jolly isn't quite the word I'd have chosen. All that chanting and stabbing. I mean one really has to be a genuine music lover to get the hang of it.

Judy You have to be prepared for a certain amount of stabbing or T.B. in most operas, just like Shakespeare. It's part of the tradition.

Stella T.B. hadn't been invented in Shakespeare's time.

Judy Well that's one thing to be thankful for anyway. He'd have been onto it like a terrier with a rat and we'd have had to watch Ophelia and Romeo and Juliet all coughing their lungs out.

27

At this point Naomi's daughter-in-law Melissa Kemble arrives, filled with righteous indignation, and tells her that Jasper, Naomi's grandson, has left his wife to live with another man, an antique dealer. Surely Naomi must intervene? She and the other ladies take the matter lightly, and Naomi refuses. When Judy and Stella have left, Melissa asks whether Naomi really believes her position as her mother-in-law entitles her to 'patronize and insult' her.

Naomi It certainly entitles me to demand that you behave with more dignity than you are behaving now. Please go away as I asked you to and give your acids time to settle. I know you are genuinely distressed and upset and, in spite of what you say, I assure you that I have not the least desire to patronize you or insult you. As far as the Jasper situation is concerned there is nothing we can any of us do at the moment beyond keeping calm and trying to regard it with as much detachment as possible. I see clearly that you are much more shocked by it than I am but that perhaps can be accounted for by the difference in our generations. I have a feeling that only the very old or the very young are capable of understanding the social and moral values of these strange times. You happen to be caught between two stools, always an agitating position in which to find oneself. Curiously enough I sympathize with you a little more than you realize. But not enough to shake my conviction that Jasper's problems are for him to deal with and not us. He is no longer a child and he is by no means a fool. Much has been learned and disclosed in our day about the waywardness of the human heart. There is nothing left for us but to profit from this and learn from it as much tolerance as possible. Please try to see what I mean Melissa, its [sic] so very very important that you should.

32

After a few more exchanges, in which Naomi makes it clear that she does not accept that her grandson's 'emotions', so long as they are genuine, are 'decadent and abnormal', and finds Melissa's attitude prejudiced and illogical, Melissa is outraged:

> Your attitude over this whole horrible affair has convinced me of something that I have suspected for years, which is that you're a cynical, wicked, mischief-making old woman, and I would like to say here and now that I never wish to see you or speak to you again until the end of my days.
>
> 37

She 'storms out, slamming the door behind her', and, 'after a slight pause', Naomi says 'I think, by and large, this is the happiest moment of my life!' This is as effective a 'curtain' as Coward ever devised, and it seems fair to assume that in whatever version of the family drama followed, Naomi's good sense and the comic tone would have prevailed.

Conclusion

Edith Evans (*as Judith Bliss, in rehearsal at the National Theatre, 1964*)   On a very clear day, you can see to Marlow.

Noël Coward (*from the stalls, directing*)   Edith, the line is 'On a clear day you can see Marlow.' On a *very* clear day you can see Marlowe and Beaumont and Fletcher.[1]

It has been pointed out that Sheridan Morley was mistaken in taking as the title for the first full-scale biography of Noël Coward, *A Talent to Amuse* (1969), a phrase that does not do justice to his subject. It is after all sung by a character in the musical play *Bitter Sweet* (1929): 'The most I've had is just / A talent to amuse. / Heigh-ho, if love were all!' (*PP1*, 124/M2, 138). The Coward who emerges from this study, as indeed from Morley's and other biographies and his own diaries and letters, was certainly amusing, but he was also a tireless and enterprising worker.

He inhabited a theatrical world that, towards the end of his life, was undergoing transformations, about which he was invariably curious, even when the playgoing experience was annoying or disappointing. Above all, as well as being formidably talented, he was resilient – in one of his favourite phrases, 'rising above' adversity – and a stickler for detail. He was able to insist, even with Dame Edith Evans, whom he had known and admired for many years, that the letter of his text had been precisely honed to convey its spirit. After 'a week of Hell in merry Manchester', during which Evans 'dried up and fluffed through all the performances' and 'took her curtain calls as though she had just been un-nailed from the cross', *Hay Fever* opened in London 'and was a triumph'.[2] This was a pattern he had learned to expect over many years, and in his diaries and letters he often lets off steam amusingly about the vagaries of his fellow actors, but he was steadfastly loyal to the theatre and to his colleagues, even those who at one time or another exasperated him.

Coward's restlessness in moving from one genre to another has been a recurring theme of this study. The archive has many examples of ideas pursued for a while and then either picked up later or abandoned. The facility with which he could write when in the vein was accompanied with an openness to the opinions of those he trusted. On 3 October, 1965, he revised *Shadows of the Evening* 'from beginning to end' in the light of comments by the director Vivian Matalon, and the actors Lilli Palmer and Irene Worth: 'Curiously enough, I enjoyed rewriting it. I respond most effectively to constructive criticism and I know my critics were right over this.'[3] From his earliest manuscripts, written in pencil, to his later drafts, composed on one or another of his many typewriters, the material drawn on in this study reflects Coward's pleasure in both writing and rewriting. Following his hand when the pencil is blunted and has to be sharpened, or his typing when a row of 'x's strikes out a word or line to make way for a replacement, gives a vivid sense of looking over the shoulder of an author who above all, despite any setbacks before and during production, enjoyed exercising his craft as a playwright.

NOTES

Abbreviations

Diaries   *The Noël Coward Diaries*, Graham Payn and Sheridan Morley, eds. (London, Macmillan, 1982).

TS diary   Typed transcripts of the diaries and journals, Cadbury Research Library (COW/4/H).

Letters   *The Letters of Noël Coward*, Barry Day, ed. (London, Methuen, 2007).

Companion Ray Mander and Joe Mitchenson, *Theatrical Companion to Coward*, updated by Barry Day and Sheridan Morley (1957; London, Oberon Books, 2000).

For unpublished archive material, reference numbers are prefixed with 'NPC' for items held in London by the Noël Coward Archive Trust, and 'COW' for those in the University of Birmingham's Cadbury Research Library.

As appropriate, senders and recipients of letters and cables are identified as follows:

NC – Noel Coward.

CL – Cole Lesley.

LL – Lorn Loraine.

JW – John C. Wilson.

Introduction

1   *Play Pictorial*, November 1932, iii.
2   John Lahr, *Coward the Playwright* (London, Methuen, 1999), 77.

3 Richard Overy, *The Morbid Age: Britain and the Crisis of Civilization, 1919–1938* (London, Allen Lane, 2009), 20.
4 John Russell Taylor, *The Rise and Fall of the Well-Made Play* (London, Methuen, 1967), 127.
5 William Archer, *Play-making, a Manual of Craftsmanship* (1912; New York, Dover, 1960), 148.
6 *Diaries*, 330.
7 *Diaries*, 436.
8 Lahr, 3.
9 Kenneth Tynan, 'Remembering Mr. Coward', in *The Sound of Two Hands Clapping* (London, Jonathan Cape, 1975), 60.
10 W. Somerset Maugham, *The Constant Wife*, in *Collected Plays*, Vol. 2 (London, Heinemann, 1931), 96–7.
11 St John Ervine, *How to Write a Play* (London, 1928), 70; 75.
12 Maugham, *Collected Plays*, Volume 3, xiii.
13 Lahr, 7.
14 Sos Eltis, 'Bringing out the Acid: Noel Coward, Harold Pinter, Ivy Compton-Burnett and the Uses of Camp', *Modern Drama*, vol.51 no 2 (2008) 211–33 (220).
15 *New Statesman*, 3 November 1928, in Martin Stannard, ed., *Evelyn Waugh: The Critical Heritage* (London, RKP, 1984), 86.
16 *Diaries*, 235.
17 Richard Huggett, *Binkie Beaumont, Eminence Grise of the West End Theatre, 1933–1973* (London, Hodder and Stoughton, 1989), 99.
18 Terence Rattigan, 'An Appreciation', in *Theatrical Companion to Coward*, updated by Barry Day and Sheridan Morley (London, Oberon Books, 2000), xix.
19 Alan Sinfield, 'Private Lives/Public Theatre: Noël Coward and the Politics of Homosexual Representation', *Representations*, 36 (Autumn, 1991), 43–63 (47); Sean and Julia O'Connor, *Straight Acting: Popular Gay Drama from Wilde to Rattigan* (London, Bloomsbury, 1997), chapter 3, 'Public Lives, Private Faces'.

Chapter 1

1 Aldous Huxley, *Point Counter Point* (1928; London, Vintage Books, 2018), 267.

2 Evelyn Waugh, 'The War and the Younger Generation' (*Spectator*, 13 April 1929) in *A Little Order: Selected Journalism*, edited by Donat Gallagher (London, Eyre Methuen, 1977), 10–11.
3 *Manchester Evening Chronicle* 'Boy Dramatist's Plays. How He Prepares Them' (undated clipping in scrapbook).
4 *Pall Mall Gazette*, 22 July 1920.
5 *Daily Telegraph*, 22 July 1920.
6 *Time and Tide*, 30 July 1920.
7 J.W. Marriott, ed. *Great Modern Plays* (London, Harrap, 1929), 5, 903.
8 *Autobiography*, 85.
9 Dan Rebellato, 'Noël Coward's Bad Manners', in Joel H. Kaplan and Sheila Stowell, eds., *Look Back in Pleasure: Noel Coward Reconsidered* (London, Methuen, 2000), 44–61 (57).
10 Cited in Steve Nicholson, *The Censorship of the British Drama, 1900-1968, Volume One, 1900-1932* (Exeter, University of Exeter Press, 2020), 260.
11 *Autobiography*, 118.
12 *Autobiography*, 136.
13 *Daily Sketch*, 26 November 1924.
14 James Agate, *The Contemporary Theatre, 1924, with an Introduction by Noël Coward* (London: Chapman and Hall, 1925), 216–19; 218.
15 *Illustrated Sunday Herald*, 30 November 1924.
16 *Autobiography*, 145; Christopher Innes, *Modern British Drama, 1890-1990* (Cambridge, Cambridge University Press,1992), 239.
17 Norman MacDermott, *Everymania: The History of the Everyman Theatre, Hampstead 1920–1926, by its Founder* (London, Society for Theatre Research, 1975), 67–9.
18 *Autobiography*, 130–1.
19 Agate, *The Contemporary Theatre, 1923* (London, Leonard Parsons, 1924), 118.
20 *The Vortex*, MSS: NPC-0260, 0261, and 0262 (Notebooks, 40, 41 and 42).
21 *Illustrated Sporting and Dramatic News*, 6 December 1924.
22 Noël Coward, *Three Plays* (London, Ernest Benn, 1925), x.
23 Steve Nicholson, *The Censorship of the British Drama, 1900-1968, Volume One, 1900-1932* (Exeter, University of Exeter Press, 2020), 231–2.

24 *Fallen Angels* MS: NPC-0266.
25 Bennett, Arnold *The Journals*, selected and edited by Frank Swinnerton, 2nd edn. (Harmondsworth, Penguin, 1971), 494.
26 *Fallen Angels* (New York, Samuel French, [1958]), 44. The edition has copyright dates of 1925, 1953 (copyright renewal) and 1958, but no details of a specific production.
27 *Diaries*, 661.
28 COW/1/A/16/1: copy of French's 1927 acting edition, pasted into foolscap notebook, with MS annotations in blue and red ink. Other changes include a prolonged tussle between Simon and Myra on the sofa in Act One, and the omission of Judith's song in Act Two. The file includes other production material, lighting plots, etc.
29 *Spectator*, 9 June 1926.
30 *Easy Virtue* MSS: NPC-0266 (Notebook 46).
31 *The Times*, 10 June 1926.
32 *Sunday Times*, 13 June 1926.
33 *Semi-Monde* MSS: NPC-0250 (Notebook 29).
34 John Lahr, *Coward the Playwright* (London, Methuen, 1999), 6–7; Michael Coveney, *The Citz: 21 Years of the Glasgow Citizens Theatre* (London, Nick Hern, 1990), 95.
35 *Autobiography*, 163.s

Chapter 2

1 TS diary, 10 June 1958.
2 Faye Hamill, *Sophistication: A Literary and Cultural History* (Liverpool, Liverpool University Press, 2010), 115.
3 *Autobiography*, 216–17. (The location of Act One was eventually shifted to Deauville, on the Normandy coast.)
4 *Autobiography*, 375–6.
5 *Autobiography*, 379.
6 NC to GL, 7 January from Hong Kong: typescript copy in *Private Lives* business file: COW/3/N/1/35.
7 This account is based on documents in the Cadbury Research Library: letters and cables in the play's business file, and a sheaf of cables and a letter to NC explaining Lawrence's alleged contractual obligations for a revue in the Legal and Financial file for André Charlot (COW/3/N/9).

8   *Private Lives*, business file.
9   *Autobiography*, 226. See *Letters*, 180 for the undated cable, quoted as 'Have read new play stop nothing wrong that can't be fixed'.
10 *Autobiography*, 226, and *Letters*, p. 180 (undated but presumably after receiving her address from Wilson).
11 Charles B. Cochran, *Cock-a-Doddle-Doo* (London, Dent, 1940), 94.
12 Christopher Innes, *Modern British Drama, 1890–1900* (Cambridge, Cambridge University Press, 1992), 253.
13 *The Times*, 15 September 1930.
14 *Era*, 1 October 1930.
15 Maria Aitken, *Acting in High Comedy* (New York, Applause Books, 1996), 105.
16 *Autobiography*, 231.
17 *Autobiography*, 232.
18 NC's cable to Cochran: *Letters*, 262–4.
19 *Autobiography*, 234.
20 *Cavalcade* MS: NPC-2044.
21 *Observer*, 26 October 1931.
22 *Illustrated London News*, 24 October 1931.
23 *Spectator*, 24 October 1931.
24 *Stage*, 15 October 1931.
25 'Mr. C.B. Cochran tells how Little Scraps of Paper became "Cavalcade", *News of the World*, 27 March 1932.
26 Robert Graves and Alan Hodge, *The Long Weekend* (1940; London, Abacus Books, 1985), 296–7.
27 *Autobiography*, 239.
28 *Autobiography*, 265–7.
29 Jared Brown, *The Fabulous Lunts, a Biography of Alfred Lunt and Lynn Fontanne* (New York, Atheneum, 1988), 203. A slightly different version is given by Cole Lesley, *Remembered Laughter: The Life of Noël Coward (*New York: Alfred Knopf, 1976) 151–2; *Letters*, 276–9.
30 *Autobiography*, 268.
31 John Lahr, *Coward the Playwright* (London, Methuen, 1999), 80; 84.
32 *Design for Living* MSS: NPC-2644, 2645 and 2646; typescript, Yale University, Beinecke Rare Book and Manuscript Library: John C. Wilson Collection, GEN MSS 608, b. 1, f. 6.

33 Outline from NPC-2644.
34 *New York Times,* 25 January 1933.
35 *New Yorker*, 4 February 1933.
36 *New York News*, 26 January, 1933.
37 See *PP1*, xvii–xviii. The article appeared on 29 November 1933: the cutting filed in the Performing Arts Division of New York Public Library lacks the full title of the paper and the article.
38 *Observer*, 11 June 1933.
39 Richard Huggett, *Binkie Beaumont,* Eminence Grise *of the West End Theatre, 1933–1973* (London, Hodder and Stoughton, 1989), 231.
40 Steve Nicholson, *The Censorship of the British Drama, 1900-1968, Volume Two, 1933-1968* (Exeter, 2020), 90–1.
41 *Stage*, 19 January 1939.
42 Punch, 8 February 1939.
43 Yale script, 336.
44 James Agate, '*Design for Living*', (25 January 1939), reprinted in *Red Letter Nights* (London: Jonathan Cape, 1944), 246–8; 248.
45 *Daily Sketch* and *Daily Mail*, 26 January 1939.
46 *Star*, 26 January 1939.
47 *Observer*, 30 January 1939.
48 *News Chronicle*, 26 January 1939.
49 *Spectator*, 17 January 1936.
50 *The Times*, 19 January 1936.
51 Quoted in *Companion*, 323.

Chapter 3

1 *Companion*, 260–1; 267.
2 NC to JW, 17 April 1943 (COW/3/N/2/58).
3 NC to JW, [?] January 1945 (COW/3/N/2/58).
4 Richard Dyer, *Brief Encounter* (BFI, 1993), 16–17.
5 *Autobiography*, 323.
6 Kevin Brownlow, *David Lean* (London, Faber, 1977), 195.
7 TS diary, 3 October 1945.

8 Noël Coward, *Screenplays*, edited by Barry Day (London, Methuen, 2015), 222.
9 *Sunday Dispatch* (undated clipping in scrapbook).
10 Sean and Julia O'Connor, *Straight Acting: Popular Gay Drama from Wilde to Rattigan* (London, Bloomsbury, 1997), 101.
11 *Present Laughter* ('Sweet Sorrow') typescript: COW/1/A/44.
12 NC to JW, 12 November 1946 (COW/3/N/2/58).
13 Quoted by the *Manchester Dispatch* (undated clipping in scrapbook), and in reviews of performances in Nottingham and elsewhere.
14 *The Times* and *Daily Herald*, both 30 July 1943.
15 *Companion*, 255: the 1947 run opened on 16 April; Hugh Sinclair took over from Coward from 14 July.
16 *Daily Telegraph*, 30 July 1943.
17 *Observer* and *Stage*, undated clippings in scrapbook.
18 *Stage*, undated clipping in scrapbook.
19 *What's On* and *Daily Worker*, undated clippings in scrapbook.
20 *This Happy Breed*, film script: COW/1/A/63 (101–2).
21 The draft speech is typed on a separate sheet of paper, dated 'Inverness, / 8th JANUARY, 1943/ (K.E.).' Kay Walsh recalled that Coward was vehement in arguing for the speech, against the advice of 'the boys', although, as Brownlow points out, Lean misremembered the dispute, claiming that at least part of it had been kept in (Brownlow, *David Lean*, 180).
22 TS diary, 3 January 1941.
23 TS diary, 13 February 1941.
24 TS diary, entries for 14 February and 5 March 1941.
25 TS diary, entries for 18 March and 11 April 1941.
26 NC to JW, 17 April 1943 (COW/3/N/2/58).
27 TS diary, 22 April 1941.
28 TS diary, 3 May 1941; *Autobiography*, 418–19.
29 TS diary, entries for 3–11 May 1941.
30 *Autobiography*, 419.
31 *Blithe Spirit* typescript: NPC-0120.
32 TS diary, 5 June 1941.
33 *Blithe Spirit: An Improbable Farce in Three Acts* (London: Heinemann, 1941), 4; *PP5*, 50/M4, 7); corrected in Fr. (1941), 3–4.

34 Cole Lesley, *Remembered Laughter: The Life of Noël Coward* (New York: Alfred Knopf, 1976), 226–8.
35 TS diary, 21 February 1941.
36 TS diary, 12 May 1941.
37 TS diary, 22 May 1941.
38 TS diary, 4 June 1941.
39 TS diary, 12 June 1941.
40 Autograph copy of speech: NPC–2032.
41 TS diary, 16, 17 and 18 June 1941.
42 TS diary, 23 and 27 June 1941.
43 NC to JW 18 July 1941 (COW/3/N/2/58).
44 NC to JW, 18 Sept 1941(COW/3/N/2/58).
45 Rebecca D'Monté, *British Theatre and Performance, 1900-1950* (London, Bloomsbury, 2015), 127.
46 *Manchester Guardian*, 17 June 1941.
47 *Star* and *Daily Sketch*, 3 July 1941.
48 *Observer*, 6 July 1941.
49 *Sunday Time*s, 6 July 1941
50 *Spectator*, 11 July 1941.
51 *Topper* (1937), *Topper Takes a Trip* (1938) and *Topper Returns* (1941).
52 See Norman Sherry, *The Life of Graham Greene, Volume Two, 1939–1955* (London, Jonathan Cape, 1994), 72–8.
53 Barry Day, *Coward on Film: The Cinema of Noël Coward* (Lanham, MD, Scarecrow Press, 2005), 91.
54 TS diary, 8 April 1945.
55 *Diaries*, 35–6.
56 Synopsis of first version at: COW/3/N/1/29; scripts at COW1/A/37.
57 *Diaries*, 52.
58 *Daily Mirror, Evening News* and *News Chronicle*, all 20 December 1946; *John O'London's Weekly*, undated clipping in scrapbook; *Tatler and Bystander*, 1 January 1947.
59 *Diaries*, 66.
60 *Diaries*, 81; 85.
61 Jeremy Lewis, *Cyril Connolly, a Life* (London, Jonathan Cape, 1997), 398–9.

62 *Illustrated*, 9 August 1947.
63 *Diaries*, 87.
64 *Daily Telegraph*, 23 July 1947.
65 *News Chron*icle and *Evening News*, 23 July 1947; *New Statesman* and *Spectator*, 25 July 1947.
66 *Sunday Times*, 27 July 1947.
67 *Spectator*, 30 July 1947
68 *Daily Worker*, 23 July 1947.
69 *Evening Standard*, 23 July 1947.
70 COW/1/A/16a. The cast list includes Moira Lister, whom Coward first encountered when she auditioned for Joanna on 24 January 1947 for the revival of *Present Laughter*, and Billy Thatcher, who played Fred in the first production of *Present Laughter* and its 1947 revival.
71 *Diaries*, 92; 93.
72 NC to LL, 30 September [1947].
73 *Long Island Sound*, typescript: COW/1/A/21.

Chapter 4

1 *News Chronicle*, 28 November 1951.
2 *Diaries*, 157.
3 *Diaries*, 167.
4 *Diaries*, 168.
5 TS diary, 24 April 1951.
6 TS diary, 27, 28 and 29 June; *Diaries* 172.
7 *Letters*, 570–1.
8 *Relative Values*, typescript: COW/1/A/47.
9 *Bournemouth Daily Echo*, 'Gladys Cooper in a Coward Satire on Social Standards,' undated cutting in scrapbook.
10 *Diaries*, 176.
11 Cole Lesley, *Remembered Laughter. The Life of Noël Coward* (New York: Alfred Knopf, 1976), 301.
12 *Diaries*, 180–1.
13 *Evening Standard*, 19 November 1951.
14 *Observer*, 2 December 1951.

15 *Manchester Guardian*, 29 November 1951.
16 *Evening Standard*, 19 November 1951.
17 *The Times*, 29 November 1951.
18 *Illustrated London News*, 22 December 1951.
19 *What's On in London*, 7 December 1951.
20 TS diary, 21 February; *Diaries* 231–2.
21 *Diaries*, 258; 259.
22 Richard Mangan, ed., *Gielgud's Letters* (London, Weidenfeld and Nicolson, 2004), 189.
23 *Nude with Violin* MS: NPC-2225; typescripts at COW /1/A/34 (two versions); synopsis in Business File; 'vocabulary' filed with NPC-2225.
24 The 'tableau' ending is described in the 1957 edition of Ray Mander and Joe Mitchenson's *Theatrical Companion to Coward* (London, Rockliff, 1957), 346.
25 (Dublin) *Evening Herald* and *Irish Times*, both 15 September 1956.
26 LL to NC 30 October 1957: COW/4/1/3; Telegram Log Book, Vol. 2: 3 November 1956.
27 *New Statesman*, 17 November 1956.
28 Caryl Brahms, 'Nude with Violin,' *Plays and Players*, December 1956, 13.
29 *Daily Telegraph*, 8 November 1956.
30 Doubleday edition (New York and Garden City, 1957), 27–8: Sébastien's entrance and the dialogue are inserted after 'Your aunt Freda wrote indecent on it in red ink and sent it back' (*PP6*, 341).
31 Doubleday edition, 42: this follows Max's remarks on critics (*PP6*, 355).
32 TS diary, 14 September 1957.
33 Doubleday edition, 64.
34 Wolcott Gibbs, 'Miss Hayes and Mr. Coward,' *New Yorker*, 22 November 1957, 77–80 (80).
35 *Diaries*, 168, 171.
36 *Diaries*, 141.
37 TS diary, 2 October 1949.
38 Examples of these are in the play's business papers: COW/3/N/1/36/1.
39 *Diaries*, 176,188; *Letters*, 551.
40 *Diaries*, 188.

41 A typescript of *Design for Rehearsing* is at COW/1/A/13; for Barry Day's adaptation for performance see M9, 295–304.
42 *Diaries*, 191; *Quadrille* business papers, COW/3/N/1/36/1.
43 Lunt to NC, 3 April 1952: *Letters*, 553.
44 *Quadrille* typescripts, COW/1/A/46; Beinecke Library, John C. Wilson Collection, GEN MSS 608, b. 2, f. 28.
45 Lunt to NC, from Paris, 11 May 1952: manuscript, *Quadrille* business papers, COW/3/N/1/36/1.
46 *Diaries*, 196.
47 Lunt to NC, from Adelphi Hotel, Liverpool, 28 August 1952: typescript copy, in correspondence file, COW/4/1.
48 Lunt to NC, 10 October 1952 (Noël Coward Archive Trust, letters file)
49 *Diaries*, 199.
50 *Letters*, 555–7.
51 Fontanne to NC, [?] July 1954: *Letters*, 557–8.
52 Coward to Lynn Fontanne, 10 August 1954 (MS and TS Farringdon). Dated from Venice and sent to Loraine to be typed, this appears to be a version of the letter dated from Paris on 4 August (*Letters*, 558–9): some passages are repeated verbatim, and it is possible Coward had kept a copy of these in hand and referred to the earlier letter when he wrote from Venice.
53 *Letters*, 560–1.
54 Lunt to NC, 18 October 1954, from New York (Noël Coward Archive Trust, letters file).
55 *Home and Colonial* and *South Sea Bubble* typescripts: COW1/A/18 and COW/1/A/58.
56 Dossier for 'Samolo' at COW/1/A/51/1.
57 *Diaries*, 125.
58 TS diary, 28 April 1949.
59 *Diaries*, 127.
60 TS diary, 23 and 24 May 1949.
61 Telegram Log, vol. 2 (COW/4/l/1): NC to Lawrence, 21 September 1949.
62 TS diary, 26 September 1949.
63 TS diary, 28 September 1949.
64 *Diaries*, 150.
65 *Diaries*, 174–5.

66 Telegram Log, vol. 2 (COW/4/l/1): 'Junior' (Max Gordon) to NC, 1 August 1951; NC to Gordon, 2 August 1951.
67 *Stamford Advocate*, 24 July 1951.
68 *New York Morning Telegraph*, 20 August 1951; *World-Telegraph and Sun*, 25 July 1951.
69 *Diaries*, 192.
70 *Diaries*, 257–8; 261.
71 Leigh to NC, 7 September 1955: ALS and typescript copy, (Noël Coward Archive Trust, letters file).
72 *Diaries*, 284.
73 *Letters*, 612.
74 Leigh to NC, 11 April 1956: Typescript with MS additions (Noël Coward Archive Trust., letters file).
75 *The Times*, 26 April 1956.
76 *Sunday Times*, 29 April 1956.
77 *Diaries*, 321.
78 TS diary, 22 May 1956.
79 Leigh to NC, 3 July 1956: ALS and typescript (Noël Coward Archive Trust, letters file).
80 *Diaries*, 327.
81 *Diaries*, 331.
82 Letters, 612–13.
83 TS diary, 16 September 1956.
84 *Diaries*, 373.
85 *Diaries*, 376–7.
86 On the Flemings and Blanche Blackwell, see Andrew Lycett, *Ian Fleming, The Man who Created James Bond* (London, Weidenfeld and Nicolson, 2020), 308–9.
87 TS diary, 10 March 1957; CL to LL 29 March 1957: COW/4/1/3; *Volcano* typescript, COW/1/A/69. A MS of the play is at NPC-2009.
88 LL to NC 18 March 1957 and 30 March 1957: COW/4/1/3.
89 TS diary, 5 May 1957.
90 NPC-3066: this is page 12 of what appears to be the earlier of two versions, written (unusually for Coward) with a green ball-point pen. A second draft, closer to the typescript in the Birmingham collection, is in black ink with stage-directions in red.
91 TS diary, 15 September 1957.

Chapter 5

1. Ray Mander and Joe Mitchenson, *The Theatres of London*, 2nd edn (London, New English Library, 1975), 322.
2. *Semi-Monde* MSS: NPC-0250 (notebook 29), 'Preface.'
3. John Russell Taylor, *The Rise and Fall of the Well-Made Play* (London, Methuen, 1967), 124.
4. *Diaries*, 377 (13 April and 1 May 1958).
5. NC to LL, 21 May 1958 (B'ham); TS diary, 1 June 1958.
6. Graham Payn, with Barry Day, *My Life with Noël Coward* (New York, Applause Books, 1995), 81.
7. *Diaries*, 405 (5 April 1959).
8. NC to LL, 6 April 1959 (COW/4); *Diaries* 407 (26 April 1959).
9. *Diaries*, 408.
10. Webster to NC, 7 February 1960, *Letters*, 664–5.
11. Webster to Sardoff, 7 February 1960, typed copy in business file: COW/3/N/1/29.
12. *Letters*, 667.
13. *Waiting in the Wings* was published by Heinemann in 1960; as a French's Acting Edition (undated); and in *Play Parade, Vol. 6* (Heinemann: 1962). Coward accepted Webster's offer to oversee the French's edition: lines for Almina, cut on account of Mary Clare's memory difficulties, were restored, and the edition reflected several minor cuts and alteration made for performance. These are present in the first edition and in *Play Parade*, but French's fuller stage directions and some functional lines added for entrances and exits were not retained.
14. *Letters*, 664–5: Webster to NC, 21 February 1960, on casting.
15. *Diaries*, 434.
16. *Diaries*, 442.
17. Webster to NC, 25 July 1960 (*Letters*, 665–7).
18. *Diaries*, 445–6.
19. *Waiting in the Wings* MSS material: NPC-2014; 'First Version' typescript, COW/1/70.
20. TS diary, 22 April 1960.
21. *Letters*, 666.
22. *Daily Express*, 8 September 1960.

23 *Daily Mail*, 8 September 1960.
24 *Guardian*, 9 September 1960.
25 *News Chronicle*, 8 September 1960.
26 *Stage and Television Today*, 15 September 1960.
27 LL to NC, 6 October 1960: COW/4.
28 LL to NC, 31 January 1961: COW/4.
29 *Diaries*, 465.
30 Steve Nicholson, *The Censorship of British Drama, 1900—1968. Volume Four: The Sixties* (Exeter, University of Exeter Press, 2020), 61.
31 LL to NC, 10 February 1960: COW/4.
32 *Stage*, 24 March 1957; *Diaries*, 431.
33 *Diaries*, 496–7.
34 CL to LL, 21 Feb 1962: COW/4.
35 *Diaries*, 512: 28 August 1962.
36 *Diaries*, 606.
37 *Diaries*, 594; 601.
38 TS diary, 2 and 14 July 1965.
39 *Diaries*, 604.
40 'Foreword' to Garson Kanin, *Remembering Mr. Maugham* (London: Hamish Hamilton, 1966), i–ii.
41 Selina Hastings, *The Secret Life of Somerset Maugham* (London, John Murray, 2009), 480
42 *Diaries*, 593–4.
43 TS diaries, 4 April: the entry differs slightly in *Diaries*, 596.
44 TS diary, 19 April; *Diaries*, 599.
45 *Diaries*, 601.
46 *Diaries*, 606.
47 *Diaries*, 608–10.
48 Scripts referred to: (a) Undated 'first versions' in the Birmingham archive: COW/1/A/57: (*A Song at Twilight*), 54 (*Shadows of the Evening*), and 9 (a) and (b) (*Come into the Garden Maud*); (b) 'October' scripts (also undated) sent to Alfred Lunt and Lynn Fontanne in Alfred Lunt and Lynn Fontanne Papers, MSS 622, Box/folders 12/9 (*Shadows*), 12/10 (*Twilight*) and 11/10 (*Maud*), Wisconsin Historical Society.

49 The directions correspond exactly to those in the October script (II-44).
50 *Diaries*, 629.
51 *Daily Express* and *Daily Telegraph*, 26 April 1966.
52 *Sunday Times*, 1 May 1966.
53 *The Times*, 26 April 1966.
54 *Spectator*, 19 April 1966.
55 *Guardian*, 26 April 1966.
56 *Stage and Television Today*, 21 April 1966.
57 *Diaries*, 645.
58 *Diaries*, 647.
59 *Diaries*, 648–9; 651.
60 COW1/A/3: *Age Cannot Wither*, 37-page typescript, unmarked except for minor corrections.

Conclusion

1 Adapted from Sheridan Morley, *A Talent to Amuse: A Biography of Noël Coward* (London, Heinemann, 1969), 305. The account is confirmed by a number of first-hand accounts: for example, Robert Stephens (with Michael Coveney), *Knight Errant: Memoirs of a Vagabond Actor* (London, Hodder and Stoughton, 1996), 80–2.
2 *Diaries*, 578: 25 October and 1 November 1964.
3 *Diaries*, 608: 19 September 1965.

BIBLIOGRAPHY

1. Works of Noël Coward

(i) Plays

(a) 'Collected Plays' (Methuen)

Volume 1	*Hay Fever*, *The Vortex*, *Fallen Angels*, *Easy Virtue*
Volume 2	*Private Lives*, *Bitter-Sweet*, *The Marquise*, *Post-Mortem*
Volume 3	*Design for Living*, *Cavalcade*, *Conversation Piece*, *Tonight at 8.30*, part one (*Hands Across the Sea*, *Still Life*, *Fumed Oak*)
Volume 4	*Blithe Spirit*, *Present Laughter*, *This Happy Breed*, *Tonight at 8.30*, part two (*Ways and Means*, *The Astonished Heart*, 'Red Peppers')
Volume 5	*Relative Values*, *Look After Lulu*, *Waiting in the Wings*, *Suite in Three Keys* (*A Song at Twilight*, *Shadows of the Evening*, *Come into the Garden Maud*)
Volume 6	*Semi-Monde*, *Point Valaine*, *South Sea Bubble*, *Nude with Violin*
Volume 7	*Quadrille*, *Peace in Our Time* and, from *Tonight at 8.30*, *We Were Dancing*, *Shadow Play*, *Family Album*, *Star Chamber*
Volume 8	*'I'll Leave it to You'*, *The Young Idea*, *'This was a Man'*
Volume 9	Previously unpublished plays: *Salute to the Brave/Time Remembered*, *Long Island Sound*, *Volcano*, *Age Cannot Wither*, *Design for Rehearsing*

(b) *Play Parade* volumes

The first volume is simply *Play Parade*. Thereafter, the volumes are numbered in the series of 'The Collected Plays of Noël Coward.' Volume 2 first appeared in 1939 as *Second Play Parade*: a revised version was issued in 1950.

Volume 1 (1934) *Cavalcade, Bitter Sweet, The Vortex, Hay Fever, Design for Living, Private Lives, Post Mortem*
Volume 2 (1950) *This Year of Grace, Words and Music, Operette, Conversation Piece, Fallen Angels, Easy Virtue*
Volume 3 (1950) *The Queen was in the Parlour, 'I'll Leave it to You', The Young Idea, Sirocco, The Rat Trap, 'This was a Man', Home Chat, The Marquise*
Volume 4 (1954) The Three Volumes of *Tonight at 8.30, Present Laughter, This Happy Breed*
Volume 5 (1958) *Pacific 1860, 'Peace in Our Time', Relative Values, Quadrille, Blithe Spirit*
Volume 6 (1962) *Point Valaine, South Sea Bubble, Ace of Clubs, Nude with Violin, Waiting in the Wings*

(c) British (Heinemann) and American (Doubleday) first editions

Blithe Spirit (London, 1941); *Cavalcade* (London, 1932); *Design for Living* (London, 1935); *Look after Lulu* (London, 1959); *Nude with Violin* (London, 1956; Garden City and New York, 1958); *Operette* (London, 1938); *Peace in Our Time* (London, 1947); *Point Valaine* (Garden City and New York, 1935); *Present Laughter* (London, 1943); *Private Lives* (London, 1930); *Quadrille* (London, 1952; New York and Garden City, 1955); *South Sea Bubble* (London, 1956); *Suite in Three Keys* (Garden City and New York, 1967); *This Happy Breed* (London, 1943); *Waiting in the Wings* (London, 1960).

(d) Samuel French (London) Acting Editions

Blithe Spirit (1941); *Hay Fever* (1927); *Nude with Violin* (1956); *Present Laughter* (1949); *Private Lives* (London, 1947); *Relative Values* (1952); *South Sea Bubble* (1958); *Suite in Three Keys* (1966); *This Happy Breed* (London, 1945); *Waiting in the Wings* (1960).

(e) Other editions

Home Chat (London, Martin Secker, 1927)
Sirocco (London, Martin Secker, 1927)
Three Plays: The Rat Trap, The Vortex, Fallen Angels. With the Author's Reply to his Critics (London, Ernest Benn, 1925)
Three Plays: Blithe Spirit, Hay Fever, Private Lives, with an introduction by Philip Hoare (New York, Vintage International, 1999)

The Young Idea, in Marriott, J.W., ed. *Great Modern Plays* (London, Harrap, 1929).

(ii) Non-dramatic Works

Autobiography (*Present Indicative* [1937], *Future Indefinite* [1954] and the uncompleted *Past Conditional*), with an introduction by Sheridan Morley (1986; Methuen, London, 1999)
Complete Lyrics, Barry Day, ed. (Woodstock, NY, Overlook Press, 1998)
Collected Revue Sketches and Parodies, Barry Day, ed. (London, Methuen, 1999)
Collected Short Stories, with a Preface by Martin Tickner (1985; London, Methuen, 1999)
Collected Verse, Graham Payn and Martin Tickner, eds. (London, Methuen, 1999)
Screenplays: In Which We Serve, Brief Encounter, The Astonished Heart, Barry Day, ed. (London, Methuen, 2015)
Pomp and Circumstance, a Novel (London, Heinemann, 1960)

(iii) Diaries and letters

Payn, Graham, and Sheridan Morley, eds., *The Noël Coward Diaries* (London, Macmillan, 1982)
Day, Barry, ed., *The Letters of Noël Coward* (London, Methuen Drama, 2007)

2. Secondary sources

Agate, James, *The Contemporary Theatre, 1923* (London, Leonard Parsons, 1924)
Agate, James, *The Contemporary Theatre, 1924, with an Introduction by Noël Coward* (London, Chapman and Hall, 1925)
Agate, James, *Red Letter Nights* (London, Jonathan Cape, 1944)
Aitken, Maria, *Acting in High Comedy* (London, Applause, 1996)
Archer, William, *Play-making, a Manual of Craftsmanship* (New York, Dover, [1912] 1960)
Bennett, Arnold, *The Journals*, selected and edited by Frank Swinnerton, 2nd edn. (Harmondsworth, Penguin, 1971)
Braybrooke, Patrick, *The Amazing Mr. Noël Coward* (London, Denis Archer, 1933)

Brown, Jared, *The Fabulous Lunts, a Biography of Alfred Lunt and Lynn Fontanne* (New York, Atheneum, 1988)
Brownlow, Kevin, *David Lean* (London, Faber, 1977)
Castle, Charles, ed., *Noël* (London, W.H. Allen, 1972)
Cochran, Charles B., *Cock-a-Doddle-Doo* (London, Dent, 1940)
Coveney, Michael, *The Citz. 21 Years of the Glasgow Citizens Theatre* (London, Nick Hern, 1990)
Day, Barry, *Coward on Film: The Cinema of Noël Coward* (Lanham, MD, Scarecrow Press, 2005)
Day, Barry, ed. *Noël Coward on (and in) Theatre*, (New York, Knopf, 2021)
D'Monté, Rebecca, *British Theatre and Performance, 1900–1950* (London, Bloomsbury, 2015)
Dorney, Kate and Maggie B. Gale, eds., *Vivien Leigh, Actress and Icon* (Manchester, Manchester University Press and Victoria and Albert Museum, 2018)
Dyer, Richard, *Brief Encounter* (London, British Film Institute, 1993)
Eltis, Sos, 'Bringing out the Acid: Noël Coward, Harold Pinter, Ivy Compton-Burnett and the Uses of Camp,' *Modern Drama*, vol. 51 no. 2 (2008), 211–233
Ervine, St John, *How to Write a Play* (London, George Allen and Unwin, 1928)
Graves, Robert and Alan Hodge, *The Long Weekend* (1940; London, Abacus Books, 1985)
Hamill, Faye, *Sophistication: A Literary and Cultural History* (Liverpool, Liverpool University Press, 2010)
Hastings, Selina, *The Secret Lives of Somerset Maugham* (London, John Murray, 2009)
Hoare, Philip, *Noël Coward, a Biography* (London, Sinclair-Stevenson, 1995)
Huggett, Richard, *Binkie Beaumont,* Eminence Grise *of the West End Theatre, 1933–1973* (London, Hodder and Stoughton, 1989)
Huxley, Aldous, *Point Counter Point* (1928; London, Vintage Books, 2018)
Innes, Christopher, *Modern British Drama, 1890–1900* (Cambridge, Cambridge University Press, 1992)
Jeans, Ronald, *Writing for the Theatre* (London, Edward Arnold, 1949)
Kanin, Garson, *Remembering Mr. Maugham*, with a preface by Noël Coward (London, Hamish Hamilton, 1966)
Kaplan, Joel and Sheila Stowell, eds., *Look Back in Pleasure. Noël Coward Reconsidered* (London, Methuen, 2000)
Lahr, John, *Coward the Playwright* (London, Methuen, 1999)
Lesley, Cole, *Remembered Laughter: The Life of Noël Coward* (New York, Alfred Knopf, 1976)
Lewis, Jeremy, *Cyril Connolly, a Life* (London, Jonathan Cape, 1997)

MacDermott, Norman, *Everymania. The History of the Everyman Theatre, Hampstead 1920–1926, by Its Founder* (London, Society for Theatre Research, 1975)
Mander, Raymond and Joe Mitchenson, *Revue, a Story in Pictures*, with a foreword by Noël Coward (London, Peter Davies, 1971)
Mander, Raymond and Joe Mitchenson, *The Theatres of London*, 2nd edn (London, New English Library, 1975)
Mander, Raymond and Joe Mitchenson, *Theatrical Companion to Coward* (London, Rockliff, 1957; updated by Barry Day and Sheridan Morley, London, Oberon Books, 2000)
Mangan, Richard, ed., *Gielgud's Letters* (London, Weidenfeld and Nicolson, 2004)
Maugham, W. Somerset *Collected Plays*, (3 vols., London, Heinemann, 1931)
Morley, Sheridan, *A Talent to Amuse: A Biography of Noël Coward* (London, Heinemann, 1969)
Nicholson, Steve, *The Censorship of the British Drama, 1900–1968*, 4 vols. (Exeter, University of Exeter Press/Society for Theatre Research, 2020)
O'Connor, Sean and Julia O'Connor, *Straight Acting: Popular Gay Drama from Wilde to Rattigan* (London, Bloomsbury, 1997), ch.3, 'Public Lives, Private Faces.'
Overy, Richard, *The Morbid Age: Britain and the Crisis of Civilization, 1919–1938* (London, Allen Lane, 2009)
Payn, Graham, with Barry Day, *My Life with Noël Coward* (New York, Applause Books, 1995)
Rebellato, Dan, *1956 and All That: The Making of Modern British Drama* (London, Routledge, 1999)
Rebellato, Dan, 'Noël Coward's Bad Manners,' in Kaplan and Stowell, eds., *Look Back in Pleasure*, 44–61
Sherry, Norman, *The Life of Graham Greene, Volume Two, 1939–1955* (London, Jonathan Cape, 1994)
Sinfield, Alan, 'Private Lives/Public Theatre: Noël Coward and the Politics of Homosexual Representation,' *Representations*, 36 (Autumn, 1991), 43–63
Stannard, Martin, ed., *Evelyn Waugh: The Critical Heritage* (London, RKP, 1984)
Stephens, Robert, with Michael Coveney, *Knight Errant: Memoirs of a Vagabond Actor* (London, Hodder and Stoughton, 1996)
Strachan, Alan, *Dark Star: A Biography of Vivien Leigh* (London, I.B. Tauris, 2019)
Taylor, D.J., *Bright Young People: The Rise and Fall of a Generation, 1918–1940* (London, Vintage Books, 2008)

Taylor, John Russell, *The Rise and Fall of the Well-Made Play* (London, Methuen, 1967)
Tynan, Kenneth, *The Sound of Two Hands Clapping*, London, Jonathan Cape, 1975)
Waugh, Evelyn, *A Little Order: Selected Journalism*, Donat Gallagher, ed. (London, Eyre Methuen, 1977)

INDEX

Agate, James 15, 16, 37, 38, 77, 102
Amherst, Jeffrey 45
Archer, William 3
Ardrey, Robert 173
Arlen, Michael (*The Green Hat*) 16, 20
Arnaud, Yvonne 120
Arts Theatre, London 125
Ashton, Winifred ('Clemence Dane') 98
Atkinson, Brooks 75, 76, 126
Austen, Jane (*Pride and Prejudice*) 155

Baddeley, Angela 119
Bagnold, Enid 3
Banbury, Frith 155
Barrie, James M. (*Peter Pan*) 158
Baum, Vicki (*Grand Hotel*) 39
Baxter, Beverley 107–8
Beaton, Cecil 127, 131
Beaumont, Hugh ('Binkie') 5–6, 76, 96, 98, 99, 108, 119, 120, 124, 140, 148, 150–1, 155, 182
Beerbohm, Max 172
Belasco Theatre, New York 126
Benchley, Robert 75
Bennett, Arnold 11, 25
Bevin, Ernest 142
Blackwell, Blanche 149
Brahms, Caryl 125
Braithwaite, Lilian 16

Brook, Peter 107, 146
Brown, Ivor 58, 78, 89, 102, 119

Calthrop, Gladys 5, 16, 57, 93, 98
Cambridge Theatre, London 48
Campbell, Judy 119
Carey, Joyce 5, 86, 96, 108, 128
Casson, Lewis 155, 157
Cecil, (Lord) David 172
censorship (Lord Chamberlain's Office) 7, 13, 76, 109, 167–8
Chamberlain, Neville 105
Chappell, William 146
Charell, Erik 57–8
Charlot, André 47–8
Chekhov, Anton 155, 166
Churchill, Sir Winston 95
Citizens Theatre, Glasgow 39
Claire, Ina 47
Clare, Mary 156, 166
class 24, 57, 113–15, 118, 119, 146, 148
Clements, John 140
Cochran, C.B. 57–8, 60
Colbert, Claudette 140–1
Coliseum, The London 57
Collier, Constance 34, 36, 172
colonialism 112, 141–6, 147
Compton, Fay 99, 100–1
Congreve, William 16, 89
Connolly, Cyril 4–5, 106
Conway, Harold 119

INDEX

Cookman, Anthony 104
Cooper, (Lady) Diana 138
Cooper, Gladys 115, 119, 168
Cornell, Katharine 93
Covent Garden (Royal Opera House) 87
Coward, Noël
 autobiographies:
  Future Indefinite 84, 96
  Past Conditional 61, 172
  Present Indicative 14, 15, 44, 47, 57, 60
 plays, musical theatre and films:
  Ace of Clubs 83, 113, 127
  After the Ball 5, 6
  Age Cannot Wither (unfinished play) 7, 181–4
  Bitter Sweet 6, 45, 160, 185
  Blithe Spirit 83, 89, 96–103, 95 (film), 113, 169
  Brief Encounter (film) 78, 83–5, 178
  Cavalcade 44, 55, 56–60, 90, 107, 147–8, 160
  Conversation Piece 6
  Design for Living 3, 7, 12, 43–4, 55, 61–78, 81, 83, 129, 130, 169, 180
  Design for Rehearsing 130
  Easy Virtue 36–8, 44
  Fallen Angels 14, 24–30, 49
  Happy Breed, This 44, 57, 82, 83 (film), 90–1 (play and film)
  Hay Fever, 4, 7, 15, 24, 30–6, 44, 82, 144, 169, 185
  Home and Colonial/Island Fling; see *South Sea Bubble*
  Home Chat 13
  Home Sweet Home (planned play) 108
  I'll Leave it to You 10–11, 15
  In Which we Serve (film) 83–4
  London Calling (with Ronald Jeans) 6, 14
  Long Island Sound 2, 108–9
  Look after Lulu 5, 44, 153
  Nude with Violin 112–13, 120–6, 149, 151, 167
  Operette 44, 160
  Pacific 1860 6, 44, 83, 104, 113, 137–8
  'Peace in Our Time' 83, 104–9, 113
  Point Valaine 112, 144, 149
  Post-Mortem 2, 42, 55–6, 101
  Present Laughter 5, 44, 81, 82, 86–9, 96–7, 108, 141, 149, 172
  Private Lives 3, 4, 7, 41–2, 44–55, 57, 62, 82, 96–7, 129, 134, 144, 169, 180
  Quadrille 111, 127–36, 141, 148, 169
  Rat Trap, The 9, 12–13
  Relative Values 44, 111–12, 113–20, 148
  Salute to the Brave/Time Remembered 82, 83, 91–6
  Sail Away 6, 155, 169
  Semi-Monde 2, 3, 7, 10, 39–42
  Sigh no More (revue) 6
  South Sea Bubble 83, 112, 136–48, 167
  Suite in Three Keys 167–81:
   Shadows of the Evening 169–72, 178–9, 186
   Song at Twilight, A 7, 171–8, 180, 181
   Come into the Garden Maud 170, 179–80
  This Was a Man 13–14
  This Year of Grace! (revue) 6
  Three for the Money (planned play or film) 168–9

Tonight at 8.30 78–9:
  Astonished Heart, The 79, 140 (film)
  Family Album 78
  Hands Across the Sea 78, 138
  Red Peppers 78
  Shadow Play 78–9
  Star Chamber 78
  Still Life 78, 79, 83; *see also Brief Encounter*
  Ways and Means 78
  We Were Dancing 78
Volcano 2, 96 112, 149–52, 179
Vortex, The 14–24, 25, 26, 30, 125
Waiting in the Wings 149, 154–67, 182
Words and Music (revue) 6
Young Idea, The 11-12
songs:
  'Dance Little Lady' 57
  'Play, Orchestra, Play' 79
  'Poor Little Rich Girl' 57
  'London Pride' 99–100
  'Twentieth Century Blues' 58
other work:
  'Consider the Public' (newspaper articles) 167
  London Morning (ballet) 155
  'Me and the Girls' (story) 169
  Pomp and Circumstance (novel) 137–8, 144, 167
  Pretty Polly Barlow (collection of stories) 169
  'Solali' (short story) 138
  'Star Quality' (story and play) 181–2
  'What Mad Pursuit?' (story, adapted as *Long Island Sound*) 108
critics, theatre 43, 124
Cutler, Kate 15–16, 24

Darlington, W.A. 89, 100, 125, 134, 181
Day, Barry 6, 95, 155, 182
de Bear, Archie 77
D'Monté, Rebecca 101
Dear Octopus (Smith) 90
Decline and Fall (Waugh) 5
Dent, Alan 107, 111, 115
Drury Lane Theatre, London 56, 104
Duke of York's Theatre, London 156
Dukes, Ashley 21–2
Dyer, Richard 84

Eltis, Sos 4
Ervine, St John 4, 76
Ethel Barrymore Theatre, New York, 75
Evans, Edith 185
Everyman Theatre, London 15
expressionism 56, 58–9

farce 26, 44, 86, 89, 96, 101–2, 115
Ferber, Edna 155
Festival Ballet, London 155
Feydau, Georges 5, 153
Fleming, Ann and Ian 149
Fleming, Peter 79
Fontanne, Lynn 61, 112, 127–36, 173
Frankau, Pamela 155
Freedley, George 140–1
French, Harold 77
Fry, Christopher 3

Garrick Theatre, London 159
Generational conflict 10, 11–12, 16–17, 30, 44
Gibbs, Wolcott 126
Gielgud, John 120, 124–5
Gordon, Max 140

Grant, Elspeth 102
Graves, Robert 60
Gray, Timothy 169
Greene, Graham 102–3
Guitry, Sacha 15

Hale, Lionel 78
Hammerstein, Oscar, III 140
Hammill, Faye 45
Hammond, Kay 98, 100–1, 103, 140
Harrison, Rex 77, 103
Hastings, Selina 172
Havelock-Allan, Anthony 83
Haymarket Theatre, London 77, 81–2, 86, 89
Helpmann, Robert 125
Henry, Joan (*Look on Tempests*) 168
High Spirits (musical version of *Blithe Spirit*) 169
Hobson, Harold 107, 147–8, 181
Hodge, Alan 60
Hope-Wallace, Philip 119, 166, 181
Howard, Leslie 98
Hunter, N.C. 3
Hurren, Kenneth 120
Huxley, Aldous (*Point Counter Point*) 10

Ibsen, Henrik 12, (*Ghosts*) 17, 36
Innes. Christopher 15, 48
Ionesco, Eugene (*The Bald Prima Donna* and *The New Tenant*) 125

James, Henry 16
Jones, Griffith 135

Kanin, Garson 172
Kerr, Walter 126

King and I, The (Rodgers and Hammerstein) 140–1
Kretzmer, Herbert 180–1

Lahr, John, 2, 4, 39, 62
Lawrence, Gertrude 44–8, 79, 138–41, 144
Laye, Evelyn 99
Lean, David 83–4
Leigh, Vivien 140, 146–8
Leighton, Margaret 140, 173
Lesley, Cole 5, 98, 113, 119, 149, 155
Levin, Bernard 165
Lillie, Beatrice 48
Littlefield, Joan 1
Löhr, Marie 157, 160
Loraine, Lorn 5, 96, 98, 109, 124, 140, 148–50, 155, 167, 168
Lunt, Alfred 61, 112, 127, 129–36, 173
Lyric Theatre, Hammersmith 107
Lyric Theatre, London 107, 147

McClintic, Guthrie 93
MacDermott, Norman 15–16
Mantle, Burns 76
Manley, Norman 138
Marriott, J.W. 11
Marriott, R.B. 166, 181
Martin, Hugh 169
Matalon, Vivian 173, 186
Maugham, Robin 172
Maugham, W. Somerset 2– 4, 15, 111–12, 115, 119, 144–5, 172
   Constant Wife, The 4
   Our Betters 16, 22
   'Rain' (short story) 178
   Writer's Notebook, A 177–8
Meiser, Edith 140–1
melodrama 59, 141, 153, 174

INDEX

Molyneux, Edward 45, 46, 99, 100
Morgan, Charles 49
Morley, Sheridan 185
Morrison, Herbert 142
Motley (design team: Margaret and Sophie Harris, Elizabeth Montgomery) 166
Mountbatten, Lord Louis and Lady Edwina, 138
Muller, Robert 165–6

National Theatre (at the Old Vic) 169, 185
Natwick, Mildred 100–1
Neame, Ronald 83–4
'new drama' (1950s–60s) 3, 111–12, 113, 118, 125, 153–4, 166, 167–8
New Theatre, London (now Noël Coward Theatre) 10
nostalgia 153–4, 165–6

O'Connor, Sean and Julia 6
Oklahoma! (Rodgers and Hammerstein) 104
Old Vic Theatre, London (as National Theatre) 169, 185
Olivier, Laurence 140, 146–7, 148
Osborne, John 3, 166, 181 (*A Patriot for Me*)
Our Man in Havana (film) 155
Overy, Richard 2

Page, Philip 77
Palmer, Lilli 172–3, 186
Parker, Cecil 98, 100
patriotism 56, 58–9, 60–1, 82, 90–1, 92–6, 104–8
Payn, Graham 5, 155, 158
Phoenix Theatre, London 48, 78, 127, 131
Piccadilly Theatre, London 82

Pinero, Arthur Wing (*The Second Mrs Tanqueray*) 36
Pinter, Harold (*The Caretaker*, *The Dumb Waiter* and *The Room*) 3
politics 90–1, 112, 117–18, 142–3 *see also* patriotism
Portmeirion 82, 96
Priestley, J.B. (*Time and the Conways*) 90
Proust, Marcel (*Sodom and Gommorah*) 36
psychoanalysis 28, 29, 68–9, 79

Queen's Hall, London 87

Rattigan, Terence 3, 6, 169 (*A Sleeping Prince*)
Rebellato, Dan 13
Redgrave, Michael 155
Redgrave, Vanessa 168
Reed, Carol 155
Reinhardt, Max 59
Restoration comedy 76, 78, 157
Rodgers, Richard 140
Royal Court Theatre, London 181
Rutherford, Margaret 99–101

Sardoff, Fred 155
Sartre, Jean-Paul (*Men Without Shadows*) 107
Savoy Theatre, London 11, 77, 81, 113
Sellars, Elizabeth 148
sex 11–12, 13–14, 16, 28, 31, 44, 46, 53, 82, 85, 149–52
  homosexuality 6–7, 20, 39–41, 62, 75, 78, 86, 109, 122, 126, 129, 167–8, 171, 178, 181–4
  lesbianism 40–1, 109, 158
Shakespeare Memorial Theatre, Stratford-upon-Avon 125

Shakespeare, William
   Hamlet 17
   Richard II 105, 107
   Romeo and Juliet 151
   Tempest, The 125
   Titus Andronicus 146
Shaw, George Bernard 11, 12
   Devil's Disciple, The 125
   You Never Can Tell 12
Sherriff, R.C. (*Journey's End*) 55
Sinfield, Alan 6
Smith, Dodie (*Dear Octopus*) 90
Smith, James Thorne (*Topper*) 102
social conventions 7, 9, 14, 32, 48, 50–1, 52–3, 62, 67, 69, 72, 75–6, 77, 89, 129, 147–8, 180, 181–4
Spurling, Hilary 181

Taylor, John Russell 2
Tennent, H.M., Ltd 5
Theatre Guild, (New York) 61
Thorndike, Sybil 155, 157, 160, 166
Travers, Ben 102
Trewin, J.C. 120
Trollope, Anthony (*Phineas Finn* and *Can You Forgive Her?*) 129
Tynan, Kenneth 4, 134

Walbrook, Anton 77
war 55–6, 58, 81–2, 91–6, 103, 104–8

Waugh, Evelyn (*Decline and Fall*) 4–5, 10, (*Vile Bodies*) 138
Webb, Clifton 100–1, 109
Webster, Margaret ('Peggy') 155–6, 160
'well-made' plays 2–3, 10, 12–13, 14, 22, 30, 31, 36, 41–2, 48, 176
Wells, H.G. 11
Wesker, Arnold 3, 166
West, Rebecca 11
Westport County Playhouse, Connecticut 136, 140
White Horse Inn (Benatzky and Scholz) 57–8
Wilde, Oscar 4, (*Lady Windermere's Fan*) 5, (*A Woman of No Importance*) 34
Wilding, Michael 125, 173
Wilenski, R.H. 120
Williams, Stephen 107
Wilson, A.E. 78, 102
Wilson, John C. 5, 46–8, 63, 77, 82, 83, 86, 92, 100–1, 115, 130–1, 136, 140
Wilson, Natasha 93
Winter Garden Theatre, London 125
wit 4-5, 9, 49, 53–4, 119, 120, 144
Wodehouse, P.G. 117
Worsley, T.C. 125, 134
Worth, Irene 173, 180, 186
Wycherley, William 76 (*The Country Wife*), 78
Wynyard, Diana 77

www.ingramcontent.com/pod-product-compliance
Lightning Source LLC
Chambersburg PA
CBHW062222300426
44115CB00012BA/2180